Advance Praise for

THE COMPLETE STORY OF THE COURSE

Now I have something I can enthusiastically give to my friends and colleagues who ask me about *A Course in Miracles*. This book is a very readable and accurate account of the important and controversial matters surrounding the Course. With careful research and journalistic skill, Patrick Miller weaves together an "on the edge of your seat" story.

> —LEE JAMPOLSKY, PH.D., author of *Healing the Addictive Mind* and *The Art of Trust* and co-author (with Jerry Jampolsky, M.D.) of *Listen to Me*

A much-needed, fair-minded and sensitive assessment of a puzzling, serious, and surprisingly influential element in the spiritual life of the twentieth century.

> —JACOB NEEDLEMAN, PH.D., author of *A Little Book on Love* and *Money and the Meaning of Life*

Miller has not only written a fascinating account of one of the most significant spiritual phenomena of our time, but his style introduces something we desperately need in these dispirited times. *The Complete Story* is a new kind of investigative journalism that draws out the spiritual side of people and movements in a fair and objective way, rather than the jaded cynicism that most journalists pawn off on us as "objectivity."

> —CHARLES T. TART, PH.D., author of *Waking Up* and *Living the Mindful Life*

Love it or hate it, *A Course in Miracles* is increasingly difficult to ignore. As a grassroots American phenomenon, the Course is deeply spiritual without being religious, and democratic rather than dogmatic. Miller's book is simply a great read, an entertaining and exquisitely accurate rendering of the stranger-than-fiction story of the Course.

> —LUCIA CAPACCHIONE, PH.D., author of *Recovery of Your Inner Child* and *The Creative Journal*

D0062354

ALSO BY D. PATRICK MILLER

The Book of Practical Faith (Henry Holt & Co., Inc.)
A Little Book of Forgiveness (Viking)

WITH TOM RUSK, M.D.:

The Power of Ethical Persuasion (Viking; Penguin)
Instead of Therapy (Hay House)

The Complete Story of
THE COURSE

The Complete Story of

THE
COURSE

The History, The People, and
The Controversies Behind

A COURSE IN MIRACLES®

D. PATRICK MILLER

FEARLESS BOOKS
Berkeley, California

First Edition

FEARLESS BOOKS

1678 Shattuck Avenue #319, Berkeley CA 94709

Copyright © 1997 by D. Patrick Miller. All rights reserved. No part of this book may be reproduced, stored in a retrieval system, or transmitted, in any forms or by any means (electronic, mechanical, photocopying, recording, or otherwise) without the written permission of Fearless Books.

Second Printing 1998

Library of Congress Catalog Card Number 97-60088
ISBN 0-9656809-0-8

Publisher's Cataloguing-in-Publication
(provided by Quality Books, Inc.)

Miller, D. Patrick, 1953–
    The complete story of the Course: the history, the people, and
the controversies behind A Course in Miracles / by D. Patrick Miller.
    p. cm.
    Includes index.
    1. Course in miracles.   I. Title.
BP605.C68M55 1977   299'.93
QBI97-40269

Cover and logo designs by Thomas Morris and D. Patrick Miller.
Interior design and typography by Linda Davis / Star Type, Berkeley.
Printed in the U.S.A.

Permissions and Disclaimers

Portions from *A Course in Miracles* copyright ©1978, 1985, 1992, 1996 by the Foundation for Inner Peace, Inc., P.O. Box 598, Mill Valley, CA 94942. Used by permission of Viking Penguin, a division of Penguin Books USA Inc.

    Portions of *Absence from Felicity, A Course in Miracles and Christianity: A Dialogue*, and the unpublished papers of Helen Schucman are reprinted by the permission of Kenneth Wapnick, Ph.D. and the Foundation for *A Course in Miracles®*.

    Transcribed portions of the audiotape "The Universal Course" are published by permission of Miracle Distribution Center and Roger Walsh, Ph.D.

    Portions of *The Guru Papers* are reprinted by permission of Frog Ltd. and North Atlantic Press.

    Portions of *Double Vision* are reprinted by permission of Celestial Arts Publishing.

A Course in Miracles® and ACIM® are registered trademarks and servicemarks of the Foundation for Inner Peace. The ideas represented herein are the personal interpretation and understanding of the author and are not necessarily endorsed by the copyright holder of *A Course in Miracles®*. This book is the result of an independent journalistic effort and is in no way financed or sanctioned by the Foundation for Inner Peace, the Foundation for *A Course in Miracles®*, or any other Course-related organization.

Brief portions of this manuscript are revised excerpts of articles originally appearing in *Free Spirit* (Brooklyn, NY) and *The Sun: A Magazine of Ideas* (Chapel Hill, NC).

Table of Contents

PART III: Living with the Course

Foreword

While writing a book on contemporary miracles I came across an article that clarified a controversial subject that was otherwise clouded in rumor, cant, misunderstanding, snide attacks, and glowing testimonials. When I read D. Patrick Miller's accounts of his own experience with *A Course in Miracles*, and his overview as a journalist of the phenomenon, I felt for the first time I'd heard an authentic appraisal of the subject and gained an understanding of its power both to attract many people and put off others. Now Mr. Miller has written a book on the subject, and it is a superb journalistic report on this popular and important phenomenon.

Miller is uniquely qualified to write this book. Early in his career he trained as an investigative reporter, co-editing an alternative newspaper in his hometown of Charlotte, North Carolina, and later reporting on environmental politics for the *San Francisco Bay Guardian*. But investigating corruption and misdeeds in the style of what Tom Wolfe has called "totem journalism" began to seem unfulfilling. After a deep questioning of his own goals — brought on by a crisis of physical illness that Miller has called "an instructive catastrophe" — he turned to the practice of what he has insightfully labeled "the journalism of consciousness." In his lucid and tough-minded volume *The Book of*

Practical Faith, he explains of his career shift that "No longer interested in documenting human flaws and failures, I felt inspired to report instead on the psychological and spiritual keys to human transformation."

In the process of doing this kind of reporting he learned that the alleged objectivity of totem journalism — the reporter as cipher who supposedly has no opinion or feeling — doesn't apply to investigating the realm of human consciousness and transformation. In fact it seems difficult, if not impossible, for journalists who have no experiential knowledge of transformational programs or practices to write about them with accuracy. Indeed, an in-bred hostility to such realms in the culture of the mainstream press has a distorting effect that can lead to outright untruth.

Miller observes correctly that the "not-so-subtle demeaning of people with spiritual or self-reforming interests is endemic in the mainstream press, reflecting the inability of most journalists to fairly assess the value of introspective and spiritual processes."

Rather than disqualify himself as an "objective observer," Miller's own experience studying *A Course in Miracles* enables him to tell the story of this phenomenon with greater insight and understanding. The fact that he benefited from the Course himself does not prevent him from asking the most critical questions about it and reporting on the most serious objections of its critics. He is not out to sell you *A Course in Miracles* but to tell you what he knows about it, both from his own experience and his investigations as a reporter, one who uses the tools of journalism with integrity and skill.

I have not studied *A Course in Miracles* myself, nor do I have any stake in how it is perceived. My interest is that of any reader who wants to know the truth about the Course as fully as an honest and able reporter can present it. That's what this book delivers.

— Dan Wakefield

DAN WAKEFIELD is a novelist, journalist, and screenwriter whose books include *Expect a Miracle, Creating from the Spirit* and *Returning: A Spiritual Journey*. He was a Neiman Fellow in Journalism at Harvard University and has been a contributing writer for *The Nation, The Atlantic,* and *GQ,* and is currently a Senior Writer for *Yoga Journal.*

Introduction

Two decades after its publication *A Course in Miracles* (ACIM) has become one of the most popular and perplexing phenomena of contemporary spirituality. With over one million English copies in print and foreign editions available in Spanish, German, Portuguese, and Hebrew, the Course has reached millions of people in its original form. Some of its principles have influenced millions more through their inclusion in several best-selling books on psychological and spiritual themes. Over two thousand Course study groups exist worldwide, as well as a profusion of eclectic ministries, teaching academies, and related service organizations. At least seven online forums and nine World Wide Web sites dedicated to the Course electronically connect students from the United States, Europe, Australia, South Africa, even the Far East.

Yet the Course remains largely a grassroots phenomenon, not yet a subject of much discussion in mainstream religion or academic theology. When it has been discussed, its various critics have described it in wildly contradictory terms.

Noted psychologist and author James Hillman, for instance, has gone on record characterizing the Course as "old-fashioned, self-deluding Christianity."[1] Yet evangelical Christian critics want nothing to do with the Course, warning their followers away from it as a satanic message disguised in Christian language. And while there is a popular recognition of the Course as a centerpiece of so-called New Age spirituality, one of its chief interpreters asserts that this is a case of mistaken identity.

"There has been some confusion of the Course with superficial New Age positivism," remarks Kenneth Wapnick, Ph.D., who helped edit the original Course manuscript and directs a major teaching center. "But the Course actually trains us to become aware of all our *negative* thoughts, in order to help us confront all the 'obstacles to the awareness of love's presence' within our minds."

Since the Course identifies the source of all such obstacles as the ego — our ordinary sense of self — the Course's unwavering prescription for surrendering those obstacles makes it an exceptionally demanding discipline. Adds Wapnick, "I find the most genuine understanding of the Course among those who are struggling with it, or whose lives became more problematic after beginning their study. When new students tell me how much happier the Course has made them already, I tend to think they're not getting it yet."

Yet even Wapnick expresses a contradictory view of the Course in terms of its potential significance. While he has frequently asserted his belief that this teaching is "not intended for the masses," he once predicted that the Course would achieve a status "equal to that of the Bible sometime in the next century."[2]

Another prominent Course student, president of the Institute of Noetic Sciences and former University of California regent Willis Harman, Ph.D., has stated that he regards the Course as "perhaps the most important writing in the English language since the Bible."[3] And the Reverend Jon Mundy, an ordained Methodist minister and religion professor who founded one of the earliest Course study groups, asserts that "*A Course in Miracles* may yet provide a Copernican revolution in Christianity."[4]

At the least, the Course's substantial and growing popularity makes it clear that it is far more than a short-lived spiritualist fad. Although the fundamental facts of the Course's nature and origin can be briefly summarized, they do not fully answer the question of what *A Course in Miracles* is. Because it can be interpreted on many levels and even some veteran students do not claim to understand it completely, an exhaustive answer to the question "What is the Course?" may actually be impossible.

By presenting an informed and balanced view of ACIM — encompassing its history, the fundamentals of its message, profiles of its major teachers and interpreters, and a survey of its diverse applications as well as the critical reactions and controversies the teaching has engendered — it is this book's purpose to present a more comprehensive answer than has previously been available from any single publication besides the Course itself.

What Is ACIM?

A Course in Miracles is a self-study curriculum that guides students toward a spiritual way of life by restoring their contact with what it calls the Holy Spirit or "internal teacher." The Course uses both an intellectual and an experiential approach within its 650-page Text, 500-page Workbook of 365 daily meditations, and 90-page Manual for Teachers. Published by the nonprofit Foundation for Inner Peace in 1976, the Course was written down in shorthand over a period of seven years by Dr. Helen Schucman, a research psychologist at Columbia University, and typed up by her supervisor Dr. William Thetford, director of Columbia-Presbyterian Medical Center's Department of Psychology.

Schucman said she heard a "Voice" that gave her an "inner dictation," and she never claimed authorship of the material, remaining personally ambivalent about its message until her death in 1981. There is no central organized religion or membership institution built around the Course, and no "guru" widely accepted as an embodiment of the teaching.

As a psychological discipline, the Course encourages the transformation of the self through the constant practice of forgiveness. As a spiritual training it insists on a complete reversal of ordinary perception, urging acceptance of spirit as the only reality and the physical world as a mass illusion (similar to the Buddhist and Hindu notions of *samsara* and *maya*, two terms designating the everyday world we see as a kind of dream).

While Christian in language, the metaphysics of the Course is thus more aligned with Eastern mysticism than traditional Western religion. In fact ACIM directly challenges significant elements of contemporary Christianity, particularly the doctrines of sin and crucifixion. For instance, it argues that the significance of the Resurrection is not that Jesus Christ died to atone for the sins of humankind but rather that, as an advanced being who was fully cognizant of the illusory nature of the physical world, Jesus neither suffered nor died on the cross. The Course further maintains that everyone shares the potential to achieve such an enlightened way of perception.

The theological challenge of the Course is intensified by the fact that the authorial "Voice" clearly identifies itself as the historical Jesus Christ, bringing a correction of traditional Christianity to the world in modern psychological language. Its corrective tone is clear in such passages as the following:

> If the Apostles had not felt guilty, they never could have quoted me as saying, "I come not to bring peace but a sword." This is clearly the opposite of everything I taught. Nor could they have described my reactions to Judas as they did, if they had really understood me. I could not have said, "Betrayest thou the Son of Man with a kiss?" unless I believed in betrayal. The whole message of the crucifixion was simply that I did not. . . . As you read the teachings of the Apostles, remember that I told them myself that there was much they would understand later, because they were not wholly ready to follow me at the time.[5]

While the Course does not identify itself as philosophically superior to any other teaching, stating that it is only one version of a "universal curriculum,"[6] it does suggest that serious students may progress faster by its use than by any other spiritual method. The Course's alleged authorship and its challenge to Western religious tradition have served to make it simultaneously popular with people seeking alternative spiritual guidance and troubling to its critics.

The Perspective of This Book

Although I have been a Course student for ten years and consider it the touchstone of my own spiritual perspective, it is not the purpose of this book to promote the Course, nor to teach it. (See "Selected Resources" in the Appendix for referrals to identified teachers of ACIM). I do hope to facilitate a more accurate impression of the Course among the general public and correct some of the misinformation about it that has been circulated over the last twenty years. It's my hope that this book will serve as a factual reference not only for current and prospective students of the Course, but also for journalists, historians, theologians, and anyone else attempting to understand the growing social phenomenon spawned by ACIM.

Some readers may question whether I can render a balanced view of *A Course in Miracles* since I already accept its teaching. There is no definitive way to answer such a challenge except to suggest that readers consider the wide range of views and voices presented in this book and come to their own conclusions. But I feel that it is impossible to write intelligently about ACIM *without* long-term study and a direct, sustained experience of the discipline it offers.

I began reporting on the Course not long after beginning my study (I was the last reporter to interview Bill Thetford before his death), and I have always incorporated contemporary criticism of ACIM in my published magazine articles (excepting some personal essays inspired by Course principles). While critical challenges to the Course are represented throughout this book, they are concentrated in two chapters, "Why the Course Is Not Christian — Or Is It?" and "Critiques of the Course."

The latter chapter includes some of my own criticism of the teaching.

The concluding chapter, "The Presence of the Course," discloses my personal experience with ACIM and offers commentary on the spiritual search in general. While I have experienced the Course as an extraordinary discipline that has dramatically benefited my quality of life in the deepest possible sense, I still regard it as it describes itself: a "teaching device" rather than a new religion. This unique status enables me to value ACIM without feeling obligated to issue a "defense of the faith."

As the manuscript of this book was nearing completion, there occurred a turning point in the history of *A Course in Miracles*. For the first time the Course publisher, the Foundation for Inner Peace, licensed the printing and distribution of the Course and related materials to a major domestic publisher, Viking Penguin, which released a hardcover edition of ACIM in the spring of 1996. (Arkana, a Viking affiliate, has previously published a Course edition in the United Kingdom.) Since the Course became a perennial bestseller without the benefit of direct advertising by the Foundation, it is difficult to predict the ultimate effects of broader distribution and publicity that this new arrangement will provide.

Yet it's safe to say that *A Course in Miracles* will reach millions more people in the near future. This widespread and ever-growing recognition would have likely stunned the reticent scribes of the material — if not so much as they were once stunned to find themselves writing down the spectacularly strange and compelling teaching now known to so many simply as "the Course."

PART I

Origins & History

1

How the Course Came to Be

Columbia University in 1965 was perhaps not the sort of place one would have expected to find the stirrings of spiritual renewal. In the College of Physicians and Surgeons, the psychology professors' struggle to affirm their discipline as a respectable branch of medical science went forward, attended by the usual amount of professional jealousy, fierce competition, and outright back-biting.

In the midst of this chaotic march of scientific progress, the reticent and scholarly director of the Psychology Department of the Columbia-Presbyterian Medical Center, Dr. William N. Thetford, one day decided that he'd had enough of the academic sparring. "There must be another way, and I'm determined to find it," he announced in an uncharacteristically forceful speech to his chief colleague, a sharp-tongued research psychologist fourteen years his senior, Dr. Helen Schucman. Moved by Thetford's commitment to a change in style, Schucman vowed to help him usher in a new era of cooperation with their peers, with a noticeable degree of success.

Over time the new outlook would prove largely ineffective in Thetford and Schucman's own severely conflicted relationship. But the momentary alignment of these two professors' sympathies seemed to catalyze an eruption of decidedly mystical energy on Schucman's part that left the rational scientist in her groping for explanations. Unexpectedly Schucman began to experience a recurrence of the symbolic visions she had witnessed in her youth — visions which had largely ceased in young adulthood when she bitterly ended her search for God.

But now, at the age of fifty-six, Schucman found herself involved in a dramatic progression of waking dreams and visions in which she was gravitating toward a mysterious duty she felt she had "somehow, somewhere, agreed to complete." In these reveries she was sometimes spoken to by an inner "soundless voice" who clarified the meaning of various events for her. Over time this voice became an authoritative presence whom she referred to as the "Voice" or "Top Sergeant." She was not unaware of the Top Sergeant's self-professed identity, but evaded acknowledging it.

In the late summer of 1965, Schucman experienced a vision in which she entered a cave by a windswept seashore and found a large, very old parchment scroll. Unrolling the aged parchment with some difficulty, she found a center panel bearing the simple words "GOD IS." As she unrolled the scroll further, more writing was revealed to the left and right of the center panel. The familiar Voice told her that if she wanted, she could read the past on the left panel, and the future on the right — an apparent offering of clairvoyant capacities. But Schucman pointed to the words in the center of the scroll and said, "This is all I want."

"You made it that time," replied the Voice. "Thank you."

After this vision Schucman's anxiety lessened somewhat and she thought with relief that her inner turbulence might be receding for good. At Thetford's suggestion, she had begun recording her inner experiences, and was about to make an entry on October 21st when the Voice spoke clearly in her mind. "This is a course in miracles," it said with authority. "Please take notes."

Schucman was soon on the phone to Thetford, her precarious emotional equilibrium once again shattered. She told Thetford what the Voice was suggesting to her and asked in panic, "What am I going to do?"

Thetford was calm and curious. "Why don't you take down the notes? We'll look them over in the morning and see if they make any sense, and throw them out otherwise. No one has to know."

Thus began seven years of difficult extracurricular labor for Helen Schucman as she faithfully though often unwillingly scribed the material that became *A Course in Miracles*, and read aloud her shorthand notes to Thetford, who volunteered to type them. The prolonged and profound inner conflict that Schucman felt about her peculiar task is clear in this excerpt from Schucman's unpublished autobiography:[1]

> As for me, I could neither account for nor reconcile my obviously inconsistent attitudes. On the one hand I still regarded myself as officially an agnostic, resented the material I was taking down, and was strongly impelled to attack it and prove it wrong. On the other hand I spent considerable time in taking it down and later dictating it to Bill, so that it was apparent that I also took it quite seriously. I actually came to refer to it as my life's work, even though I remained unconvinced about its authenticity and very jittery about it. As Bill pointed out, I must believe in it if only because I argued with it so much. While this was true, it did not help me. I was in the impossible position of not believing in my own life's work. The situation was clearly ridiculous as well as painful.[2]

In fact, early in her work Schucman argued with the Voice about the purpose of the undertaking and her role in it:

> I soon found I did not have much option in the matter. I was given a sort of mental "explanation," though, in the form of a series of related thoughts that crossed my mind in rapid succession and made a reasonably coherent whole. According to this "information" the world situation was worsening to an alarming degree. People all over the world

were being called on to help, and were making their individual contributions as part of an overall, prearranged plan. I had apparently agreed to take down a course in miracles as it would be given me. The Voice was fulfilling its part in the agreement, as I would fulfill mine. I would be using abilities I had developed very long ago, and which I was not really ready to use again. Because of the acute emergency, however, the usual slow, evolutionary process was being by-passed in what might be described as a "celestial speed-up." I could sense the urgency that lay behind this "explanation," whatever I might think about its content. The feeling was conveyed to me that time was running out.

I was not satisfied. Even in the unlikely event that the "explanation" was true, I did not regard myself as a good candidate for a "scribal" role. I stated my opposition silently but strongly.

"Why me?" I asked. "I'm not even religious. I don't understand the things that have been happening to me and I don't even like them. Besides, they make me nervous. I'm just about as poor a choice as you could make."

"On the contrary," I was assured. "You are an excellent choice, and for a very simple reason. You will do it."

I had no answer to this, and retired in defeat. The Voice was right. I knew I would do it. And so the writing of the "course" began.[3]

Thus, in addition to her full-time job as a professor at Columbia-Presbyterian, Schucman had taken on the almost-daily challenge of writing down dictation from a most unconventional superior.

I would feel the writing coming on almost daily, and sometimes several times a day. The timing never conflicted with work or social activities, starting at some time when I was reasonably free to write without interference. I wrote in a shorthand notebook that I soon began to carry with me, just in case. I could and very often did refuse to cooperate, at least initially. But I soon learned I would have no peace until I did. Even so, I maintained my "right to refuse" throughout. Sometimes I refused to write for over a month, during which I merely became increasingly depressed. It always required my full conscious cooperation.

Evenings turned out to be a favored time for "dictation," especially for additional "assignments." I objected bitterly to this and often went to bed defiantly without writing anything, but I could not sleep. Eventually, I got up in some disgust and wrote as directed. . . .

The writing was highly interruptable. At the office I could lay the notebook down to answer the telephone, talk to a patient, supervise a junior staff member, or attend to one of our numerous emergencies, and return to the writing without even checking back to see where I left off. At home I could talk to my husband, chat with a friend, or take a nap, going back to the notebook afterwards without disturbing the flow of words in the slightest. . . . It was as if the Voice merely waited until I came back and then started in again. I wrote with equal ease at home, in the office, on a park bench, or in a taxi, bus, or subway. The presence of other people did not interfere at all. When the time for writing came external circumstances appeared to be irrelevant.[4]

Among those who knew her there is a general agreement that Schucman exhibited a dramatic dissociation of personality around the issue of the Course. Bill Thetford always felt, in fact, that this split was essential to her work in recording it.

"She was usually in some degree of conflict," Thetford told me in a brief meeting about a year before his death in 1988. "In order to do this work Helen had to be in a rather dissociated mental state. She had to shift to the appropriate focus for taking down the Course material, and she was very precise and accurate about it, very much as if she were tuning into an FM channel. She frequently said to me, 'I don't want to know what it says. I'm only concerned with its grammar and syntax. If it starts making errors in syntax, then I refuse to continue with it.' She could get the material down without much difficulty, because it came to her quite clearly. But when she stopped, she would shift back to her ordinary state of ego awareness. Those states didn't necessarily connect. She was quite aware that what the Course had to say was not how she experienced the world.

"This was obviously a very unusual situation," Thetford added, "but perhaps it's the only way it could have happened given Helen's personality. She really stayed out of the way and certainly didn't try to become a high priestess. She didn't want that role."

When I asked Thetford if some of that reluctance had to do with the professional identities that both of them had to protect during the years of transcription, he laughed emphatically. "Yes, the Course was our guilty secret!" he admitted. "Professors at Columbia didn't *do* this kind of thing, particularly in the Department of Psychiatry. Can you imagine? — hearing voices, taking down material of this kind . . ."

In fact, as Thetford often reported, Schucman's anxiety about the Course material was such that he had to keep one calming hand on her and the other on the typewriter as she read aloud her notes. Occasionally her resistance to the meaning of the material would break down, as Schucman admitted:

The writing continued over years, and although the acute terror I felt at the beginning gradually lessened over time I never really got used to it. Yet despite periods of open rebellion, it never seriously occurred to me to give it up even though the whole thing struck me as a major and often insulting interference. There were, however, a few rare times when I felt curiously transported as I wrote. On these occasions the words seemed almost to sing, and I felt a deep sense of trust and even privilege. I noticed afterwards that these sections turned out to be the more poetic ones. But these were brief periods of respite. For the most part I was bleakly unbelieving, suspicious, and afraid. Yet distressing as the writing generally was, reading the material to Bill afterwards was infinitely more so. We had agreed that I would read my notes to him at the end of the day, and he would type them. I hated to hear what I had written. I was sure it would be incoherent, foolish and meaningless. On the other hand I was likely to be unexpectedly and deeply moved and suddenly burst into tears.[5]

Although Schucman's personal notes were vague about the identity behind the Voice, the overt historical references made in the material itself were unmistakable. In a discussion of the meaning of the crucifixion, the Voice said:

I elected, for your sake and mine, to demonstrate that the most outrageous assault, as judged by the ego, does not matter. As the world judges these things, but not as God knows them, I was betrayed, abandoned, beaten, torn, and finally killed. It was clear that this was only because of the projection of others onto me, since I had not harmed anyone and had healed many.

. . . My one lesson, which I must teach as I learned it, is that no perception that is out of accord with the Holy Spirit can be justified. I undertook to show this was true in an extreme case, merely because it would serve as a good teaching aid to those whose temptation to give in to anger and assault would not be so extreme. I will with God that none of His Sons should suffer.[6]

At the close of one version of her autobiography, Schucman disclosed a telling assessment of this mystical authority who had so dramatically intervened in her conflicted life.

Where did the writing come from? It made obvious use of my educational background, interests and experience, but that was in matters of style rather than content. Certainly the subject matter itself was the last thing I would have expected to write about. . . .

I have subsequently found out that many of the concepts and even some of the actual terms in the writing are found in both Eastern and Western mystical thought, but I knew nothing of them at the time. Nor did I understand the calm but impressive authority with which the Voice dictated. It is largely because of the strangely compelling nature of this authority that I have referred to the Voice with a capital "V." I do not understand the real authorship of the writing, but the particular combination of certainty, wisdom, gentleness, clarity and patience that characterized the Voice made that form of reference seem perfectly appropriate.

At several points in the writing the Voice itself speaks in no uncertain terms about the Author. My own reactions to these references, which literally stunned me at the time, have decreased in intensity and are now at the level of mere indecision. I do not understand the events that led up to the writing. I do not understand the process and I certainly do not understand the authorship. It would be pointless for me to attempt an explanation.[7]

Kenneth Wapnick, author of a detailed history of the Course scribing entitled *Absence from Felicity*, issues a disclaimer about this statement of Schucman's. Noting that she began her autobiography at Bill Thetford's suggestion — he thought it could serve as an introduction to be published with the Course — Wapnick feels that Schucman was writing to shore up her facade as "a hard-nosed scientist who suddenly woke up one day and started writing down words from a mysterious voice." In fact, Wapnick says, Schucman had been hearing the Voice for some time before October 21, 1965, and knew exactly to whom she was listening.

"I challenged Helen about this image of herself she wanted to put out there," recalls Wapnick. "I told her, 'This is what people are going to have as a legacy, and you know it's not true. Why don't you write it the way it really happened?' She agreed and started over, but it brought up such anxiety that she ended up making what she had written even worse! So I said I'd never mention it again. That's how the autobiography ended up the way it is." (In the version of her autobiography in my possession, Schucman never clearly identifies the author of ACIM.)

Lessons in Relationship

As Helen Schucman and Bill Thetford labored at their secret task, revealing it only to a few intimates over the seven years of transcription, they were not sure of its ultimate purpose beyond a private and prolific lecture on the betterment of their relationships to each other and their professional colleagues — an unexpected answer to Thetford's commitment to "another way." And no one who knew them would have denied that their particular relationship, which had begun seven years before the Course's inception, sorely needed help.

As Wapnick relates, a "tremendous animosity" existed between the assertive, abrasive Schucman and her passive-aggressive boss. "They would argue throughout the day, and then in the evening would often spend another hour or so on the phone going over their mutual grievances, each of them desperately convinced of the correctness of his and her position. Constantly critical of each other, their discussions were seemingly endless."[8]

In a two-hour film documentary about the Course released by the Foundation for Inner Peace in 1987, Bill Thetford alluded to the fact that Helen Schucman "wanted more from our relationship than I felt I was able to give"[9] — likely an oblique reference to Schucman's romantic attraction to Thetford, who was homosexual. But the relationship between Schucman and Thetford seemed a good deal more complicated than unrequited affection could explain, particularly in light of the fact that the one thing they reportedly never argued about was the Course.

Wapnick, who met the two of them while they were working

jointly on a chapter to be published in the *Comprehensive Text-book of Psychiatry*, says Thetford and Schucman were at "total war" over that professional project, but suffered no bitterness or competition when the subject matter turned to the Course. "The difference was astonishing," he recalls.

According to *Absence from Felicity*, the first five chapters of the Text of ACIM were heavily edited (by the explicit direction of the Voice) in order to remove earlier personal instructions to Schucman, many of them giving specific advice about her relationship to Thetford and clarifying their mutually supportive roles. But Schucman's resistance to guidance was intense and she did not hesitate to challenge the inner authority she heard. Wapnick's book reveals the following internal dialogue recorded in Schucman's notes but not included in the Course:

> [Jesus]: Everyone experiences fear, and nobody enjoys it. Yet, it would take very little right-thinking to know why it occurs. Neither you nor Bill have [sic] thought about it very much, either.
>
> [Helen]: I object to the use of a plural verb with a properly singular subject, and remember that last time in a very similar sentence, He said it correctly and I noted it with real pleasure. This real grammatical error makes me suspicious of the genuineness of these notes.
>
> [Jesus]: What it really shows is that you are not very receptive. The reason it came out that way, is because you are projecting . . . your own anger, which has nothing to do with these notes. You made the error, because you are not feeling loving, so you want me to sound silly, so you won't have to pay attention. . . .
>
> You and Bill have been afraid of God, of Me, of yourselves, and of practically everyone you know at one time or another.[10]

While such personal directives were excised from the Course itself, their existence helps explain some of the odd passages remaining wherein the author seems to be personally chiding the reader: "You may insist that the Holy Spirit does not answer you, but it might be wiser to consider the kind of questioner you are."[11]

Regardless of how much personal instruction Schucman was to receive internally, her resistance to applying the message of the Course appeared substantial to the end of her life. In his later years Bill Thetford seemed better able to integrate the teaching into his attitudes and behavior. While Schucman could explain the Course intellectually and would leap to its defense if she felt it was being challenged or distorted, neither she nor Thetford could fulfill its lessons in the very relationship to which it seemed, at first, to be solely directed.

As Wapnick writes, "By the time I met them in the late fall of 1972, right after the Course was completed, their relationship was at an all-time low, and it only seemed to worsen from there. It was almost as if Helen were determined to prove that the Course was ineffective at least, and deleterious at worst, enabling her to feel more justifiably bitter about her life."[12]

Nonetheless this unlikely team did complete its task. The massive Text was fully recorded by October 1968, almost exactly three years since it had begun. The Voice had earlier told Schucman that the material would be complete when she heard the word "Amen." The last paragraph of the Text reads:

And now we say "Amen." For Christ has come to dwell in the abode you set for Him before time was, in calm eternity. The journey closes, ending at the place where it began. No trace of it remains. Not one illusion is accorded faith, and not one spot of darkness still remains to hide the face of Christ from anyone. Thy will is done, complete and perfectly, and all creation recognizes You, and knows You as the only Source it has. Clear in Your likeness does the Light shine forth from everything that lives and moves in You. For we have reached where all of us are one, and we are home, where You would have us be.[13]

For all of her resistance and skepticism, Schucman's devotion to the original Text manuscript was remarkable. She retyped it twice on her own, then worked with Thetford to enter chapter and section headings into what had been one long, unbroken discourse. Tempted often to change the wording to suit her own predilections, Schucman always thought better of it. "Any changes I made were always wrong in the long run, and had to be put back," she admitted. The material "had a way of knowing what it was doing, and was much better left exactly as it was."[14]

For about a week after the final editing and typing of the Text had been completed, Schucman felt relaxed and released from her task. But soon she began to experience a sense of purposelessness. "There was lots of work to do, but somehow it did not fill the void in my life that became increasingly large and oppressive."[15] At the end of six months, Schucman was both emotionally depressed and physically ill, and the thought crossed her mind that there might be more dictation work ahead of her. She mentioned the idea to Thetford, but it was her husband Louis — who had generally paid little attention to the Course project — who seconded her notion that the writing might not be finished. Schucman reacted with predictable exasperation, but six weeks later she began to record the Workbook.

> It was not so hard as the text had been. In the first place, I liked the general format even though I found the first few "lessons" rather trivial. Nevertheless, I thought it swung rather quickly into good style and very acceptable blank verse, a realization which helped me a good deal. Also, the process of writing itself was no longer particularly strange to me. And finally, I approved of the precision of the arrangement of the workbook. It said at the outset exactly what it was going to do, and then proceeded to do it. Even its end was predetermined. It stated at the outset that there would be one lesson a day for a period of one year, and that was exactly the way it turned out.[16]

Schucman's reference to blank verse denotes the fact that large portions of the Course apparently adhere to the Shakespearean meter of iambic pentameter. According to Ken Wapnick, this is true for the two last chapters of the Text in their entirety, as well as everything following Lesson 99 in the Workbook.

Clive Matson, a well-known writing teacher in northern California who earned his MFA in poetry from Columbia University, scanned some pages from the last chapter of the Course Text at my request and reports that the prose he examined showed a consistent iambic rhythm but was not technically pentameter since the form is in prose paragraphs, not ten-beat lines of verse. However, when he picked the following paragraph at random:

> Only the self-accused condemn. As you prepare to make a choice that will result in different outcomes, there is first one thing that must be overlearned. It must become a habit of response so typical of everything you do that it becomes your first response to all temptation, and to every situation that occurs. Learn this, and learn it well, for it is here delay of happiness is shortened by a span of time you cannot realize. You never hate your brother for his sins, but only for your own. Whatever form his sins appear to take, it but obscures the fact that you believe them to be yours, and therefore meriting a "just" attack.[17]

and converted it to ten-beat lines, he discovered that the paragraph broke precisely into sixteen lines of iambic pentameter — "with not one syllable too few or too many," Matson reports. "I was astonished." Another paragraph he selected fit the form exactly as well.

In a rare public appearance at a 1976 panel discussion, Helen Schucman confirmed that the literary style of the Course was one thing that helped make the experience of scribing it tolerable to her: ". . . it is quite a literary thing and it does require a certain background . . . I happen to like this stuff from a literary viewpoint. I'm kind of a snob, but there are many of us. You know, salvation really shouldn't cut us out simply because we're snobs."[18]

With little upset or delay on Schucman's part, the scribing of the Workbook took place from May 1969 to February of 1971, followed by the Manual for Teachers beginning in April 1972 and ending about five months later. From that time until 1978, Schucman would receive dictation for a number of religious poems and two pamphlets, "Psychotherapy: Purpose, Process, and Practice" and "The Song of Prayer." She also received information gathered under the title "Notes on Sound."

A fragmentary technical treatise describing the construction of a device to convert light waves to sound waves in order to measure physical healing, the Notes were expressed in a very different voice from that of the Course. Bill Thetford once theorized that the source of the "Notes on Sound" might have been Schucman's late father, an accomplished metallurgist, from whom Helen had been alienated while growing up. The device proved impossible to build based on her incomplete notes begun in 1972, and she successfully resisted completing the dictation.

How the Course Went Public

In the first few months following the Course's completion, Bill Thetford showed the material to four people: two close friends, a Catholic priest, and Hugh Lynn Cayce, son of the famed psychic and channel Edgar Cayce. According to Robert Skutch's brief Course history *Journey Without Distance*, Cayce felt the work to be "tremendously important" with the potential for changing "millions of lives."[19] Thetford had begun reading the work of Edgar Cayce long before, during the eruption of visions Helen Schucman had experienced just prior to the initial scribing of the Course. When Thetford prevailed upon Schucman at that time to examine the Cayce legacy, she initially dismissed most of it as "spooky." Over time she would positively revise her opinion. In fact Hugh Lynn Cayce became close enough to both Thetford and Schucman that one of the earliest copies of the manuscript would be dubbed "the Hugh Lynn version." (Cayce was not involved in the editing of the Course.)

That was the copy of the manuscript first read by Kenneth Wapnick, Ph.D., who would eschew his chosen life as a monk to work closely with Schucman on further rounds of editing (see Chapter 5) until the end of January 1975. At that point the Course recorders and Wapnick no doubt felt a sense of satisfaction that their extraordinary project was completed. But had it been left up to Schucman, Thetford, and Wapnick — each of them introverted in a different way — the Course might never have progressed beyond a bulky, photocopied manuscript shared gingerly with their confidants. If the Course was to reach a wider audience — and none of the principals felt certain that it should — a different kind of personality would have to enter their small circle.

With Judith Skutch that different personality arrived, as well as what might be called the "third force" of the Course phenomenon. The first force, that of *academic psychology and psychotherapy*, was originally conveyed by the mindset and professional background of Helen Schucman and Bill Thetford, and is still evidenced today by the strong presence of professional therapists and counselors in the Course constituency. The second force of *mystical spirituality* was primarily conveyed by the voice of the Course itself, augmented by the influence of Ken Wapnick, and echoed in the contemporary popularity of ACIM with many ministers and teachers of various faiths. Skutch would facilitate the joining of these forces with the ill-defined, much-maligned social current of the last several decades called the *New Age*.

While these three forces overlap in a number of ways — both within the Course community and within the culture at large — they are sufficiently dissimilar in essence to have spawned a great deal of confusion about the true nature of *A Course in*

Miracles. Their confluence in one phenomenon has made the Course appear to be a variety of things to students, critics, and the public at large.

Skutch's connection to New Age culture lay in her long-standing involvement in parapsychology. The Brooklyn-born daughter of Samuel Rothstein, a prominent figure in organized world Jewry, Skutch was raised in a busy household full of people having meetings, discussing intriguing ideas, and founding organizations — a social condition that she has apparently replicated throughout her adult life. (In my visits to the publishing office of the Foundation for Inner Peace, housed in the home of Judy and her third husband William Whitson[20], it was unusual for there *not* to be at least two meetings going on simultaneously.)

Prior to encountering ACIM, Judy and her second husband Bob Skutch ran a sort of ongoing "consciousness salon" in their spacious apartment on Central Park West, as well as an organization called the Foundation for ParaSensory Investigation. Judy taught continuing education courses at New York University, and the Skutch household guested the likes of psychic showman Uri Geller, guru Baba Muktananda, alternative oncologist Dr. Carl Simonton, and a host of other prominent and esoteric personalities.

A few weeks before she would encounter the Course, Skutch felt herself painfully trapped in a paradox of opposite emotions. "It looked like I had a perfect, exciting life," she recalls. "We had a house in Connecticut and a large apartment in New York with plenty of rooms for all sorts of meetings to go on at once. It was a fulfilling and electric time to be alive. But deep down inside I could feel myself sinking into a real pit of despair. Somehow I knew I wasn't really fulfilled, and I didn't even know what that meant. I was talking about healing all the time and didn't feel the least bit healed myself. One night I locked myself in the bathroom and started pounding my head against the wall, asking in tears, 'Won't somebody up there please help me?' I know now that what I was experiencing was spiritual deprivation. But I didn't know that at the time."

Soon Skutch consulted with a numerologist who told her that she would shortly meet a much older woman who would be the most important teacher of her life, and also that she would become involved in publishing a highly significant spiritual document. With only a little publishing experience in her background, Skutch was skeptical of the prediction. Nine days later she met Bill Thetford and Helen Schucman at the Columbia-Presbyterian Medical Center's cafeteria, introduced by a mutual friend who thought the two psychologists might be interested in Skutch's explorations of holistic healing. As Skutch has described the meeting:

> After the usual small talk, I brought up the subject I had wanted to discuss, but neither of them showed any interest in holistic health. Bill and Helen kept talking about research in general, and the more they talked the more I wondered what I was doing there. Then I began to feel there was something on Helen's mind that she was not revealing, though for the life of me I couldn't imagine what it might be. All I knew was that it didn't have anything to do with the research designs she was discussing. And then, as we were eating our desserts, I heard myself saying something I couldn't believe. I turned to Helen, and out of my mouth came "You hear an inner voice, don't you?"
>
> Helen blanched, and there was a strained look on her face as she said, very faintly, "What did you say?"
>
> Bill pushed his chair back from the table, saying, "Why don't we all go back to our office? I think we'd be a lot more comfortable there."[21]

In the office Skutch was introduced to Ken Wapnick and told, over the ensuing two hours, the story of the scribing of ACIM. She left their office awkwardly hefting the entire manuscript in a shopping bag, already intuiting that the Course might well become her life's work. She began reading the manuscript that night, never stopping to sleep.

That was how Judy Skutch entered the small circle of Course intimates for whom the material was the focus of their lives. Meeting with Schucman, Thetford, and Wapnick three or four times weekly in her apartment, Skutch asked them to do the Workbook exercises with her for a year. (That would make the third time through for Thetford and Schucman, and the second for Wapnick.) Some of the effects of the Course on the Skutch family — as well as some unintended uses — are portrayed in the following diary excerpts written by Tamara Cohen, Skutch's daughter by her first marriage, when she was sixteen:

> I find the Course very interesting but I have to admit that I'm getting tired of the whole thing. Mom's always talking about changing perceptions, being guiltless and seeing everything through love . . .
>
> A real miracle is that Mom has been reading and practicing the Course for about a year now, and I hate to admit it but she's actually changed a lot. . . . at the beginning of her work with the Course, I knew how to get her to fight with me. I'd follow her around the house and gripe and grumble. Then, just when she would start to get furious with me, I'd say "Ah-ah-ah, remember the Course! This is all an illusion. You're not practicing love!" Boy, that would infuriate her! . . .
>
> Now she's been working with the material for a year, and when I come home looking for a fight, I don't get one . . . Although *A Course in Miracles* has inhibited the good scraps around here, it's also helped me gain more independence . . . When I'm going out late, I make sure to tell my mother while she is in front of other people. When she expresses her fears, I reply directly from ACIM: "In my defenselessness, my safety lies."[22]

(Cohen survived her own adolescent manipulations of the Course teaching, and in recent years has worked for the Foundation for Inner Peace conducting archival interviews with contemporaries of Helen Schucman and Bill Thetford.)

If Schucman, Thetford, and Wapnick lacked a certain public-relations savvy, it's obvious that Judy Skutch made up for all of them and then some. Thetford once joked that Skutch was taking their little group to a New Age gathering in order to meet five thousand of her closest friends. In fact, Skutch's enthusiasm for spreading the word about the Course induced Schucman, Thetford and Wapnick to engage in a brief period of traveling and speaking about the Course, from California (where they met Jerry Jampolsky; see Chapter 4) to London. This phase would not last long, however, as Schucman did not enjoy the limelight, and both she and Thetford did not wish to shoulder the burden of ACIM's "public life."

That was clearly the work of Judith Skutch. Distributing several hundred photo-reduced versions of the Course under the auspices of the Foundation for ParaSensory Investigation, Skutch became aware that interest in the Course was growing "exponentially." Several offers to publish the material professionally in abridged forms surfaced but were refused; as Skutch has written, "As [the Course] had not been edited for simplification, it seemed it should not be edited for profit-making, and we knew we had not yet come across the appropriate method for printing and distributing it."[23]

Finally, on Valentine's Day 1976 the ACIM inner circle met to discuss the need to publish the Course quickly. Deciding to consult the Voice of the Course as a group, Skutch, Wapnick, Thetford, and Schucman silently asked for guidance, and as Skutch relates, each received a different directive:

Helen had heard that those who will devote their lives to this alone should do the job. I had heard that it should be a nonprofit organization, so those who could not afford the price could receive scholarship copies as a "gift of love." Bill added that the Course should not be changed in any

way from the original, and Ken's directive was that somehow or other we must all be involved.[24]

In short order the group realized that they constituted the
only group who fit all these criteria, and that must mean that
they were destined to publish it. When they further asked
where the money was to come from, neither Thetford nor Wapnick heard an answer. Schucman reported that she felt "Judy
will be told what to do," and indeed Skutch received the unspecific message: "Make the commitment first." Realizing that this
could mean the commitment of all her assets to the publication
of the Course, Skutch nonetheless assented.

But the next morning Skutch received a phone call from Reed
Erickson, a wealthy industrialist in Mazatlán, Mexico, who was
studying a photocopied manuscript of the Course. He urged
Skutch to print a hardcover edition of the Course as soon as possible, and she informed him that the decision to do so had been
made without knowing where the money would come from.
Erickson then revealed that he had called to offer the proceeds of
a real estate sale to cover the printing of five thousand hardcover copies of ACIM. Erickson subsequently sent a check for
$20,000 (the first third of the total expense) directly to Long Is-
land printer Saul Steinberg, who shepherded the production of
the Course through typesetting, printing, and binding in a remarkably short time. The entire project was completed by June
22, 1976, the official publication date of *A Course in Miracles*.

By that time the name of Bob and Judy Skutch's nonprofit organization — the Foundation for ParaSensory Investigation —
had been changed to the Foundation for Inner Peace according
to guidance received by Helen Schucman. On this point at least,
Schucman apparently felt no resistance to the instruction she
received. After all, as Ken Wapnick recalls, she regarded psychics
and channelers and the like as "funny people."

William Thetford and Helen Schucman in New York City, 1975 (Photo courtesy of The Foundation for Inner Peace)

2
Who Were Schucman and Thetford?

At least fifteen percent of the general population sooner or later "hears" an inner voice offering information or guidance, according to psychologist Arthur Hastings, author of a study of channeling entitled *With the Tongues of Men and Angels*. "Regardless of the validity of the claims of supernatural agency, the fact remains that mentally healthy individuals experience these phenomena," he writes. "Moreover, a large number of these messages contain meaningful information and exhibit knowledge and talents of which the channeler is completely unaware." [1]

The whole notion of channeling has an irreducible arguability to it: either you find it credible or you don't. While virtually every prominent channel has claimed to be surprised by the initiation of his or her exotic talent, Helen Schucman appears to be unique in her long-term resistance and resentment of an extraordinary channeling task that she nonetheless completed — not to mention her unwillingness to become a spokesperson for the message she recorded.

If one finds it credible that the historical Jesus Christ would choose anyone to record a lengthy lecture to the modern world, it's worth examining the characters of Helen Schucman and Bill Thetford to investigate the sort of question Schucman herself posed: Why them? If one finds it credible only that these two sophisticated psychologists worked for seven years in service to Schucman's conscious design or subconscious ideation, the source of the Course certainly appears less supernatural — but all the more enigmatic.

Helen Schucman, the Angry Mystic

The first major critical examination of ACIM appeared in *Psychology Today* in September 1980, in an article by former *Time* magazine writer John Koffend entitled "The Gospel According to Helen." Characterizing the Course as the latest item in a "veritable supermarket of cults, religions, and psycho-mystical movements" arising in America, the article cast doubt on the veracity of the Course's genesis story and questioned the reluctance of Schucman and Thetford to take personal credit for their labor.[2] At the time, Schucman was still alive but declined to be interviewed. "If Christ was so willing to identify himself to a mere mortal named Helen," the article charged, "why are she and Bill Thetford so reluctant to admit their complicity in the Lord's work?"[3]

Written before the rise to celebrity of such publicity-conscious channelers as J.Z. Knight (Ramtha) and Kevin Ryerson, this dated criticism now reads almost like praise. But a substantial degree of perplexity has existed over the paradoxical character of Helen Schucman, leading to the spread of misinformation about her personality and religious background. In a skeptical examination of channeling appearing in *The Fringes of Reason*, a 1989 special edition of the Whole Earth Catalog, editor Ted Schultz raised the possibility that the Course is a massive artifact of "cryptomnesia," or hidden memory. Using quotes first published in Jon Klimo's book *Channeling* (St. Martin's Press), Schultz cited two well-known sources from the counterculture of psychology:

. . . Esalen co-founder Michael Murphy points out: "[Schucman] was raised on that kind of [spiritualist] literature.

Her father owned a metaphysical bookshop." And transpersonal psychologist Ken Wilber says, "There's much more of Helen in the Course than I first thought. She was brought up mystically inclined. At four she used to stand out on the balcony and say that God would give her a sign of miracles to let her know he was there. Many ideas from the Course came from the new thought or metaphysical schools she had been influenced by . . ."[4]

Both Murphy and Wilber were incorrect. According to Schucman's autobiography, her father Sigmund Cohn, a successful career chemist and metallurgist whose parents had been Jewish and Lutheran, evinced no spiritual inclinations himself. In the longest talk she could remember having with him, he answered her childish questions about God with a studied neutrality. Although Schucman's mother dabbled in both Theosophy and Christian Science at different periods, the young Helen was emotionally estranged from both parents; the chief religious influences on her early life were a Roman Catholic governess and a black Baptist maid. Helen was actually baptized in the maid's church in early adolescence, but was disappointed to feel nothing change within her afterwards. In adulthood Schucman would develop a lifelong fascination with the rituals of the Catholic church, but never considered conversion to the faith.

It was Helen's husband Louis Schucman who owned a bookshop featuring rare books and Americana. According to Helen he "riffled through some material on mysticism on and off, finding the subject of some interest though hardly worthy of scientific investigation."[5] Thus there is little evidence of "new thought" or metaphysical schools exerting significant influence on Schucman before the transcription of the Course, as noted in her own writing in Chapter 1.

In response to the mystical experiences that Schucman had begun sharing with him, Bill Thetford was developing an interest in esoterica in the months before transcription of the Course. He convinced Schucman to accompany him to the Virginia

Beach headquarters of the Edgar Cayce foundation, the Association for Research and Enlightenment, in the late summer of 1965, shortly before the first words of the Course were taken down. As noted earlier, the Cayce connection made Schucman uneasy at first, and she resisted examining that material then. Thetford continued an exhaustive study of comparative religion and mysticism after the Course transcription had begun, but Schucman read only sparingly in the field, usually at Thetford's insistence.

Once on a family trip to Lourdes at age twelve, Schucman actually did stand on a balcony one evening and ask God for the miracle sign of a shooting star which, to her amazement, she received. But an inner conflict between religious faith and scientific rationality that would characterize Schucman's later life was apparent even then, for the adolescent girl promptly debunked her own mystical experience:

> I stood quite still until the stars had faded away and the sky was dark again. And then I remembered. Our guide had told us that this was the time for meteor showers in this part of the world, and they would be coming pretty often soon. It was not really a miracle at all . . . Perhaps, I said to myself, the water and the healings and the crutches were all like the meteor shower. People just thought they were miracles. It all could happen that way. You can get fooled so easily.[6]

By the time Schucman reached college, her adolescent religiosity was waning as she became "happily involved in systems of thought, the laws of reasoning, and logic in particular." She also experienced a secret ambition which she found herself unable to fulfill. While pleasing her mother with the announced plan to become, like her, an English teacher, Schucman actually "had no doubt that some day I would be a great writer, probably an internationally famous novelist. I would live by myself and write. I would be different from other people, but distinctly better. In view of my secret goal, the intense difficulty I had in writing anything was particularly trying to me."[7]

Also trying for Schucman was a life-threatening illness not long after her college graduation that initiated an anger with God that would never entirely abate. Overweight, insecure, and very lonely as a child — her brother was fourteen years older — Schucman developed a severe eating disorder in her teens that resulted in a serious gall bladder condition by her early twenties. Having put off inevitable surgery for months while living in increasing pain, Schucman decided to give God a try on the night before her operation:

> There was a chance, I supposed, that he existed after all. Certainly the fact that I did not believe in him had nothing to do with his existence one way or another. In any case, there could be no harm in attempting a reasonable compromise. I would put the operation in God's hands in case he existed, and if things turned out all right I might even be able to believe in him again. There was nothing to lose by trying. I said the Lord's prayer, put my operation in the hands of God, and went to the hospital the next day with my medal of the Blessed Virgin around my neck.[8]

But Schucman nearly died, and she would not be able to leave the hospital for four months. Unconscious for a long time after the surgery, she awoke to find herself in the care of a deeply religious nurse who said that it was a "miracle" Schucman had pulled through — a miracle for which the nurse had already offered a mass of thanksgiving.

"I did not see it that way myself," recalled Schucman. "If this was God's idea of making things turn out all right, I thought, he certainly had a nasty sense of humor . . . I told the nurse I could not stop her from praying, of course, but added that I would appreciate her not asking God for another miracle until I was at least strong enough to cope with this one."[9]

In later years, as Schucman took up post-graduate work in

psychology, she "shifted from agnosticism to angry atheism," arming herself with "scientific weapons, prepared and even eager to do battle with ideas even remotely religiously toned. . . . I firmly believed I had overcome superstition at last, and was finally looking at things realistically."[10] By Schucman's account, this was her anti-religious and decidedly bitter state of mind by the time she became a colleague of Bill Thetford.

But Ken Wapnick, a near-constant companion of Schucman in her later years, was never convinced that she so thoroughly divorced herself from God. "Helen's atheism makes a good story," he suggests, "but it's not really true. You can't be that militant against something unless you believe in it at some level. There were periods of Helen's life when she went to Mass every day; she was attracted to it without believing in it. She had two purses full of Catholic rosaries and medals, accumulated prior to the Course. She had a deep knowledge of the Bible. Helen really adopted a pose, because she was a psychologist who *had* to be an atheist."

She was also a natural-born visionary periodically entranced by mystical experiences that left her breathless. Having married the bookish Louis Schucman in 1933 at the age of twenty-three, Helen found a reassuring stability in their dependable if somewhat dispassionate relationship. That did not mean she was above resenting him fiercely. When he once insisted that they take a subway instead of a cab to a social engagement on a wintry evening, she sulked angrily in her seat as Louis sat calmly reading the paper:

> I grew increasingly sure I would come down with a pneumonia, probably in both lungs. As an additional hazard, people were coughing and sneezing all around us, and I could almost see the germs attacking. I became convinced that my husband's thoughtlessness would probably have a fatal outcome. His contented absorption in his newspaper did not help matters, either. Besides being dangerous, the whole situation struck me as thoroughly revolting. The

train smelled of garlic and peanuts, and the people looked shabby and dirty. Across the aisle a child with hands streaked with chocolate patted his mother's face and left smudgy fingerprints on her cheek. Next to her, another mother was wiping off her coat where her baby had thrown up. A child a few seats down picked up some chewing gum from the floor and put it in his mouth. At the far end of the train a group of old men were arguing heatedly and perspiring freely. I closed my eyes in disgust, feeling sick to my stomach.

And then a stunning thing happened. It was as though a blinding light blazed up behind my eyes and filled my mind entirely. Without opening my eyes, I seemed to see a figure of myself walking directly into the light. She seemed to know exactly what she was doing. It was, in fact, as if the situation was completely familiar to her. For a moment she paused and knelt down, touching the ground with elbows, wrists and forehead in what looked like an Eastern expression of deep reverence. Then she got up, walked to the side, and knelt again, this time resting her head as if leaning against a giant knee. The outline of a huge arm seemed to reach around her and she disappeared. The light grew even brighter, and I felt the most indescribably intense love streaming from it to me. It was so powerful that I literally gasped and opened my eyes.

I saw the light an instant longer, during which I loved everyone on the train with that same incredible intensity. Then the light faded and the old picture of dirt and ugliness returned. The contrast was truly shocking. It took me several minutes to regain a semblance of composure. Then I reached uncertainly for my husband's hand.[11]

At that point Helen tried to explain her stunning experience of light and all-encompassing love to Louis. Patting her hand and assuring Helen that it sounded like "a very common mystical experience," Louis then told her not to give it another thought —

a response that would remain characteristic of Louis' attitude toward all spiritual matters, including the Course, in the years to come.

Meeting "The One I'm Supposed to Help"

Schucman was undecided about a profession all the way through her thirties. She tried more than once to partner Louis at his bookstore, but they tended to quarrel. Even after she decided to pursue graduate work in psychology, she expressed doubt about the choice and hesitated to enact it. Finally she did return to New York University in 1952, where she had done her undergraduate studies, and earned a Ph.D. in clinical psychology by 1957. The fact that she finished near the top of her class was remarkable considering that she was phobic about both reading and writing; Ken Wapnick would later tease her about being nearly a "functional illiterate."

Nonetheless her term papers earned high compliments from her professors, and soon after graduation she wrote a successful grant proposal based on her doctoral thesis about the learning abilities of children with severe mental retardation. With the offer of a teaching position at NYU, Schucman's long-delayed vocation seemed to be shifting into gear. Envisioning herself at the head of a large research department, Schucman submitted several additional grant proposals that would definitively launch her career.

Finding herself highly anxious on the day the grants were being considered, she wandered into a Catholic church, lit a candle, and presented God with a "non-negotiable demand" that her proposals be approved. But she walked angrily out of the church knowing somehow that her plans would not play out as she wished. Indeed, the grants were rejected that evening and Schucman spent the next several weeks feeling bitter and depressed, refusing to exploit any number of professional connections that could have easily landed her a job.

When she finally roused herself to call a colleague, he immediately provided her with a list of promising leads. But that same colleague then took a call from William Thetford, a recent arrival at Columbia-Presbyterian Medical Center, asking if he knew of a good research psychologist for a project Thetford had to staff. Schucman then received an urgent call from her contact, who told her to forget the list he'd just given her and call Thetford immediately. As Schucman recalled their meeting:

> As I walked into his office a few days later I made the first of a series of silent remarks that I did not understand myself, and to which I paid little attention at the time.
>
> "And there he is," I said to myself. "He's the one I'm supposed to help."
>
> I was to make a somewhat similar remark a few days later, after Bill and I got to know each other better. It was another of those odd, unrelated things that somehow began to break into my consciousness without any connection with my ongoing life. For a brief interval I seemed to be somewhere else, saying, as if in answer to a silent but urgent call, "Of course I'll go, Father. He's stuck and needs help. Besides, it will be only for such a little while!" The situation had something of the quality of a half-forgotten memory, and I was aware only of being in a very happy place. I had no idea to whom I was speaking, but I somehow knew I was making a definite commitment that I would not break.[12]

Like herself, Schucman's new boss had ended up at Columbia-Presbyterian by an unexpected route. Previously employed at the Cornell University Medical Center, Thetford had been urged by a friend to apply for the position of head of the Psychology Department at Presbyterian Hospital. Ambivalent about the opportunity, Thetford attempted a characteristically indirect maneuver. He requested that he also be appointed an associate professor, thinking that his presumption would make him an undesirable candidate. But his request was eventually granted, and Thetford joined Columbia-Presbyterian in February 1958.

When Helen Schucman met Thetford a few months later, she thought he looked haggard and in need of supportive company. But she found her new position "ghastly," and they were both extremely uncomfortable working in a highly competitive academic and medical environment. Over the next seven years Schucman felt that things got worse instead of better; she described their professional predicament this way:

> Bill was apt to withdraw when he perceived a situation as demanding or coercive, which he frequently did. . . . He rarely attacked openly when he was angry or irritated, which he frequently was, but was much more likely to become increasingly aloof and unresponsive, and then openly angry. I, on the other hand, tended to become over-involved and then to feel hopelessly trapped and resentful. . . . Bill and I seemed to be trapped in a relationship which, although we hated it in many ways, could not be escaped.[13]

In retrospect, these unlikely partners would conclude that their relationship could not be escaped because it was there to serve a purpose other than their worldly profession. When Thetford finally made his "There must be another way" speech to Schucman in June 1965 — admitting later that every word of it felt trite and sentimental — Schucman unexpectedly found herself filled with the conviction that he was right, and that she would join him wholeheartedly in the attempt to look at their personal and professional difficulties in a new light, and pursue cooperation over competition.

Ultimately the better way to which these two committed themselves reaped greater benefits between them and their colleagues than between the two of them. But almost immediately Schucman began to experience frequent episodes of what Thetford later described as "heightened visual imagery."[14] Since childhood Schucman had always seen clear mental pictures, like black-and-white snapshots, whenever she closed her eyes: "The pictures could be of anything; a woman with a dog, trees in the rain, a shoestore window, a birthday cake with lighted candles, a flight of stairs down the side of a cliff."[15]

Between June and September 1965, however, these mental pictures took on new qualities of color, motion, and sometimes plot. They were essentially dreams except that Schucman did not have to be asleep to see them. Some occurred during Schucman's early attempts to meditate, a discipline that Thetford was reading about at the time. Irritated by his enthusiasm, Schucman "did not feel that our agreement to try a new approach to problems justified entering into 'crackpot' areas."[16] Nonetheless, she consented to meditating with Thetford for a short period each day, and to doing it on her own in the morning and just before bed.

The "dreams" that Schucman experienced during these and other periods of repose constituted a progressive recognition of an inner metaphorical and spiritual life — a life in which she often appeared to be some kind of priestess from ancient times, as well as other figures in a variety of historical periods. Thetford sometimes appeared in them as well.[17]

In the dream perhaps best known to Course aficionados, Schucman found herself floating down a stream in a small boat, deciding to use a grappling hook to recover what she knew must be "buried treasure" on the stream bed. She pulled up a large chest, which to her disappointment contained neither jewels nor coins, but only a large black manuscript binder with the word "Aesculapius" (the Greek god of healing) on the spine. Only much later, well after transcription of the Course had begun, did Schucman and Thetford realize that the dream book resembled the binders in which they secured the transcription of Schucman's dictation from the Voice.

Along with the dreams also came a number of psychic experiences. Schucman once found herself certain that a distant friend was considering suicide, and tried to mentally send him the message that "the answer is life, not death." That evening Thetford called the man and learned that he had indeed been so severely depressed that afternoon as to pick up a gun and consider shooting himself. But some feeling he couldn't describe had changed his mind.

At another time Schucman became convinced that she and Thetford would see a church — whose details she could precisely describe from an inner vision — when they went to visit the Mayo Clinic in Rochester, Minnesota. But the church was not in the area near the clinic where she had expected it. Finding it became so "outrageously important" to Schucman that she and Thetford hunted down twenty-four churches in the town before giving up. On their way out of town, Thetford picked up a historical guidebook at the airport that showed a picture of Schucman's church; it had been torn down years before to accommodate the Mayo Clinic.

What Schucman later called this "magic phase" of waking dreams and psychic intuitions essentially ended with the vision in which she saw the words "GOD IS" on an ancient scroll and accepted that message as "all I want." Shortly thereafter, the dictation of *A Course in Miracles* would begin.

A Forceful Helper

The plentiful stories of Helen Schucman's phobias, mystical experiences, and religious ambivalence could suggest a portrait of a dotty, anxiety-plagued woman who achieved little of substance in her life besides the scribing of an esoteric spiritual manuscript. In fact she was an accomplished academic who held down a demanding position in a high-pressure atmosphere for most of twenty years, progressing from the rank of assistant to associate professor and impressing many with her intellect and her direct, sometimes forceful advice to friends and associates. Never desiring children of her own, she nonetheless developed a special fondness for the severely retarded children with whom she worked for years at a New York clinic. And she was unarguably devoted, sometimes to the point of possessiveness, to the new "family" of spiritual intimates delivered to her by ACIM.

Judy Skutch was one recipient of Schucman's focused attention. "I have to preface everything about Helen by saying that she was the greatest teacher I have ever known," declares Skutch. "And I was forty-four when I met her, and had a lot of life experience as well as a good bit of schooling and graduate work." Still, Skutch admits, Schucman "was not an easy teacher. She didn't mince words. She went right to the heart of things, sometimes so fast that it took your breath away. You felt as if someone had thrown a basketball hard in your stomach, because the wind had been knocked out of you by something she said, and she was right.

"This didn't make her the easiest person in the world to be with," adds Skutch. "But that forcefulness was tempered with loving advice, discussions about family members, shopping trips together, that kind of thing. I was clearly a junior, and she was an elder; I called her Mama and she called me Kitten."

Skutch recalls that Schucman did not try to influence her personal decisions except as they pertained to the Course. While clearly relieved and appreciative that Skutch was assuming the public-relations duties associated with publication of the Course, Schucman was nonetheless "a little apprehensive about the Course being brought into a community interested in psychism, because Helen did not feel that was what the Course was about. I think my having taught at NYU gave me the right credentials, in Helen's mind, for bringing the Course to public awareness.

"She was very concerned about my appearance as a Course representative," Skutch continues. "There was still some hippie stuff going on in the seventies, and although I was really too old for it, I still liked it. But this was not a style Helen liked on me, and she asked me not to wear it when I spoke about the Course. She also didn't like high heels; she thought they were unsafe and too suggestive in a sexual way. One day she said we were going shopping for new shoes, and she made me buy a pair of shoes exactly like hers: totally flat with round toes and crêpe soles, the Mary Jane style. Personally I wouldn't have been caught dead in shoes like that, but she insisted this was a better style for me."

Like the other Course principals, Skutch saw two Helen Schucmans: "There was the Helen who was fearful, contracted, controlling, suspicious, judgmental, and at times irrational. That was the Helen I felt uncomfortable with, because I never knew where I was at with her. And then there was the Helen who handed me *A Course in Miracles*, who took it down in as pure a form as possible, and gave it to me to give to the world. That was the Helen whom I revered, and my real teacher.

"The fact that there were those two Helens reminded me that I am equally split," reflects Skutch. "There's the personality that I consider myself to be — the ego — and there's the higher consciousness that I consider my Self. Helen allowed me to see which one was taking charge at different times."

It should also be noted that many people outside Helen Schucman's intimate circle saw only her helping aspect, whether they were Course students or not. Jon Mundy, who met Schucman about a month before Judy Skutch, received "a lot of personal counseling from Helen, and I always found her very helpful, very intuitive. I don't think I was close enough to experience her difficult side."

In telephone conversations and a few face-to-face encounters, Schucman counseled Mundy on such subjects as whether he should break up with a girlfriend — "she said, 'I think you'd better let her go,' which was something I didn't want to hear at the time but it soon proved to be right on target" — to breaking with the Methodist church, where he served as a minister for fourteen years. "Every time I was ready to chuck the whole thing, Helen thought it was important that I stay." (Mundy did eventually break with the Methodists to start his own eclectic ministry, the Interfaith Fellowship in New York City; see Chapter 3).

Finally, there were many people — relatives, parents of retarded children, academic colleagues — who turned to Helen Schucman for advice and never heard of ACIM. In fact it appears that the majority of people who directly encountered her in her professional and daily life in New York City did not know of the monumental task that she ambivalently referred to as her true "life's work." As Ken Wapnick has observed:

To practically all who knew her, then, Helen was a brilliant research psychologist, witty conversationalist, a friend eager to be of professional help to those in distress, a woman immaculate in appearance and prone to excessive shopping (with a weakness for jewelry and shoes), and a somewhat neurotic person preoccupied with sickness and the threat of inclement weather; but hardly one whose internal life centered on religious concerns that directly involved Jesus: a well-kept secret indeed.[18]

Bill Thetford, the Shy Professor

Born in 1923, William Thetford was the last of three children in a middle-class Chicago family traumatized by tragic losses. A brother died in infancy, and when Thetford was nine, his eleven-year-old sister contracted streptococcus. Although his parents were Christian Scientists, they consulted both medical doctors and church practitioners for their daughter, to no avail. After her death Thetford's parents renounced their religion and became socially withdrawn, curtailing their son's religious experience in childhood. His parents were still grieving their daughter's death when Thetford himself contracted a severe case of scarlet fever, soon compounded with rheumatic fever. In recovery he suffered a cardiac infarction, and his survival looked doubtful.

Several months of intensive care preserved the young boy's life, but he would not be able to rise from bed for two years. Missing three years of schooling altogether, he was tutored by his mother in arithmetic and spent most of his time reading voraciously. Although he returned to school as a fourth-grader, he was moved ahead and graduated from the eighth grade within two years, and would later finish high school with honors. He majored uncertainly in psychology at DePauw University in Indiana, also enrolling in premed in case that proved to be a more definitive career opportunity. Deferred from military service because of his childhood illness, Thetford graduated from DePauw

45

in 1944 with an acceptance of his application to the University of Chicago Medical School in hand, although he was still uncertain about his future vocation.

At that point a pattern of accelerated opportunities began to take shape in Thetford's life. Because World War II had created a shortage of talented manpower in many professional areas, Thetford's first college job carried considerable responsibility. He was placed on the University of Chicago's faculty payroll as an administrative officer overseeing buildings that served as testing areas for top-secret atomic research. At one point Thetford was in charge of a decontamination team that tried to "clean" radioactive areas, and he wore a Geiger counter at work from morning til night. Excited by the strategic urgency of this work and still ambivalent about his prospective career, he decided not to pursue medical school in the fall of 1944, remaining in his position with the atomic research project.

But with the dropping of the first atomic bomb on Hiroshima in August 1945, Thetford's sympathies reversed abruptly. "I think all of us were aghast at the extent of the devastation," he wrote, "and I felt clearly that my participation on the project had come to an end. Since I no longer felt a moral commitment to continue, I resigned that same month."[19]

A few weeks later Thetford took the suggestion of some friends in graduate school to sign up for a course on "Client-Centered Psychotherapy" being offered by a new professor on campus, Dr. Carl Rogers. "For reasons which are as obscure to me now as they were then,"[20] wrote Thetford, Rogers quickly appointed Thetford as an instructor in the course and also asked him to become a research assistant at a new counseling center. Thetford protested that he was unqualified, but Rogers insisted that he accept these roles in the study and development of a new psychotherapy founded on the premise of "unconditional positive regard." As Thetford recalled, "for me to have gone directly from being involved with total annihilation to a professional practice based on perfect love seemed, to say the least, ironic."[21]

After receiving his Ph.D. in psychology in 1949, still feeling "thoroughly unqualified for practically anything," Thetford took a position with the Michael Reese Hospital in Chicago, working on a project under the direction of Dr. Samuel J. Beck, the leading authority on Rorschach testing. It was during his two and a half years there that Thetford developed the conviction that he should never be a university professor, despite several academic job offers, because "I felt I had nothing to profess, and was unwilling to put myself in a position where this might become apparent to others."[22]

Thetford later enrolled at a school of psychiatry in Washington, D.C., that emphasized the importance of interpersonal relations in therapy. This was followed by a directorship at a psychiatric institute in Hartford, Connecticut, and then an appointment as chief psychologist under Harold G. Wolff, a leading specialist in psychosomatic medicine, at Cornell University. Thetford's antipathy to the academic life had eased by this time, and "before I knew it I became an instructor and a year later I was promoted to assistant professor."[23] About a year later, in 1957, Thetford would ambivalently but successfully pursue the position at Columbia University that would lead to the intersection of his life with Helen Schucman's.

Whether one views it as happenstance or predestined preparation, several major elements of Thetford's character made him suitable to become Schucman's helper in the recording of the Course. Perhaps most significant was his reluctance to "profess" a distinct philosophy of his own. It's safe to assume that few academics of his status could have resisted the temptation to revise, add to, or even co-opt a major project on which they were assisting a junior colleague, regardless of the project's nature or origin.

Second, Thetford's intellectual curiosity and flexibility would counterbalance Schucman's judgmental tendency, and help both of them deal with a system of psycho-spiritual thought that substantially challenged their psychoanalytic training. Thetford's brush with humanistic psychology may have also prepared him for the transpersonal dimensions of the Course material.

Finally, the younger professor's passivity is probably what

made it possible for him to tolerate Helen Schucman's contrariness, albeit not happily. It remains a sad irony that the tenuous balance of the relationship between the two Course recorders never matured into a healthy reciprocity. In 1977, the year following publication of ACIM, Schucman was forced to retire from Columbia-Presbyterian at age sixty-eight, having managed to remain on staff two years past retirement age. In 1978 Thetford took an early retirement and moved to California along with Bob and Judy Skutch and the Foundation for Inner Peace. Although they spoke often by phone and occasionally saw each other, Thetford and Schucman essentially parted ways without directly resolving the many difficult issues of almost twenty years of professional relationship.

In California, where he often said he was practicing forgiveness full-time, Thetford became a dedicated student of the Course in various venues while steadfastly refusing to become identified as a teacher or spokesman. Schucman progressively withdrew from both Course-related activities and society in general until the terminal illness that struck her in 1980, leading to her almost complete isolation before she died the following year.

Frances Vaughan, a leading figure in transpersonal psychology (see Chapter 6), got to know Bill Thetford well after he moved to Tiburon, a peaceful and affluent bayside town in Marin County that is home to the Foundation for Inner Peace as well as Vaughan, her husband Roger Walsh, and Jerry Jampolsky. Meeting with Thetford in a small Course study group every day for two years, and then twice a week for several years thereafter, Vaughan was always impressed with his sincerity, self-effacing quality, and serious commitment to personal change through the application of Course principles.

"Bill felt that the Course was a sacred trust that he and Helen had been charged with," Vaughan recalls. "He really did commit himself to using it, whereas Helen always maintained a certain resistance. Bill was able to transform all the other relationships he'd had at Columbia that had been so problematic, and by the time he retired he felt that he had made peace with those people." Vaughan says that he also resolved his differences with others close to the Course, such as Ken Wapnick.

"Bill and Ken were polarized at times," Vaughan remembers, "because they did not have the same interpretations of the Course on a number of points. For instance, Ken always emphasized that the source of the material was the historical Jesus; Bill thought of it more as the universal Christ-mind or consciousness that we all share."

Also unlike Wapnick, Thetford would become increasingly open to a liberal variety of Course applications. Vaughan credits Thetford with teaching her "to take my judgments more lightly, because I was prone to get upset when I thought somebody was distorting or misinterpreting the Course. He accepted that everybody has a different perception of the Course, and that's okay because we can't know how the teaching will affect people working with it in different ways."

Indeed, during the last two years of his life spent in La Jolla, near San Diego in southern California, Thetford became affiliated with a social set of Course students whom his New York academic colleagues doubtlessly would have perceived as New Age and "touchy-feely." While Ken Wapnick has written that the Bill Thetford of northern California was always "a slight shock" for him to see — "Bill in sneakers and blue jeans, he who while in New York was almost never without a jacket and tie"[24] — the Bill Thetford of southern California loosened up even further. In a lengthy interview published in *Miracles Magazine*, La Jolla Course teachers Jack and Eulalia Luckett recalled how Thetford learned to accept group hugs, try hands-on healing, enjoy singing in a group, and even wear a silly party hat at a birthday party he had initially refused to allow for himself.

"Nobody in Tiburon had ever seen this face of Billy . . ." Jack Luckett remarked. "Jerry [Jampolsky] would call every now and then, or he would come down, and would see the growth in Bill. And he would thank everybody, for he could see the opening up, the blossoming . . . the comfort Bill had with himself." Luckett also recalled that Thetford allowed he was getting "too old not to be flexible," and in a demonstration of his lifelong love of puns, thereafter referred to himself often as "flexi-Bill."[25]

"I always appreciated Bill's sense of humor," Frances Vaughan recalls, "and his lack of pretension about being forgiving or even particularly good. He was shy, a very private person and contemplative by nature. He could live a very monklike existence and be at peace with that."

Although Thetford was reportedly often depressed and there are indications that his intimate life was quite troubled at times — it was probably not easy to be a gay man in East Coast academia from the fifties to the seventies — his private nature seems to have limited how much was known by others about his personal struggles. It is known that he lived with a male lover in New York for ten years, and with a woman in northern California for four; one close observer opines that Thetford was "mentally straight but biologically gay." What seems most likely is that his almost overwhelming tendency toward ambivalence permeated every aspect of his life. Frances Vaughan says, for instance, that despite her long friendship with Thetford she couldn't hazard a guess about his politics — "there were aspects of life on which Bill just didn't make a statement," she recalls.

While Thetford consistently resisted adulation or the assignation of "Course expert" status by other students, he is widely remembered for how he settled a spat between two men who had disagreed long and vociferously over the meaning of a particular passage in the Course. Finally they asked Thetford to settle the dispute with an authoritative reading.

"He told them, 'If you can't agree, just tear the page out,'" Vaughan reports. "For Bill the message of the Course was not in the letter of it but in the spirit of love and forgiveness."

"Getting Out of Its Way"

A final contrast between the characters of Helen Schucman and Bill Thetford can be observed in the different ways they experienced their final days. Struck by pancreatic cancer in 1980,

Schucman progressively withdrew from the world and became increasingly despondent and dependent on her husband Louis, Ken Wapnick, and a devoted housekeeper. Some acquaintances were so disturbed by Schucman's deterioration that they curtailed their own visits; as Wapnick observed, "the discrepancy between the Helen they knew — impeccably groomed and socially appropriate, wise and helpful . . . and the Helen they now were experiencing — physically disheveled, preoccupied with her own disturbing thoughts, and totally unresponsive to anyone beside herself — was so glaring as to be disturbing, painful, and even frightening."[26]

Judy Skutch remembers a poignant encounter with Schucman in her last months that suggests her dying constituted a process of spiritual surrender she had steadfastly resisted all of her life. "I was sitting with Helen one day when she seemed completely removed from the world. She was making repetitive motions and drumming her fingers on the couch, not interacting with me at all even though I was holding her hand. I was beginning to feel useless, wondering if I should leave, when she suddenly turned to me and said, 'Do you know why I'm dying?' I said, 'No, mama, I don't.' Then she looked me straight in the eye as if to say, *stupid girl*, but instead she said, very forcefully, '*To get out of its way*,' and then she retreated inside herself again. That was one of the last things she ever said to me."

Schucman was probably referring to a conversation with Ken Wapnick from a few days earlier, when he remembers suggesting to Schucman that in the process of dying her ego-self would finally get out of the way of the Course's message. On her last night, Wapnick and Louis Schucman left the hospital when Helen's condition, now obviously terminal, seemed to be stabilizing; three hours later they received a call that she had died. As Wapnick writes,

We returned to the hospital, and Helen was still in her bed. Her face had a remarkably quiet expression of peace, so different from the tortured disquiet we had grown so

accustomed to seeing those many months. I suddenly recalled what Helen had shared with me on several occasions,
a thought that always brought her great comfort. Jesus had
told her that when she died, he would come for her personally. Who can really know what was in her mind in those
closing instants? Yet, her peaceful face was unmistakable,
and spoke convincingly for an experience of knowing, at
the very end, that her beloved Jesus had indeed kept his
promise, as she had kept hers. The priestess had returned
home.[27]

Seven years later Bill Thetford was staying at the home of
Judy Skutch and Bill Whitson while on a trip north to Tiburon.
His La Jolla lifestyle had resulted in a visibly different Bill —
more playful, more forthcoming, less formal than anyone there
could remember seeing him before. In fact, on the day before a
July Fourth party that Judy Skutch was planning for thirty people, she was startled to see Thetford dance a little jig in the living room, exclaiming "I'm free, I'm finally free. I'm flexible!"

Worried that he might be having some kind of manic episode,
Skutch asked him what he meant. "He looked me in the eyes,"
Skutch recalls, "put his hands on my shoulders and said, 'I am
not holding any grievances.' I said, 'Oh, come on,' and then I
asked him about several problematic people from his past. He
had a specific answer for every one, that he'd written to so-and-
so, and gone to meet someone else, and extended his love and
forgiveness to everyone.

"Then I said, 'And what about Helen?' He laughed and said,
'How could I not forgive Helen? She was the opportunity for
me to *learn* forgiveness.' While Bill had a great sense of humor, I
don't think he was trying to be funny. I thought he said this
with real joy."

The next morning Skutch asked Thetford if he still felt so
ebullient. "He said, 'Sure, it's freedom day. It's my freedom day.'
And I said, 'Well, I'm glad it's still working,' because I was a little suspicious of all this." When she asked him if he wanted to

come along with her to the grocery store, Thetford said he would walk and catch up with her.

"I must have made a face," Skutch recalls. "I guess he could see I was worried about having to wait for him, because he said 'Don't worry dear, if I'm not there in time you go home without me.' Well, a chill went through me and I put my arms around him and said, 'I'll *never* go home without you.' He just patted me on the head and smiled, and off he went." Skutch then gathered her shopping list, purse, and keys, and went to her car. She had driven a short distance down the driveway when she saw Thetford collapsed there, dead from a heart attack.

The dramatic difference in how Helen Schucman and Bill Thetford were able to make use of the spiritual teaching they brought into the world points up yet another of that teaching's paradoxes. While it consistently urges a surrender of ego-driven perception and motivations upon its students — promising that the ego's voice will be replaced by the beneficent guidance of a mystical agency called the Holy Spirit — *A Course in Miracles* also stresses that surrender cannot be forced upon anyone. "The power of decision is my own," the Course suggests in Workbook lesson #152 — a principle that could not be more clearly demonstrated than by the example of Helen Schucman.

In his foreword to *Journey Without Distance*, Institute of Noetic Sciences president Willis Harman tells yet another story of Schucman's deliberate resistance to the spiritual teaching she gave the world.

Helen hardly seemed to embody the inner peace that the Course puts forth as its goal. She found much to complain about, and her life seemed to contain more than the usual amount of pain. I once asked her how it happened that this remarkable document she had been responsible for had brought wisdom and peace to so many, and yet it was seemingly ineffective for her. I will never forget her reply. "I *know* the Course is true, Bill," she said — and then after a pause, "but I don't believe it."[28]

53

3
How the Course Teaching Has Spread

O f all the distinctions that set *A Course in Miracles* apart from other spiritual teachings, one of the most noteworthy is its *timing*. Most teachings of similar depth and complexity, be they mainstream or esoteric, originated hundreds if not several thousand years in the past. Major teachings such as Christianity, Buddhism, and Islam originated with sole prophets whose messages were later written down, revised, and translated. Virtually every spiritual tradition was initially shepherded by a small band of followers, taking many decades or even centuries to evolve into forms that would earn the devotion of large numbers of people.

But the Course sprang into being, complete and self-contained, in the middle of the latter half of the twentieth century — just as mass worldwide communications were increasingly achieving the speed of light. Even before the Course was published as a book, thousands of people gained access to its message through photocopies, a modern complement to the "word of mouth" by which ancient traditions were first disseminated. As the millennium approaches, many people are discussing the Course and sharing its lessons over the worldwide electronic network known as the Internet — for which there is no historical analogue unless one gives a lot of credence to long-distance telepathy.

Another significant factor in the rapid spread of the Course is its *accessibility*. Unlike most religious teachings, the Course has no central orthodoxy controlling who can become its students, requiring any sort of initiation, collecting dues or requesting tithes, keeping an eye on the faith of followers or issuing rules for their comportment. Anyone can buy the book (or request a free copy from the original publisher; see Appendix) and study it, in whole or in part, alone or with company, as one wishes. Students can also drop it or speak ill of it without fear of excommunication or retaliation by any religious authority.

On the other hand anyone can decide to start teaching the Course without certified training or official approval. As the *Manual for Teachers* asserts,

> A teacher of God is anyone who chooses to be one. His qualifications consist solely in this; somehow, somewhere he has made a deliberate choice in which he did not see his interests as apart from someone else's. Once he has done that, his road is established and his direction is sure. A light has entered the darkness. It may be a single light, but that is enough. He has entered an agreement with God even if he does not yet believe in Him. He has become a bringer of salvation. He has become a teacher of God.[1]

Elsewhere the Course specifies that teachers of its particular curriculum must have finished the Workbook exercises. Since the dictation of these lessons to Helen Schucman were preceded chronologically by the Text — and followed by a self-evident *Manual for Teachers* — completion of the entire Course would seem to be an implied and reasonable requirement for its instructors. But there is no one anointed or appointed to verify anyone's qualifications.

The net result is a free-for-all in the style and quality of teachers, study groups, schools, and service organizations inspired by the Course. One friend of mine was surprised to learn I was writing a book on ACIM because he had once encountered a study group that convinced him all Course students were "total flakes." I've encountered a wide disparity in the quality of Course groups myself. The first one I attended, for a period of about six weeks early in my personal study, was both intellectually challenging and emotionally supportive. Later I dropped in on a group monopolized by an organizer who seemed content merely to read the Course in a droning voice, without comment or questioning from anyone else, for at least forty-five minutes. (I don't know how long he continued after that because I left at that point and never returned.)

Established teaching programs range from the collegiate environment of the Foundation for *A Course in Miracles* (FACIM) in Roscoe, New York, to the certificate-granting California Miracles Center in San Francisco, to the controversial residential institute in Wisconsin called Endeavor Academy. A number of Course teachers support themselves in whole or in part by lecturing and leading groups on their own. In fact one of the surprising aspects of the Course story is how many careers (scores, if not hundreds) have been spawned and supported by a spiritual teaching still too young to be called a tradition.

An exhaustive survey of Course study groups and academies could easily take a book in itself. This chapter will offer a brief overview of the field and "snapshots" of a few significant organizations. First, a short history of the dissemination of *A Course in Miracles* itself.

A Perennial Best-seller

After photocopied versions of the Course were supplanted by a quality hardcover edition in 1976, the first-year sales were modest, about 5000 copies. In 1977 *Psychic* magazine editor James Bolen changed his publication's name to *New Realities*, partly to overcome Helen Schucman's resistance to a story about the Course appearing therein. The first issue of *NR* featured an interview with Judy Skutch, and helped boost second-year sales of the Course to 7500.

In 1980 a largely hostile story on the Course appeared in *Psychology Today* (see Chapter 2), but helped sales nonetheless. Publisher Judy Skutch says that's when she realized that "it didn't matter what anybody said about the Course as long as they spelled the name right. People were just drawn to it." By 1984 sales of the Course were approaching 30,000 copies annually; with the release of the softcover edition in 1985 that figure rose to 60,000 and the Course was on its way to becoming a perennial best-seller. During the mid to late 80s the Course and its study groups began to receive press coverage from major regional newspapers including *The Oregonian, San Francisco Examiner, Dallas Times Herald, Anchorage Daily News, Philadelphia Inquirer, The Atlanta Journal, The New York Times, The Guardian* of London, and *The Record* of Perth, Australia.

The largest single leap in Course sales occurred after the 1992 publication of Marianne Williamson's *A Return to Love* (see Chapter 4), when sales rose from 70,000 to 105,000, an increase of fifty percent. Thereafter the numbers leveled off to about 85,000 copies annually, prior to release of the new Viking edition of the Course in the spring of 1996. Viking announced a release of 100,000 copies supported by a $75,000 publicity campaign, the first time the Course has ever been advertised directly by its publisher (Helen Schucman received guidance that the Foundation for Inner Peace was not to advertise the Course itself).

Because the Course has become so widespread and well known, some people have concluded that the Foundation must be a large and well-heeled organization. In fact it employs only five people and operates out of two private residences in Marin County, California. The headquarters are at the home of William and Judith Skutch Whitson; Bob Skutch, Judy's second husband, has run the daily operations related to book distribution out of his home. When I interviewed him there, he recounted a call from someone who wanted to come by and visit FIP's "center" and "research department." Gesturing around his kitchen and living room, the laconic Skutch told me that "this is pretty much it, counting in Judy's place."

According to FIP President Judy Skutch, salaries for FIP staff range from the low to high five figures, although no salaries at all were paid during the first seven years of operation. Members of the FIP board of directors receive no compensation. In the two years prior to licensing of the Course to Viking, FIP's average gross revenues were just under $2 million, with a net of about $75,000. The Foundation has generally plowed all revenues into its ambitious translation program, supervised by William Whitson. Bob Skutch has characterized FIP's cash flow as "giving us just about what we need to operate, and no more."

Judy Skutch adds that the net effect of the licensing deal with Viking (which included a $2.5 million advance against royalties) will be to halve the Foundation's annual income. The licensing arrangement is limited to five years on a renewable basis.

Copyrights and Coffee Mugs

In recent years copyright protection of the Course has become one of the hotter "intramural" controversies of the Course community, as FIP has strengthened and threatened to enforce a previously laissez-faire policy regarding excerpting of the Course and the use of its name in other publications or commercial endeavors. The tighter policy resulted from an increasing trend toward reprinting parts of the Course in other media without FIP permission or conventional citations of the source — particularly Marianne Williamson's 1992 best-seller *A Return to Love*, in which a number of Course excerpts were quoted without citation. (FIP requested quote citations in subsequent paperback editions of *A Return to Love*, and the author and publisher, HarperCollins, cooperated.)

The new policy has generally not been well received by major Course groups, teachers, and writers, most of whom feel it amounts to an attempt to control how the Course is disseminated and taught — an attempt suspected of originating with Kenneth and Gloria Wapnick of FACIM. Although FIP and FACIM share directors and have always jointly made most of the decisions concerning ACIM's worldly affairs, they have strengthened their ties lately; FACIM is now referred to as the official "teaching organization" of the original Course publisher. Thus, some people fear that FIP and FACIM are gradually consolidating themselves into the sort of religious orthodoxy that the Course has always been free of in the past. (In fact, it's not uncommon to hear Ken Wapnick sardonically referred to as "the pope" by those who are most disgruntled with the copyright policy and FIP/FACIM alignment.)

For their part, both FACIM and FIP maintain that they have acted only to maintain the identity and integrity of the Course in the face of increasing usage of its ideas, name, and text without proper acknowledgment. At different times Judy Skutch of FIP and Gloria Wapnick of FACIM reported to me that they are sometimes asked by students why more has not been done to protect the Course from infringements and misinterpretations. FIP and FACIM also assert that copyright protection of the Course was always part of Helen Schucman's guidance about how the teaching was to be presented to the world — although it is clear that their sense of how to apply that guidance has changed throughout the years.

For instance, in 1989 Judy Skutch told me that "we were guided to give the copyright freely without questioning or judgment. If people want to make Miracles coffee mugs, they can."[2] While I was researching this book in 1995, Ken Wapnick explained to me that the new copyright policy included trademarking of the title A Course in Miracles and the acronym "ACIM" because both were increasingly being used to promote commercial ventures neither affiliated with nor approved by FIP. "We don't want people making Miracles coffee mugs," remarked Wapnick.

With the assumption of Course publishing duties by Viking Penguin, the issue of copyright protection intensified considerably. In mid-1996 Penguin Books USA filed an infringement suit against Endeavor Academy (see page 66) for their publication and distribution of a number of booklets that reprinted portions of

ACIM without permission or acknowledgment of the copyright, now assigned to Penguin by its licensing arrangement with the Foundation for Inner Peace. Endeavor answered with a motion to dismiss the suit based on a challenge to the original 1975 copyright in the name of Helen Schucman and FIP. If the real author is Jesus Christ, Endeavor argues, the copyright should be voided — an argument that is not without some precedent, according to Los Angeles attorney Jonathan Kirsch, a specialist in publishing law with whom I informally reviewed the dispute.

"If a spiritual entity is presented by an author as a 'person' with an objective existence of its own, then the author cannot claim to own a copyright in the words and expressions dictated or channeled through her by the spiritual entity," opines Kirsch. He cautiously concludes that the suit "will make for an interesting bit of litigation" — not to mention a significant chapter in Course history regardless of the suit's outcome.

Major Course-Related Organizations

Although the very first study groups consisted of the Course principals and their friends, many more were rapidly spawned from the dissemination of Course photocopies in a pattern like that of seeds thrown randomly to the winds. It's impossible to determine how many have come into being, dissolved, or reformed since the Course literally came out of the closet in the mid-seventies.

Following is a brief rundown of some of the current, better-known Course organizations in this country, most of them featuring teachers familiar to the general Course community. A major teaching academy run by FACIM is profiled in detail in Chapter 5. (See the Appendix for addresses, telephone numbers and online contacts for all these groups.)

Miracle Distribution Center (Fullerton, California)

The most exhaustive directory of all Course study groups is kept by Miracle Distribution Center (MDC) in Fullerton, California, founded by former actress Beverly Hutchinson McNeff and her brother Richard in 1978. MDC, a nonprofit organization, is the oldest clearinghouse for Course media, answering over 300 calls, letters, and orders weekly. Originally founded to support Southern California Course students, MDC gradually grew into a multi-purpose organization with an international outreach that today provides a wide range of free services — including a prayer ministry, pen pal project, counselor referral service, study group and prison project referrals, and 24-hour "lesson phone line" — in addition to its healthy mail-order business in books, audiotapes, and videos. A free bimonthly newsletter entitled *The Holy Encounter* is sent to 10,000 people.

Hutchinson says that MDC "has been a lifesaver for those who think they're all alone in studying the Course, especially those in remote areas of the world or the Bible Belt regions of the United States." Hutchinson also lectures on the Course and leads study groups at MDC's spacious but nondescript facility in an industrial section of Orange County, as well as periodic weekend workshops in the mountains outside Los Angeles.

According to MDC computer printouts, in mid-1996, there were at least 2100 Course study groups worldwide. In America they can be found in all fifty states plus Puerto Rico and the Virgin Islands. There are ninety groups in Australia and seventy-five in England, seven in Scotland, three in Japan, two in the West Indies, two in Nigeria, and one each in such countries as Argentina, Botswana, Israel, the Philippines, and most recently Slovakia. Most are English-speaking but the number of foreign-language groups is growing with the spread of the various Course translations.

Even in the United States, Hutchinson notes that it's impossible to track the demographics of Course students, who seem to come from all classes, races, lifestyles, and prior religious backgrounds. (During my research I encountered students who are or have been Jewish, Catholic, Episcopalian, Mormon, Christian Scientist, mainline Protestant, Christian fundamentalist, American Buddhist, Islamic, agnostic, and atheist.) There is a strong concentration of Course groups in Southern California, which has over two hundred groups, roughly ten percent of the world-wide total.

The Foundation for Life Action (Los Angeles, California)

This organization represents the teaching of Tara Singh, a native of India who was a close student of the famed philosopher Krishnamurti for thirty years before meeting Helen Schucman. Singh recounted in a *Miracles Magazine* interview that Schucman rebuffed his initial expressions of respect for her as a spiritual teacher, even going so far as to call him "a pest." Nonetheless he persisted in calling Schucman almost nightly for years and "no matter how many stones she threw at me, it didn't matter. I just collected them and set them by her feet."[3]

Singh went on to give lectures, write books, and lead seminars on the Course, including a "One-Year Non-Commercialized Retreat" in 1983, in which he led forty-nine people through the Course Workbook in exactly 365 days. A pamphlet from the Foundation for Life Action summarizes its philosophy:

> We do not accept charity or seek donations, nor do we own a community. Because the Name of God cannot be commercialized and ill-earned money begets other vices, the School charges no tuition. It has its own integrity of bringing the student to: Being Self-Reliant and Productive, Extending His Own Intrinsic Work and Not Working for Another, Having Something of His Own to Give and Never Taking Advantage.[4]

The FLA has also developed a charitable service organization called the Joseph Plan Foundation. With four of his many books being distributed by major publishers — including the 1997 Ballantine title *Encounters with Eternity: My Relationships with J. Krishnamurti and Helen Schucman* — Singh's work has become well known in Course circles. Some observers feel that Singh's teaching of the Course has a "Krishnamurti flavor" owing to his long affiliation with that teacher.

The Interfaith Fellowship (New York City)

The Reverend Jon Mundy, who taught the Course from a Methodist pulpit for fourteen years (see Chapter 7), calls the organization that he and the Reverend Diane Berke administer "the seekers' church in New York City. We have a lot of old hippies and people who have looked for wisdom in many places."

With a membership of 150 people and 200 showing up for Sunday morning services across from Carnegie Hall, Interfaith offers a Course-based spirituality that embraces many other perspectives. For instance, Interfaith's monthly periodical *On Course* (which bears a passing resemblance to the Methodist magazine *The Upper Room*) regularly chronicles "the Interfaith year" for its 3500 subscribers by listing religious holidays from the traditions of Christianity, Buddhism, Shinto, Zoroastrianism, Islam, and others. Interfaith also publishes a quarterly catalog of Course media. In the fall of 1995 Interfaith started offering a Sunday school class that Mundy says "is probably one of the first anywhere to appreciate different religious traditions while teaching Course principles at the kids' level — like the importance of being generous and telling the truth."

Both Mundy and Berke have authored books about the Course teaching and lecture at various workshops nationwide.

The Circle of Atonement (Sedona, Arizona)

Located in the Southwest's hotbed of New Age culture, this organization hews to a fairly conservative rendering of the Course philosophy. "My belief is that the author intended the Course as a very serious, demanding and transformative spiritual path," says founder Robert Perry, "rather than merely an inspiring and eye-opening collection of ideas." Perry is the author of a brief "Introduction to A Course in Miracles" that has 200,000 copies in distribution.

The Circle's co-teacher Allen Watson (see Chapter 9) is an on-line Course activist who distributes commentaries on Course lessons through several electronic forums and "newsgroups." Although the Circle of Atonement is presently headquartered at a rented private residence in Sedona, Perry and Watson have long-range plans for a "three-wing" center pursuing Teaching, Transformation, and Healing activities. In 1994 the Teaching wing was established with a Course school called the Learning Circle. Robert Perry notes that "one of our primary objectives is to spawn a 'support system' for ACIM students analogous to the Twelve Step support groups." A quarterly newsletter entitled *A Better Way* is circulated to a mailing list of two thousand, along with a quarterly series of booklets.

The California Miracles Center (San Francisco, California)

Although many Course followers question the idea of founding formal ministries, the Reverend Tony Ponticello cast aside such doubts when he incorporated the California Miracles Center (CMC) as a state-approved church in 1987. Tucked away in a small second-story space in San Francisco's Castro district, CMC not only offers Sunday morning services complete with singing, sermons, and a passing of the plate, but also administers training programs for ACIM "Practitioners," ACIM "Teachers-of-God," and legally recognized ACIM "Ministers."

CMC's gaily-decorated *Miracles Monthly* newsletter is one of the livelier Course-related periodicals, complete with classified ads, news of bake sales and CMC retreats, and the occasional picture of Ponticello sporting a jaunty Santa cap. While the CMC bookstore does not deal in volume like the Miracle Distribution Center, it lists a broader variety of Course-related media (over 200 titles) than MDC or most other sources. CMC's online home page irreverently suggests such revelations as "Wow! I just suddenly received the guidance that I want to give a *Donation* to the California Miracles Center" — but it also posts a detailed financial statement revealing that CMC is a break-even proposition paying its founding minister well under $10,000 annually.

Endeavor Academy (Baraboo, Wisconsin)

The most controversial of all Course-related teaching centers is undoubtedly the Endeavor Academy, an educational facility and permanent community of about two hundred people in southern rural Wisconsin, not far from the state capital of Madison. Endeavor differs from the norm of Course groups in several major respects, including its residential status, its aggressive evangelical outreach, and most notably its focus on a "Master Teacher"— a former real estate broker and recovered alcoholic named Chuck Anderson, whom Endeavor residents refer to as "Dear One." In the larger Course community Endeavor Academy is often described as a "cult" that seriously misrepresents the Course teaching.

Not surprisingly, Endeavor insiders don't see it that way. Distinguishing Endeavor's approach from that of FACIM, the oldest Course teaching center, Academy administrator Ted Poppe asserts that "Ken Wapnick is teaching the Course like it was English, where you learn to decline words and diagram sentences. To him it's just something that you study. We're saying that's not it at all. People come here to undergo an actual experience of communion with God, at which point they see the futility of trying to be a human anymore. Then they make a decision as to what they should do with the rest of their lives. A lot of them who get to that point decide to stay on here."

Endeavor's cult reputation apparently got started because some people who decided to stay on at Endeavor changed their minds after a while, and soon began letting others know of their concerns about what they experienced there. Their strongest charges revolve around the behavior of the Master Teacher (MT) himself.

Val Scott, a Canadian Course student since 1979 who did two stints at Endeavor, published an eighty-page booklet about his experiences there in which he claimed that he had been harangued and physically assaulted by MT.[5] Kalie Picone of Massachusetts, who spent three weeks at Endeavor, wrote in an open letter circulated in Course circles that MT "commonly attacks

66

people for having questioning minds and for asserting their identities."[6] And Robert Lilly of Las Vegas, Nevada, described MT in an online posting as an "egomaniac who used circular reasoning and silly logic. I saw him yelling and confronting people, including me . . . I heard him saying things that even as metaphors were clearly not in line with the Course. His sessions were monologues with no allowance for discussion or questioning."[7]

Equally problematic for many Course veterans is Endeavor's apparent attitude of superiority toward other groups and teachers. Ted Poppe asserts that Endeavor is "doing something completely different" from other groups and that it is "more advanced" in terms of its members' spiritual progress. The Endeavor journal *out of time* goes even farther, satirizing typical Course study groups in this fictional "news bulletin":

> There's wonderful news from the "Let's All Practice Forgiveness" Group of *A Course in Miracles* in Selroy, California. The group leader, Ms. Margarette L.L. Thurston II, reports that at their last regular meeting a member successfully, and much to the delightful astonishment of all, whistled *La Marseillaise* out of a portion of his rear anatomy. Group members, George and Alma Finstly, pledged to "really get out there and 'Forgive' in earnest this week." He's a bass and she's an alto. They are determined to form a trio and whistle "Hark the Herald Angels Sing" by Christmas. Good Luck Miracle Workers![8]

Whatever its attitude toward the rest of the Course community, Endeavor has not caused any appreciable upset in its own neighborhood in rural Wisconsin. While Endeavor maintains a residential facility called God's Country Place plus several renovated motels for some of its students, others live, work, and operate businesses in the surrounding community of Wisconsin Dells. "We live a normal life in the community just like everybody else," asserts Poppe. Regional press coverage of Endeavor has been slight and neutral, although a local ministers' association did question the Christianity of the New Christian Church of Full Endeavor in a 1992 article appearing in the *Baraboo News Republic*.

Reports from Endeavor expatriates are not all negative. Jim Lane, a lecturer in management and marketing at Southern Cross University in New South Wales, Australia, says that the month he spent at Endeavor in 1995 "accelerated my understanding of the Course by decades." And a number of people have left Endeavor to begin their own groups that are more or less inspired by the Master Teacher's interpretation — including Ted Poppe's wife, Victoria, who facilitates what she calls the "leading Course group in the Boston area."

Endeavor Academy itself has not been satisfied to limit its teaching to its Wisconsin center, staging ambitious outreach programs in Western Europe and Australia, and starting several satellite centers in various locations. In 1995 the Academy bought a 15,000-seat convention center near its headquarters in Wisconsin, which Ted Poppe says will be used as "a place where spiritual healing based on *A Course in Miracles* takes place."

Clearly, then, Endeavor Academy evinces an intent to stay and spread its version of a Course gospel. But it's safe to say that the larger Course community perceives Endeavor Academy just as ex-resident Val Scott does: "a pure and simple cult-guru trip hitch-hiking on *A Course in Miracles*."[9] Likewise, several prominent Course veterans privately challenged my inclusion of Endeavor Academy in this survey of teaching organizations.

The Course in Unity and Recovery

One of the places that people discover *A Course in Miracles* is at their local Unity church. Sometimes called "New Age Christianity," Unity was founded in 1889 by an American couple, Charles and Myrtle Fillmore, who "sought health by changing their ideas about God and themselves."[10] Although sometimes identified as part of the New Thought movement — which promotes the idea of the divinity of humankind — Unity distinguishes it-

self from New Thought by its explicit endorsement of the teachings of Jesus Christ. In practice, however, Unity churches generally embrace a wide range of spiritual beliefs and perspectives.
While not officially endorsed by Unity, the Course seems to have
become one of its frequent companions.

Joan Gattuso of Ohio has been a Unity minister for sixteen
years and a Course student for even longer, and is the author of
the 1996 HarperCollins book *A Course in Love*. While she notes
that the Course is not universally accepted by Unity churches,
she finds the principles of the two spiritual approaches to be "essentially the same . . . The Course actually increased my respect
for the wisdom and foresight of the Fillmores." Gattuso's book
on relationships is chiefly Course-inspired but also draws on her
multi-faceted spiritual experience, including Buddhism. She remarks that a central message of her book is the necessity to
"forgive, forgive, and forgive — without exception — because
our guilt goes so deep that we're out of touch with it."

The Course is also showing up with increasing frequency in
recovery groups of every description. That connection has become sufficiently well-known that one of the leading publishers
of recovery materials, Hazelden, released a book in 1995 by recovery and meditation writer Karen Casey entitled *Daily Meditations for Practicing the Course*. Not intended as a substitute for
the Course's own yearbook of meditations, Casey's book offers
365 daily thoughts and essays that echo the general Course philosophy, including "Change the mind and the behavior follows,"
"Joining with others is how healing occurs," and "God knows no
wrath."[11] A recovery sponsor herself, Casey says that she believes *A Course in Miracles* offers a form of "graduate studies for
people working the Twelve Steps."

The Course in Business, the Professions, and Politics

"There is no TV show called 'The Lifestyles of the Balanced and
Loving,'" comments North Carolina businessman Robert Roskind in his 1992 book *In the Spirit of Business*, a guide to apply-

ing the principles of ACIM to the business world. "Fear-based accomplishments will not lead to peace of mind and a true sense of self-worth, life's greatest rewards. . . . If we can begin to eliminate the fears that motivate and control our actions, we will find that we accomplish just as much but with clarity and balance."[12]

Roskind is not the only Course-inspired writer and business activist proposing a new perspective on the meaning and pursuit of prosperity. Willis Harman, president of the Sausalito, California-based Institute of Noetic Sciences and a former regent of the University of California, helped found the World Business Academy, an affiliation of business leaders and futurists who meet to discuss how business can help prepare for the worldwide transition to a "positive, sustainable society." In 1993 the Academy published an anthology of its ideas under the title *The New Paradigm in Business* that concluded with Harman's commentary on "business as a vehicle for global transformation."

Although Harman does not cite the Course specifically, his list of indicators for a "new paradigm" contains several concepts that echo the ACIM philosophy, including "peace and common security," "nonviolent change," "empowerment of people," and "trans-materialist beliefs . . . The new emphasis includes self-realization, transcendent meaning, and inner growth leading to wisdom and compassion."[13]

Because of its earthly roots in academic psychology and psychotherapy, the Course has had a significant and increasing presence in those professional fields, particularly on the West Coast and in the field of psychology termed "transpersonal" (see Chapter 6). While there are no statistics available, my own journalistic survey over the years suggests that there is also an increasing presence of Course students in the medical professions and, somewhat surprisingly, in the law. During my research I heard of several small law firms that attempt to put Course principles into practice, including ones in San Rafael and Carmel, California.

In his book *Seeing Law Differently*, Canadian attorney Alan Reid attests to six Course-inspired principles that he follows in order to turn the practice of law toward the purpose of healing:

- Let go of all grievances I am holding towards the person I am dealing with, whether it be my client, another lawyer, a witness, another party, the judge or the court administrator.
- Never use the law to reinforce a judgment I have made about another person.
- Never use my legal rights or my legal skills to attack another person or to seek vengeance.
- Make all decisions that have legal implications for myself or for someone else while I am in a state of peace, not in a state of fear or anger.
- Trust that the process will open up opportunities for me and for others to make choices that will bring healing, if we make them in a loving, not a fearful state of mind.
- Seek only the justice that is the gift of healing for all who are involved in a legal proceeding.[14]

Reid acknowledges the difficulty of seeing the law so differently by admitting the equal importance of a seventh guideline: "to be aware of my resistance to the other six."[15]

If there is any realm where one might expect extreme resistance to a message of inner work and spiritual transformation, it's that of politics — yet *A Course in Miracles* has made inroads there as well. Some of its principles have at least been introduced to President Bill Clinton and First Lady Hillary Rodham Clinton, who have consulted with popular Course teacher Marianne Williamson (see Chapter 4). ACIM publisher Judy Skutch reports that there has been at least one Course study group composed of Congressional wives, and several members of Congress have apparently studied the teaching at one time or another. Former California Governor Jerry Brown was also introduced to the Course.

In a film documentary about the Course, a former presidential speechwriter named Milton Friedman (not to be confused with the prominent economist) spoke about the potential of the Course message for national politics. Assigned dual tasks during the presidency of Gerald Ford — to editorially advocate the defense budget and write the chief executive's religious speeches — Friedman found himself caught in a contradiction not atypical for those involved in public policy. He was helping "to spread fear" on one hand while penning public declamations of brotherly love with the other.

"I saw something of a dichotomy there," Friedman admitted. "I also saw what was going on in government and international affairs, and I became so troubled that by the time I left office with Carter's election, I turned to prayer and meditation. Then the Course appeared, delivered to me by Judy Skutch . . .

"The Course can't bring peace to the world, but people can. First, inner peace must come before anything externally. . . . Fear is dealt with by the Course with great insight, and what can be a teaching instrument for the individual could be applied on a national scale. The leadership of a nation is only the mirror image of its citizens. When enough citizens begin opening and changing, and seeing without fear . . . we can have national change."[16]

The Course in Prisons

The central Course themes of forgiveness and personal responsibility are increasingly reaching into the growing national subculture of the incarcerated. In 1982, an attorney named Bob Plath started a Miracles study program inside San Quentin Prison in Marin County, California. At its peak the program encompassed four different weekly ACIM group meetings of inmates at all security levels, and continued for five years. One San Quentin Course student was David Magris, who served sixteen years on charges of murder, kidnapping, armed robbery, and burglary, and who sat on Death Row before California temporarily repealed the death penalty in 1972.

Encountering the Course about seven years into his term, Magris was already involved in rehabilitative programs and says that he "had already decided I had the power to change. But I needed more avenues for growth. I had resolved the basic motivations for my crimes, but I was still carrying a considerable amount of guilt. To talk about the past always left me strained, drained, and sad. The Course was essential to me in gaining a better understanding of self-forgiveness."

Magris also observed the effects of regular Course meetings on his fellow inmates: "I think everybody in the group was substantially moved and changed. They all became more comfortable in expressing themselves, and the Course lessons helped them learn to take criticism from their peers. This definitely changed their decisions and behavior on the yard, and improved their relationships to the staff."

Off parole since 1985, Magris lives and works near San Quentin and is active in the decidedly unpopular movement to abolish the death penalty. In public appearances for that cause he is sometimes accompanied by Dennis Tapp, whom Magris shot and nearly killed during the youthful crime spree that landed him in San Quentin. They were reconciled after Magris left prison.

In Boston, Course student Robin Casarjian has undertaken an ambitious prisoner education project under the auspices of her National Emotional Literacy Project for Prisons. Author of a successful trade book entitled *Forgiveness: A Bold Choice for a Peaceful Heart* (Bantam), Casarjian found an unexpected receptivity to her message when she first visited a prison in 1988, and began working with the incarcerated on a regular basis. In 1995 she self-published a book entitled *Houses of Healing: A Prisoner's Guide to Inner Power and Freedom*, which is distributed free to prisons nationwide, with an ultimate goal of disseminating 65,000 copies including a Spanish translation. This work is supported entirely by donations to Casarjian's nonprofit organization, whose board of directors includes popular health writer Joan Borysenko, Ph.D., whose work has also been influenced by the Course.

The first self-help book devoted entirely to prisoners, *Houses of Healing* couches some of the fundamentals of the field — including relaxation, self-observation, anger and grief work, and meditation — in simple, accessible terms. Scattered throughout the book are adaptations or direct quotes of Course Workbook lessons: "There is another way of looking at the world,"[17] "I could see peace instead of this,"[18] "The power of decision is my own."[19]

A rape victim and opponent of the death penalty who advocates a complete reversal in prison objectives — from the present emphasis on punishment to a focus on rehabilitation and re-education — Casarjian feels that the psychospiritual solution to the prison problem is also the most practical one. "We have a million and a half people incarcerated today," she observes, "and ninety percent of them are coming back into society no matter how many prisons we build. The kind of experience people have in prison is going to determine their success or failure when they return to society.

"People change," adds Casarjian, "and people in prison change. They are either going to change for the better in terms of emotional healing, maturity, and personal responsibility, or they are going to become more wounded, more despairing, and more likely to strike out against others in the future."

Another Course-related prison project is Visions for Prisons in Costa Mesa, California, founded by Dan Millstein, an abandoned child of teenage parents who grew up to become a self-identified "criminal who never got caught." An adherent of Transcendental Meditation who encountered the Course in 1987, Millstein later met Jerry Jampolsky and asked him how to start an Attitudinal Healing group (see Chapter 4). Jampolsky told him simply, "Go do it. You're it!" and Millstein soon began taking the principles of yoga, meditation, and Attitudinal Healing into prisons and schools. In 1995, Millstein and Visions for Prisons won one of three International Jampolsky Awards given to honor exceptionally successful and innovative applications of the Attitudinal Healing principles.

Course-Related Media

Raised by atheist, socially activist parents in New England, Paul Ferrini was brought up to believe that "science had all the answers and would eventually solve all the problems of human existence." But Ferrini began to feel spiritual influences in his mid-teens, and at 23, during a very low point in his life, he heard what he believed to be the voice of God telling him to walk into the next room with his eyes closed and pick up a book. The book turned out to be *I and Thou* by Martin Buber, who helped Ferrini realize that "it was my choice about what kind of world I wanted to see — the spiritual world of I-Thou or the material world of I-It. Before that time, I thought the world was only about exploitation and struggle."

When Ferrini encountered *A Course in Miracles* in the early eighties, he felt that he grasped it immediately and knew it would become his primary spiritual path. The only problem was that "I didn't like the Christian, patriarchal language of the Course." Still, Ferrini felt a "deep, intuitive relationship" with the teaching and noticed that he didn't have to labor over its meanings as much as other students he observed. "I think the Course is a path given to intellectuals to help bring them into their hearts," Ferrini comments.

Ferrini has a long history of organizing Course conferences and retreats, and was also the editor of *Miracles Magazine*, which he founded in 1991 and folded five years later. "My vision for the magazine was something that could sit next to the *National Enquirer* in every grocery store but tell only positive stories about the miracles and transformations in people's lives," relates Ferrini. "People would read it and feel inspired and hopeful about their own lives." The first few issues of *Miracles* were devoted strictly to ACIM-related stories; thereafter Ferrini diversified its subject matter. Later issues featured cover stories on such personalities as Elisabeth Kübler-Ross, John Bradshaw, and Raymond Moody, M.D., and explored themes like "Death, Dying and Life after Death" and "Childhood Trauma and Sexual Abuse."

With a peak circulation of 15,000 and anemic revenues, the 100-page, irregularly published glossy magazine was always a long way from sitting beside every display of *The National Enquirer*, admits Ferrini. But Ferrini's varied experience in organizing Course-related activities has made him philosophical about the success or failure of any particular venture.

"At the height of my ego's participation in the Course community, I wanted to fix everything I thought was wrong," Ferrini remembers. "Now I realize that whenever I think that way, I'm the one who's suffering the most. I don't have to be Don Quixote and take on every windmill."

While *Miracles Magazine* has been the only full-size magazine dedicated to the Course, there are scores of newsletters originating with Course groups and individual writers. FACIM's newsletter *The Lighthouse* reaches over 10,000 readers. ACIM students appear to be a highly verbal bunch, prone to self-publishing and discussing among themselves in a wide variety of media, including the newer electronic ones. During my research for this book I monitored ACIM discussion groups available on America OnLine, Compuserve, and Prodigy. An Internet "list serve" discussion group facilitated by James Hale of La Trobe University in Australia enables Course students worldwide to share e-mailed thoughts with each other. This electronically linked group's discourse often comprises over fifty missives daily. (See the Appendix for a guide to on-line Course resources.)

Other Course media include taped readings and related musical offerings by a wide variety of Course-inspired artists. Beverly Hutchinson has done several collections of Course readings set to the music of New Age composer Steven Halpern. The Course even has its own symphony, *Journey Without Distance*, available on CD along with two other modern classical pieces by Richard Danielpour, a Juilliard-trained composer and pianist, recorded with the Seattle Symphony (Delos International Recordings).

And for those who may tire of spiritual seriousness, there's some comic relief available in *A Course in Marigolds*, an ACIM parody written and published by student Michael Stillwater.

Purportedly approved by the "Foundation for Dinner Peas," this booklet-length course in home horticulture claims to be "quite consistent in what it presents, with the seeming goal of leading an incompetent gardener into a state of psychological torment by mentally fabricating a war of epic proportions with the snails. Why it wants to do this is unclear."[20]

Students of the thicker ACIM will appreciate the familiar style of *Marigolds'* Workbook lessons, including such inspiring meditations as "What I see in my garden is a form of vengeance," "I am upset because I see snails everywhere," and "In better fences my safety lies."[21] The witty accuracy of Stillwater's satire has been appreciated even by Course purists; *Marigolds* bears an endorsement from Ken Wapnick declaring that "Gloria's gardening will never be the same!"

Alternate Channels

Michael Stillwater is not the only one channeling a Course-like alternate message. In an entirely serious vein, several people have authored books and recorded tapes with the claim that they are channeling the same source of wisdom that dictated the original Course. Tom Carpenter of The Carpenter Press in Princeville, Hawaii, says that his book *Dialogue on Awakening* was dictated by Jesus, and Brent Haskell, Ph.D. recorded a series of tapes dictated by "Jeshua" from January 1990 to January 1991 that became *Journey Beyond Words* (DeVorss), "a companion to the Workbook of the Course." In general terms, both of these books display a much simpler language than ACIM itself while echoing its central themes. Just how consonant these teachings are with ACIM depends upon whom you ask about them, but Carpenter and Haskell each have a following without sparking any significant controversy.

Such is not the case with Paul Norman Tuttle of the Northwest Foundation for *A Course in Miracles* in Kingston, Washington. Tuttle channels an entity called Rajpur, or "Raj," who has been particularly active on electronic forums. Raj was once blocked from participating on Compuserve's New Age Forum (by its sysop, or moderator) for identifying himself as "the one known as Jesus" and the author of the original Course. Thereafter Raj surfaced in the ACIM section of Compuserve's Religion Forum, which is populated mostly with his followers. But the authenticity of Raj is occasionally challenged by new participants even there, "about every six months" according to one on-line observer.

Michael Brewer, an American-born Course student living in Switzerland (see Chapter 9), learned of Raj from the Compuserve forum and thereafter listened to some Raj tapes that gave him a "gut reaction"the source might be less than divine. "He sounds arrogant," says Brewer. Several Raj critics told me privately that they believe the voice is only that of Paul Norman Tuttle, whether by conscious or unconscious design. Nonetheless Raj has a following sufficient to mount twice-monthly lectures attended by about twenty-five people, and periodic weekend workshops that may draw a hundred or more.

While the notion of multiple channels of Jesus Christ strikes some Course students as dubious, it's really no stranger than the idea of Jesus speaking through Helen Schucman in the first place. As one Course student suggests, "it forces us all to discern the real quality of these messages, including the Course itself, rather than believing blindly in whatever authority claims to be behind them." But Paul Ferrini has observed firsthand the lure of authority at Course conferences where workshops by Tom Carpenter or Brent Haskell would draw standing-room-only crowds while the Reverend Jon Mundy, who claims to channel no one, might have a considerably smaller audience. "But Jon has just as much to say that's worthwhile as Tom or Brent," opines Ferrini.

Ironically, what authenticates the wisdom of the original Course for many students is the fact that they initially *disbelieve* and resist its authority — only to become convinced of its power through sustained study and practice of Course principles. Such a test of usefulness is probably the best determinant of the real "authority" behind any spiritual teaching.

Who is the Course Student?

Ten or fifteen years ago it might have been reasonably accurate to typify ACIM students by their psychotherapeutic or New Age connections. Those constituencies remain significant elements of the Course audience today. But these correlations have more to do with where the Course originated and how it was first publicized than with any particular appeals of its message. As Beverly Hutchinson has noted, the demographics of Course students have become impossible to characterize, increasingly crossing all borders of class, race, nationality and pre-existing spiritual orientations. Robert Perry says that he feels "the only thing that all Course students have in common today is owning a blue book."

Apart from sociological indicators, are there any psychological factors common to all Course students? Are they all "total flakes," as my friend suspected? From my experience of talking to many Course students over the years, I would say they seem to be at many different levels of psychological growth and spiritual progress, from the flakiest to the most sophisticated.

Thus to gauge the value and effectiveness of the Course requires more evidence than a first impression of a student's or group's maturity. It also requires learning something about what students' lives were like *before* they encountered the Course, and what sort of changes have been wrought in their characters and consciousness since that time.

For a while I entertained the theory that the Course tends to attract especially dynamic people whose own misguided ego strength has led them into calamitous life situations — situations from which ACIM proves to be the means of a narrow but ultimately transformative escape. I thought that theory particularly fit the subjects of the next chapter, well-known Course popularizers Jerry Jampolsky and Marianne Williamson, until I mentioned it to Williamson herself.

"I have to disagree," she replied. "I don't think that Jerry and I, or any other Course students, are especially intense or have had tougher problems than anyone else. I think everybody's life is on the way to peace or shipwreck, depending on where we direct our energy." From that perspective, perhaps a common identifying factor among serious ACIM students is their decision to follow a new course away from the typical shoals of human shipwreck, and toward peace.

4
Extending the Message:
*Talking to Jerry Jampolsky
and Marianne Williamson*

T he ever-increasing popularity of *A Course in Miracles* has
   always been something of a mystery given that it's so difficult to read and understand, much less practice. While the
Course has found many students on its own, much of its widespread recognition derives from the popularization of some of
its principles by psychiatrist Jerry Jampolsky, M.D., and popular
spiritual lecturer Marianne Williamson. Although both admit
that they are not Course "purists," Jampolsky and Williamson
have each played a significant role in extending the general message of the Course into diverse venues and specific social applications. They also helped bring the Course itself to a level of
public notice that no one could have predicted twenty-five years
ago, when the teaching was still hidden in bulky thesis binders
in a corner of Bill Thetford's office.

"Physician, Heal Thyself"

It was around the same time, the early seventies, when Jerry Jampolsky appeared to have it made. His lucrative psychiatric practice had brought him a comfortable living and the reputation as
the most effective therapist treating alcoholics in Marin County,
just north of San Francisco. Busy at success, Jampolsky nonethe-

less dutifully kept up with his two sons' school and Little League activities, trying to spend at least some evenings at home to fulfill the role of the good family man. And indeed people who knew them generally regarded the Jampolskys as a model family.

But things were not really going as well as they appeared; in fact things were not going well at all. As Jampolsky relates in his autobiography *Out of Darkness Into the Light*:

> I had a Dr. Jekyll and Mr. Hyde personality. In the haven of my office I could be loving and receive love. But at home I was quite capable of being a tyrant, denying it even as I was doing it. At the office I could talk about unconditional love with parents; at home, I was always nagging my sons to get good grades in school. In spite of my good intentions, I was doing exactly those things that I had so sharply criticized in my parents.[1]

Even in the "haven" of his office, reality failed to match appearances. His reputation as a specialist in treating alcoholism would certainly have suffered had it been known that Jampolsky was denying his own drinking problem.

In 1973 Jampolsky was divorced from his wife of twenty years, and life became even worse. "I was extremely agitated," he recalls now, "and continued my psychiatric practice even though I was deeply depressed." Despite all his training in troubleshooting other people's psychological problems, Jampolsky could not seem to treat the central wound of his own childhood: the conviction that he was fundamentally unlovable. As he relates in *Good-bye to Guilt*, Jampolsky had developed a personality founded on a self-punishing compensation:

> I discovered . . . that I could make others right by becoming more guilty. The more guilty I became, the better they liked it. Becoming guilty became a way of pleasing others. Consequently, I became a storehouse of guilt, and the store-

house expanded and grew beyond anything I could possibly imagine.

Since I believed I was a second-class citizen, I concentrated on being a first-class pessimist — at least that was something I felt I could control. I decided to fulfill the negative expectations others had of me by doing things to make myself wrong in order to make them right. It gave me a crazy sense of power finally to be right about something. Although I couldn't succeed at making people love me, I became an expert at making people angry. By provoking anger, I reinforced my belief that I could control something by demonstrating convincingly what an unworthy and unloving person I was.

I experienced the world as a precarious place where I might be attacked at any moment. . . .[2]

Thus Jampolsky was predictably skeptical when Judy Skutch called him from New York one day in 1975, describing her meeting with Helen Schucman and Bill Thetford and informing Jampolsky of a manuscript she thought could change his life. When he asked Skutch what it was about, she spoke of God and spiritual transformation, and the decidedly atheistic Jampolsky said no thanks. When Skutch was in Marin days later, she asked him again if he might take a look at *A Course in Miracles*.

"In a very snobbish way I said I'd look at one page, but that was it," Jampolsky recalls. "So I read one page, and for the first time in my life I heard an inner voice saying, 'Physician, heal thyself. This is your way home.' I've never been able to articulate this exactly, but I had a feeling of oneness with all the world, and oneness with God. I knew that my whole life was going to be different."

Still, Jampolsky undertook his Course study with some suspicion, wondering if he was being hoodwinked in some way. It was not until several months into his study — when he first met Schucman and Thetford and was "convinced of their integrity and ordinariness" — that Jampolsky could accept that "Jesus must have really talked through Helen in order for this book to come into being. For one thing, the message and the way Helen behaved were not consistent; she still had a lot of conflicts. So did I, but it was becoming clear by then that the Course was helping me in ways beyond what I thought was possible."

Not long after meeting Schucman, Jampolsky was consulting at the University of California Medical Center in San Francisco when he observed a young child with terminal cancer asking a doctor what it was like to die. Instead of answering, the physician changed the subject. Jampolsky relates that soon afterward he "received guidance to start a center that would be based on the healing principles of *A Course in Miracles*, but in such a way as not to use any religious language. We would start with children who were dying. My guidance was that these children were very wise spirits who could help each other and everyone who volunteered to help them."

Thus was born the first Center for Attitudinal Healing, operating out of Jampolsky's small office in bayside Tiburon, California. From an experiment devised to help children and their parents face catastrophic illness — "and help myself find peace of mind," Jampolsky admits — has grown a worldwide network of over one hundred centers that provide support to people facing a wide array of physical, social, and cultural crises. Although Jampolsky continued to work as a psychiatrist for several years, he provided the Center as a free service to its participants, also establishing the philosophy that helpers should "leave their credentials at the door" and facilitate attitudinal healing as equals with the other participants.

"The Course makes it very clear that everyone is equally a student and teacher," explains Jampolsky, "something that had never occurred to me as a psychiatrist trained to believe that I knew more than my patients. So I started calling my patients co-workers at that point." Another change of mind occasioned by the Course was the surrender of "the psychotherapeutic idea that certain kinds of guilt are not good and other kinds are healthy," says Jampolsky. "The Course taught me that no kind of guilt is healthy."

Noting that the entire psychiatric model is built on descriptions of pathology rather than health, Jampolsky proposes a dramatic reorientation of psychological diagnosis and treatment. "If I had to rewrite the American Psychiatric Association nomenclature, a great big book with hundreds of diagnoses, I'd replace the whole thing with one concept: *Insanity is when you are not experiencing yourself as the essence of love, and giving that love away.* Of course that means most of us are insane, including myself, a good deal of the time. But the Course asks us to achieve sanity only one instant at a time, because that 'holy instant' is really an eternal moment. As you begin to achieve these instants, something very different begins to happen in your life."

As the Center for Attitudinal Healing grew and Jampolsky continued his Course study with a "family" that included Judy Skutch, Frances Vaughan, and Bill Thetford, he eventually reached a turning point in his career. In 1979 he decided to stop charging fees for therapy, trusting that his strengthening sense of inner guidance would somehow provide for his needs. About a year and a half later, Jampolsky remembers his secretary suggesting that perhaps he should see a psychiatrist himself. "She said that listening to God's voice was fine, but I had a lot of bills stacking up and would soon be in real trouble. I did wonder if I might be slipping into some sort of spiritual psychosis."

Soon afterward Jampolsky's book *Love is Letting Go of Fear* was published. "I thought it might help some people," Jampolsky recalls, but otherwise his expectations were low. After all, he had once received a D-minus in a college English class from a professor who told him, "Jampolsky, I don't know what you're going to do with your life, but for God's sake don't ever try to write a book." On top of that he had been dyslexic since childhood, a problem that he now believes worked to his advantage. "Otherwise I wouldn't have written so simply and appealed to as many people."

Whatever the reason, *Love* was a near-instant hit. After the actor Orson Bean enthusiastically endorsed it during an appearance on the Johnny Carson show, the book took off and has sold over three million copies to date. Jampolsky's subsequent Course-inspired titles *Goodbye to Guilt* and *Teach Only Love* also did well, providing Jampolsky with a livelihood from royalties and lecture fees. Remarried in 1990 to former businesswoman Diane Cirincione, who would soon become a speaking partner, Jampolsky has recently performed about thirty-five paying lecture dates yearly and appears for free at numerous benefits as well. Although he does not practice psychiatry formally, Jampolsky often counsels individuals, couples, and small groups by request, and does not charge.

Despite his own transformational experience with the Course, he rarely recommends it directly to those who come to him for help. "I don't think the Course is right for everyone," explains Jampolsky. "I refer people to therapists or psychiatrists when it seems appropriate. That doesn't mean I wouldn't suggest that someone look within to open a door. The difference is that as a psychiatrist I used to try pushing or pulling people through the doors I thought they should go through. Now I ask the Holy Spirit what to say, and sometimes I'm surprised as hell by what comes through me. Sometimes I'm directed to use a psychiatric technique. But I never know ahead of time what I'm going to say."

Lately both Jampolsky and Cirincione have reduced their speaking schedule, "feeling guided to go for more simplicity in our lives." Although he asserts that neither his books nor the principles of Attitudinal Healing should be regarded as Course teachings, Jerry Jampolsky's influence on the spread and "real world" application of ACIM is unmistakable. The continued growth of the Centers for Attitudinal Healing — sometimes in surprising places, always in response to daunting challenges — suggests that this legacy will continue for decades to come.

Facing Life, Death, and Pain

The existence of 110 Centers for Attitudinal Healing contradicts a common criticism of *A Course in Miracles:* that its philosophy will encourage students to withdraw from worldly concerns or deny the most unpleasant facts of life (see Chapter 8). Jerry Jampolsky's Course-inspired concept of "attitudinal healing" was in fact born from an exactly opposite motive, as a way to counter the denial of death he observed in professional medicine. From its earliest days, Attitudinal Healing has been widely lauded as a boon to people in severe crisis and distress.

Even the CBS investigative news show *60 Minutes,* normally a tough customer, recognized Attitudinal Healing as "a way of looking life, death, and pain squarely in the eye" in a 1979 report that identified Jampolsky's first center as "a place where trust and understanding happen, rather than pity or institutional therapy."[3] Other press coverage of the original and subsequent centers appears to be consistently positive, even though Jampolsky allows that "I'm sure we've had our dirty laundry just like anyone else."

In a sense, the Centers could be regarded as the first and most widespread "missionary work" inspired by *A Course in Miracles.* The twelve principles of Attitudinal Healing, providing the framework and philosophy by which Center groups operate, are expressed more simply than the Course itself, but are unmistakably rooted in its teaching:

Attitudinal Healing Principles

1. The essence of our being is love.
2. Health is inner peace. Healing is letting go of fear.
3. Giving and receiving are the same.
4. We can let go of the past and of the future.
5. Now is the only time there is and each instant is for giving.
6. We can learn to love ourselves and others by forgiving rather than judging.
7. We can become love finders rather than fault finders.
8. We can choose and direct ourselves to be peaceful inside regardless of what is happening outside.
9. We are students and teachers to each other.

10. We can focus on the whole of life rather than the fragments.
11. Since love is eternal, death need not be viewed as fearful.
12. We can always perceive ourselves and others as either extending love or giving a call for help.

In another important sense, however, Attitudinal Healing is not a missionary extension of the Course because ACIM itself is neither promoted nor offered to people who attend Center workshops and programs. At the spacious Center headquarters (now in Sausalito, California) where over thirty groups meet regularly to provide mutual support for those dealing with catastrophic illness and loss, the bookstore does not even sell the Course. People who wish to found centers in their own locales are not expected to be familiar with the Course, although adherence to the principles of Attitudinal Healing is required and training for facilitators is offered.

Although the traditional emphasis of the Centers is on catastrophic illness, suffering, loss and grief, recent years have seen the development of Attitudinal Healing groups dealing with the challenges of broader sociopolitical crises. A 1995 edition of *The Rainbow Connection,* a newspaper published by the Center headquarters in Sausalito, noted the formation of a Center in Oklahoma City after the bombing of the federal building there, and the work of centers and affiliated support groups in Moscow and Bosnia. In Oakland, California, a Center focusing on the challenge of "racial healing" has been founded by Aeesha Abbabio, a long-time Course student and former Nation of Islam member.

In 1995 Jerry Jampolsky received a call from Chief Ann Bayne, a Kaska Indian and leader of the Liard First Nation in the Canadian Yukon. A Course student, Chief Bayne had just read *Out of the Darkness Into the Light,* and felt that Jampolsky might be able to offer her tribe some assistance in dealing with a daunting array of sociopolitical problems, including family and tribal infighting, sex and drug abuse, alcoholism, and high suicide rates.

Originally a nomadic people whose children were forced into a residential schooling system by the Canadian Department of Indian Affairs in the early 1950s, Chief Bayne's nation became "spiritually bankrupt," as she puts it, due to the cultural disruption caused by the mission schools, whose administrators were largely Catholic. "They banned our ceremonies and practices," says Chief Bayne, "and referred to us as heathens, savages, and pagans. Today we need so much healing from what has happened to us. We need to find our way back to our Creator."

For Chief Bayne, what Jerry Jampolsky and Diane Cirincione brought to the Kaska people in the autumn of 1995 was the beginning of exactly the healing she seeks. "Jerry and Diane were the most loving and generous people to come to our community for a long time. These were two strangers, who came to us at no expense and gave us a lot of literature and ideas. But mostly they brought us hope and faith."

Chief Bayne, who is now planning a center for her people based on Attitudinal Healing, says that she finds a strong harmony between its principles, the Course, and the teachings she received from her elders. "My parents and ancestors always taught the ideas of forgiveness and not getting angry. My dad also said that you shouldn't judge people. We don't even have the word *judge* in Kaska, but the idea was that you never put people down. And of course faith in Creator was always our way."

When I mention to Chief Bayne that the Course has sometimes been criticized as a self-serving, feel-good philosophy for New Age types, it seems to be news to her. "No, I don't think that's true at all," she replies. "To me the Course is the same as the honorable way of the Kaska people. It feels like coming home."

A Girl with an Edge

The powerful and mixed effects that Marianne Williamson has had on the public awareness of *A Course in Miracles* were aptly demonstrated to me in a conversation I had with a friend just before interviewing Williamson herself. My friend, a well-read, churchgoing Episcopalian who has studied Buddhism and the Workbook of the Course, told me he had mentioned the Course to a new acquaintance who immediately replied, "Oh yes, I saw her on Oprah the other day." After recounting this exchange, my erudite friend asked me quizzically, "So who is Marianne Williamson?"

The short answer is that Williamson is the foremost popularizer of the Course, owing chiefly to the success of her first book *A Return to Love: Reflections on the Principles of* A Course in Miracles, which became a mega-best-seller almost immediately upon its release in 1992. Also known as a spiritual lecturer, Williamson attained during the early nineties the kind of celebrity usually accorded Hollywood movie stars (among whom she counts many friends).

Indeed Williamson's fame has eclipsed that of the Course itself, creating not a little chicken-and-egg confusion about her relationship to it. Just before I talked with her, Williamson had appeared on a Larry King television special devoted to the subject of miracles — where she hastened to correct King's offhand reference to "her course in miracles."

"I could just imagine all those Course students out there screaming '*What?*' or thinking that I told him to say that!" Williamson exclaims. "There are ideas out there that I wrote the Course or have some sort of monopoly on it. I don't even consider myself a representative of the Course, nor an advanced student. I think I'm a good intermediate student. But I talk about a lot of things that are not from the Course at all, and my last two books are on different subjects. I'm a popularizer of spiritual themes, and I certainly don't think the Course has a monopoly on spiritual truth."

Even if Williamson doesn't consider herself a Course representative, she is clearly a major figure in the spread of the Course, her first book having spurred a 50% increase in sales of ACIM itself (see Chapter 3). Her lectures, tapes, TV appearances and high media profile have brought at least the notion of a "course in miracles" to the awareness of millions.

That all this exposure has led some people to mistake Williamson as the earthly source of the Course is especially ironic. Attractive, outspoken, and comfortable in the spotlight, Williamson seems to be everything that Course scribe Helen Schucman was not — including the fact that Williamson has accepted the Course as a guideline for living in a way that Schucman always resisted. When I ask Williamson how she thinks her life might have gone without the Course, she says, "It's funny that you ask because I ask myself that question regularly, and always with a laugh and a shudder. Let's put it this way: before the Course, I was not on the road to peace and happiness."

Raised for Revolution and Propriety

The daughter of liberal, middle-class Jewish parents in Houston, Williamson has said that she was "raised to raise hell whenever hell needed to be raised."[4] Her father Sam was an outspoken immigration attorney, an "armchair revolutionary" who earned a lifetime achievement award from the Center for Human and Constitutional Law. In 1965, when Marianne was in the seventh grade, she reported to her father that one of her teachers had said the United States must fight in Vietnam in order to keep communism from the shores of Hawaii. Sam Williamson's response was to take his 13-year-old daughter to Vietnam to see war for herself. As she wrote in *A Return to Love*, "he wanted me to see bullet holes firsthand. He didn't want the military-industrial complex to eat my brain and convince me war was OK."[5]

But along with such lessons in challenging authority and conventional assumptions, the young Marianne was also expected to hew to certain customs of social propriety. "I was raised to forge a revolution, but I was supposed to do it in an organdy dress with white gloves."[6] These contrasting influences of rebellion and correctness seem very much in evidence in Williamson's adult style as a popular spiritual teacher who draws her primary inspiration from a radical discipline while often speaking in a strong moral tone to her audiences. Unafraid to challenge social conventions in her message and her lifestyle, she would nonetheless never be mistaken for an anarchist.

In fact in early 1995 there was a flurry of press attention about the invitation extended to Williamson and several other human potential speakers to confer with the President and First Lady at Camp David. It also became news that Williamson had lunched a number of times with Hillary Clinton. One rumor went that Williamson tried her hand at presidential speechwriting, prompting disclaimers from the White House.

Long before Williamson might have imagined such connections and influence, her ambitions were indistinct and much less far-reaching. After leaving Pomona College in 1972, her sophomore year, Williamson wandered the country following romances, temporary jobs, and doomed plans for the future. "There are a lot of things from those years I can't remember," she confessed in *A Return to Love*. "Like a lot of people at that time — late sixties, early seventies — I was pretty wild. Every door marked 'no' by conventional standards seemed to hold the key to some lascivious pleasure I had to have. Whatever sounded outrageous, I wanted to do. And usually, I did."[7]

By 1977 Williamson was living in New York City for the second time, working temp jobs in order to finance her fledgling career as a cabaret singer. Some listeners thought she wasn't bad, others thought she should hold on to her day job, and still others enjoyed her patter between numbers more than the songs themselves.

Williamson first saw the Course in 1977, but was put off by its Christian language; her serious study began a year later. She volunteered her services at the Foundation for Inner Peace when it was still in New York, working there for three months and later helping out for a few weeks at FIP's new home in Tiburon, California. Following a pattern not uncommon among serious students of the Course, Williamson's life would become much more difficult as her study intensified, leading her into a "dark night of the soul" spanning several years after she moved back to Houston in 1979.

"Nervous breakdowns can be highly underrated methods of spiritual transformation," Williamson has written. "They certainly get your attention."[8] Williamson's occurred not long after a brief, failed marriage to a Houston businessman. Soon Williamson was seeing a psychiatrist (who was also a Course student) five times a week, and she has credited that therapeutic relationship with helping her survive a tumultuous period during which she ran a bookstore/coffeehouse with an ambitious cultural arts program while still trying to launch a singing career. During this time Williamson remained an avid Course student, sometimes counseling bookstore customers on its teaching. In a reference that every Course student would appreciate, her back-up band onstage was called the "Little Egos."

Finally Williamson approached a spiritual surrender, a "grandiose, dramatic moment where I invited God into my life . . ."

> After that, nothing felt the way I expected it to. I had thought that things would improve. It's as though my life was a house, and I thought God would give it a wonderful paint job — new shutters perhaps, a pretty portico, a new roof. Instead, it felt as though, as soon as I gave the house to God, He hit it with a giant wrecking ball. "Sorry, honey," He seemed to say, "There were cracks in the foundation, not to mention all the rats in the bedroom. I thought we better just start all over."[9]

By 1983 Williamson was indeed starting all over. With her bookstore closed and a thousand dollars to her name, Williamson pointed her mother's Oldsmobile toward the mecca that has drawn so many other natural-born performers with nothing left to lose: Los Angeles. This time she would not be seeking a nightclub gig, however. After taking a secretarial job with the Philosophical Research Society, Williamson soon became the society's weekly lecturer on the principles of *A Course in Miracles*.

Becoming an Overnight Sensation

With the publication of her first book in 1992 and a blizzard of press notices that began shortly before, Williamson seemed to spring full-blown into America's celebrity culture. But in fact her climb to fame was built on years of steadily increasing popularity as a spiritual lecturer, as well as a demanding schedule of unpaid service and charity organizing.

Williamson's effect on her lecture audiences was dramatic, as attested to by Hollywood producer Howard Rosenman:

> "The first time I went to see her it was like the Liberty Bell fell on my head. . . . Here was this gorgeous Jewish chick who obviously came from a sophisticated, neurotic Texas Jewish background, talking in the argot of my generation, bringing together strands of sociology, politics, anthropology, history, science, and the Bible. The community she's addressing is a group that partied and drugged and sexualized through the sixties and seventies, and here comes this woman who looks like one of us, who you know could have been at Studio 54 or dancing at Fire Island Pines with a tambourine on her hip — and yet she's talking like Jesus Christ. She's talking about the most fundamental precepts. She's talking about the Golden Rule."[10]

Williamson's fast-paced, funny, sometimes strident lectures quickly outgrew the confines of the Philosophical Research Society, but would not provide her with a living wage for two more years, during which time she continued to do temporary secretarial work. By 1986 she was speaking to full houses in various venues in both Los Angeles and New York. Listening to tapes of her talks was becoming almost *de rigueur* for southern

California baby boomers turned off by conventional religion but seeking more profound motivations than the affluent material-ism and professional success that were largely in their grasp already.

Williamson's Course-inspired but multi-faceted philosophy seemed to hit a particular chord with gay men facing the specter of the AIDS epidemic, leading to the inspiration for the Center for Living — a combination hospice/cultural center for people facing catastrophic illness — that she helped found in Los Angeles and later in New York.

Forceful, hyperactive, and by all reports remarkably generous in contrast to the me-first mentality of the 1980s, Marianne Williamson spawned a phenomenon that seemed to be moving faster, and on a larger scale, than she could by herself. While charging five to seven dollars per head for her lectures — with free admission for anyone who could not afford that — Williamson also began organizing high-yield, star-studded benefits for the Centers for Living and a Los Angeles subsidiary, Project Angel Food, a free home-delivery meal service for AIDS sufferers. She was also a frequent visitor to bedridden hospital patients, and was increasingly asked to officiate at weddings and funerals. In 1989 she became pregnant by a father whom she has never publicly identified, adding single motherhood to her list of self-created obligations.

On top of all that, New York literary agent Al Lowman had convinced Williamson to do a book, and sold the proposal for *A Return to Love* in 1988. But the project was delayed by the difficulty of translating Williamson's rapid-fire oratory into a literary form; Williamson has said that learning to write has been one of her greatest personal challenges. Editor Andrea Cagan has recounted what it was like to work with the busy author:

"She works in a tremendous amount of maelstrom. Phone calls are coming in, the baby jumps on her in the middle of everything. So there's no time to have quiet — no phone calls, no interruptions. I never get a chance like that to work with her. Ever. Her life is not set up that way. She works in fits and starts. She's out of the room, she's in the room, she's eating something — it's her personality. So I had to adapt to that. . . .

"It's hard to deal with full-throttle intensity all the time. A lot of people get frightened of it. When she's happy, she's happy. When she's angry, she's angry. You have to be in your own center around her."[11]

Hand in hand with Williamson's intensity came a fierce loyalty, Cagan revealed. When Cagan once called her with a personal problem, Williamson "stopped what she was doing to do a prayer for me on the phone. She would do anything for me."[12]

By the early 1990s, even before the release and immediate success of her first book, Williamson was becoming a celebrity in her own right. The June 1991 issue of *Vanity Fair* carried a feature article, "Marianne's Faithful," that opened with a dramatic photo of Williamson reclining languorously in a fashionable pink suit on a lawn divan, her face set in a firm, no-nonsense expression that seemed to be saying, "Don't mess with me." Perhaps she was momentarily anticipating the attitude she would need to face all the public notoriety yet to come.

Marianne, Meet the Press

When I ask Williamson if she would have posed for *Vanity Fair* if she knew then what she knows now, she replies without hesitation: "Absolutely not. I was incredibly naive then. I was like a lamb to slaughter." But at first Williamson appeared to be the beneficiary of an almost divine reception by America's pop culture. Shortly after the *Vanity Fair* story, *Time* magazine headlined her as a "Mother Teresa for the '90s" in a largely friendly story noting that no other Course teacher had the "show-biz pizazz that Williamson brings to the lecture circuit." (For balance the article quoted an unidentified "expert on new religious movements in California" who panned the Course itself as "the perfect disconnected religion of the 90s. It allows driven, self-absorbed, narcissistic people to continue in their ways.")[13]

Shortly thereafter, Williamson officiated at the highly publicized wedding of Liz Taylor to Larry Fortensky, raising her media profile by a significant notch. Then came *Oprah*. Shortly after publication of *A Return to Love* in February 1992, America's most popular daytime talk show host invited Williamson onto her show and announced that she had bought copies of the book for everyone in her studio audience. This endorsement sparked a bookselling frenzy, moving 750,000 copies of the HarperCollins title in just a few months. Soon Williamson seemed to be showing up everywhere, from the Larry King show on CNN to the tabloid press. But the predictable backlash of sudden fame was already under way.

As both *People* magazine and the *Los Angeles Times* would reveal shortly after Williamson's *Oprah* debut, the year before publication of *A Return to Love* had seen considerable dissension and turmoil in the Centers for Living on both coasts. Williamson's administrative style and personality were reportedly deeply embroiled in a series of controversies that involved everything from her interpersonal difficulties with Los Angeles staffers to her predilection for public prayer, a tendency that made fundraising colleagues in New York nervous.

The fallout from all these problems would be significant: resignations by Center for Living staffers and board members on both coasts, followed eventually by Williamson's full retreat from involvement in both organizations. Today the New York center no longer exists, and the Los Angeles chapter is focused on Project Angel Food, which granted Williamson their first Founder's Award in 1995. Williamson has also participated in benefits for other Centers for Living that have been started independently in Palm Beach, San Francisco, and Denver. She says that the growth of the idea she initiated gives her "the pride of a mother in a grown-up child who's doing good work in the world."

But the public charges made against her in the early nineties — which included hypocrisy, self-promotion, an over-controlling managerial style, and an ungovernable temper — clearly stung Williamson and no doubt played a part in the temporary roll-back of her public profile. Although she published two more best-selling books, *A Woman's Worth* and *Illuminata* during the mid-nineties, she reduced her public appearances and made herself less available to the press. When I ask Williamson how she would critique her own performance during the heady and conflicted period of her organizational activism and peak of fame, she is largely unapologetic:

"This is not to say that I don't ever have a temper. But those stories were of a time when I was pregnant and producing charity events grossing well over a million dollars, for which I did not earn a dime. People often charge thousands of dollars for this kind of work. Here I was a single woman, pregnant, struggling to make ends meet on my own, and dealing with subterfuge and sabotage. Did I ever break under the pressure? Yes. But I don't think many people could have held it together as well as I did."

In a 1993 interview with *Miracles Magazine* editor Paul Ferrini, Williamson admitted that "I'm a girl who does have an edge . . . [but] the press wasn't angry because I'm a bad girl; the press was angry because I'm a good girl."[14] When I ask Williamson to expound on this remark three years later, she explains that "people would say to me back then that the press just couldn't stand that I had weaknesses like everyone else. But I don't think my weaknesses angered them; what angered them were my strengths. That's what misogny is based on: the power of a woman, not her weakness."

As a high-profile messenger of spirituality and personal transformation, Williamson certainly made an irresistible target for the chronic cynicism of contemporary journalism — an attitude that has only recently begun to be confronted by some members of the press itself. As *Atlantic Monthly* Washington editor James Fallows notes in his book *Breaking the News*, "If 'investigation' was the word for journalism in the Woodward and Bernstein era, attitude and snarl are the words now. . . . The 'toughness' of today's media is mainly a toughness of demeanor rather than real toughness of reporting, investigation, or substantive change."[15]

In the reporting done on Marianne Williamson in the early nineties, such a tough demeanor is not hard to find. Typical of the writing about her is the following passage from a 1993 *Mirabella* magazine feature that rhetorically asked, "So why did Marianne's faithful suddenly turn on her?"

> The story has a lovely fablelike quality. Young, beautiful woman with creamy, transparent skin and Natalie Wood looks and a passionate nature comes to Los Angeles wanting to be a songwriter and singer . . . and ends up teaching God to thousands of sad gay men, recovering substance abusers, New Age vegetarians, spiritually blocked yuppies, Hollywood producers and a bunch of others whose est training was wearing off.[16]

Such not-so-subtle demeaning of people with spiritual or self-reforming interests is endemic in the mainstream press, reflecting the inability of most journalists to fairly assess the value of introspective and spiritual processes.

One result is that the story of a teacher like Williamson gets covered as a win-lose popularity contest, and some facts are inevitably distorted in the process. For instance there is no evidence that any significant number of Williamson's faithful listeners ever "turned" on her. It would be more accurate to say that Williamson alienated some colleagues who were once close to her, and that many people who knew of Williamson only through her press clippings gained a negative impression of her.

After reviewing several years of those clippings, it becomes clear that the press never managed to dig up as much dirt on Marianne Williamson as they might have liked to, given that they had assigned her the charged (and unwanted) label of "guru." Because she always made her problems and foibles public knowledge in her lectures and tapes, she ultimately appeared to be simply flawed and perhaps overreaching her capacities rather than hypocritical. Despite making substantial sums of money from her book advances, Williamson has never been tainted by allegations of greed or financial impropriety; her personal and financial expressions of generosity remain almost legendary. And like nearly all Course-inspired teachers, she has never claimed to be a "guru" or a perfect embodiment of the spiritual message she conveys.

"None of us claim to be role models," comments Beverly Hutchinson of the Miracle Distribution Center, who has worked with Williamson in workshops and benefits. "I think the first sign of a real Course teacher is someone who says she's still a student and always will be." Or as the Course itself says of "teachers of God": "They are not perfect, or they would not be here."[17]

Trading Pizazz for Depth

Twelve years after she began lecturing on *A Course in Miracles*, Marianne Williamson observes that she's in "a very different phase of a woman's life. I have less pizazz, and I'm probably less superficially impressive. I would like to think that my insights are deeper, if not so quick as they used to be."

Having recently completed her fourth book (*The Healing of America*) and launched an ambitious Internet project (see the Appendix for website address), Williamson still maintains a steady lecture schedule and recently began appearing in high-profile venues like the *Oprah* and Larry King shows again. As the Course has become better known on its own, Williamson has become the focus of a comparatively mild-mannered controversy within the Course community over how "pure" her interpretations are. Long credited with a keen capacity to lend spiritual significance to people's typical problems, Williamson is sometimes faulted by other Course veterans for not conveying the "heavier" meanings of ACIM in public venues — including the issue of its spiritual authorship — and for mixing in other ideas, such as astrology, with Course philosophy.

"I don't talk about the authorship or Course theology unless I'm asked," Williamson admits. "But look at some of the venues I'm in. Larry King isn't going to ask you about the heavier theological principles of the Course, nor is Dick Cavett or Lauren Hutton. I'm sure that Carl Sagan talks about science in a different way on television than he would at a scientific conference. And in my lectures it's been years since I was specifically teaching Course principles; it's just like being a Buddhist who might not always lecture on Buddhism."

Williamson also recognizes that the broader principles of the Course are universal. "A rabbi once told me that I could have found everything I like about the Course in Judaism. So I said, 'Well, then you should have taught me that.' If I'd been shown the mystical source of Judaism when I was young, I'd probably be lecturing on the Kabbalah today. It's just that nobody told me about it when they had the chance."

Will the Course always be important to Marianne Williamson? "For those of us who view it that way, *A Course in Miracles* is the word of Jesus," she says softly. "Once Jesus has arrived in your heart, I don't think there's a question that he will always occupy a place there. He becomes your heart; he is your heart." By now the characteristic urgency of Williamson's voice has subsided; it sounds as though she is speaking from an inward peacefulness that apparently eluded her throughout her youth.

"I didn't find some peace in my life simply because I found the Course," Williamson explains. "I found peace because I found a way to experience conscious contact with God."

PART II:

Understanding
the Course

5
Higher Learning:
Talking with Kenneth and Gloria Wapnick

Watching an ethereal mist drift across broad Tennanah Lake during a summer sunrise, it seems to me that the Course might be right about the inauthenticity of the material world — especially after coming here by way of New York City, two and a half hours to the southeast. Compared with the nonstop clamor of the metropolis, this restful scene in the gently rolling Catskills seems almost too simple and serene to be real. One has the feeling of being near the end of a tranquil morning dream that may abruptly dissolve with the slightest jostle or a faintly heard call.

It is by Tennanah Lake, within the study and retreat center of the Foundation for *A Course in Miracles* (FACIM), that the original manuscript of the Course is secured — once removed but not very distant from the urban center where it was scribed. Here also resides the last surviving participant in the shaping of the Course. Kenneth Wapnick was thirty-one in 1973 when he first examined the typed volumes that would later be known as the Course and was, he recalls, "bowled over. I thought it was the most beautiful thing I'd read since Shakespeare, and that it really said something. It took only days for me to decide what my life would be." Wapnick spent the next year editing the manuscript line-by-line with Helen Schucman, and gradually assumed the role of a full-time teacher of the Course over the next several years, leading to the formation of FACIM with his second wife, Gloria.

FACIM occupies a five-story former resort hotel and a small office building nearby, both facing Tennanah Lake. Across the narrow country road lie six buildings for students in temporary residence while taking classes given by the Wapnicks and a few other teachers under the auspices of FACIM's Institute for Teaching Inner Peace Through *A Course in Miracles*. (ITIP-ACIM was incorporated under the New York State Education Law and chartered by the state Board of Regents in 1995. While it does not offer academic credits or degrees, it can cooperate with colleges and universities to offer credits, including credits in continuing education for working professionals.)

With room for more development on its 95 acres, FACIM can presently house as many as 150 people for stays lasting anywhere from a weekend to one year in duration. The staff, usually numbering about twenty, is composed entirely of Course students who work for a stipend plus room and board. Although a few students have lived on campus for up to a year and a half — and a long-term study program of up to twelve months is offered — the Wapnicks dissuade students from attaching to the retreat as a permanent community. "We don't have a cult atmosphere here," remarks Gloria, "and we actively discourage it."

Indeed, the general ambience of FACIM is more like that of an intimate college than a spiritual enclave. While pictures of Jesus and other religious symbols are in evidence, the retreat does not have a chapel or meditation room, and no religious services or prayer meetings are held. In fact there are hardly any organized activities besides the classes conducted mostly in two spacious rooms on the ground floor of the main building. Although classes and workshops of various lengths have specific titles such as "The Nature of the Dream," "From Time to Timelessness," and "Exploring Our Relationship with God," most sessions follow a general discussion format. Overnight "homework" assignments are made in the longer classes, and the general atmosphere of classes and workshops might best be described as casual but nonetheless studious.

Students have access to various recreational facilities including tennis, hiking, swimming, paddleboating, and shuffleboard, but anyone looking to FACIM for a luxurious vacation stay will be disappointed. While the rooms are comfortable, they are minimally appointed and no daily linen service is provided. Children and pets are not accommodated. Only two public phones are available on campus. Most of the rooms feature a kitchenette; the Institute also operates a dining room. Typical fees average less than sixty-five dollars per day for tuition, lodging, class materials, and some meals on campus.

The conservative accommodations of FACIM occasionally induce complaints from students, which the administrators respond to by further defining what FACIM is in terms of what it is not. "We have to remind people sometimes that this is not a hotel," says Gloria, adding slyly that "we've had to tell a few folks that we're not running a *motel* either."

In general, however, FACIM experiences few problems with the conduct of its students, probably owing to the fact that most of them are middle-aged or older and have often come to the retreat for a period of intense reflection and study. Gloria recalls a woman in residence for a few months who came to FACIM after weathering a divorce, the death of a parent, a bitter estrangement from her children, and the death of her beloved horse — all within six months prior to her arrival.

"A lot of people who come here are in pain," Gloria explains, "because people everywhere are in pain due to the upheavals in our culture. Marriages are collapsing, people are losing jobs and are worried about their children, and so on. Many students are asking, 'What's it all about?' because their lives seem to be crumbling."

But Ken issues a disclaimer to anyone who might look to FACIM as a spiritual rescue mission. "We try to make it clear that we're not here to solve anyone's personal problems. What we offer is a clarification of Course principles for students. Their own study of the Course may ease their crisis, but we can't do that."

Thus, compared to many other Course schools and churches offering everything from prayer groups to weekly services, there is a distinctly intellectual and contemplative ambience at FACIM. After considering the life story of Kenneth Wapnick, this should come as no surprise to anyone.

"A Very Funny Christian"

Raised in a Jewish home and sent to a Hebrew school, Wapnick nonetheless thought of himself as an agnostic by high school, recognizing only Mozart and Beethoven as his "spiritual teachers." Still, for his doctoral thesis in psychology Wapnick was drawn to study the mystic Saint Teresa of Avila, understanding "all her references to God and Jesus as metaphors for something else."

After his first marriage ended bitterly in 1970, Wapnick realized that his life was becoming increasingly solitary and monastic, and he took to reading the works of Thomas Merton. This study led to visiting the Abbey of Gethsemane where Merton had lived, and it was there that Wapnick decided to become a monk. Eventually baptized as a Catholic, he later visited two monasteries in Israel, choosing one in Galilee as the place he would settle. It was this paradoxical spiritual path — an agnostic Jew converting to Catholicism in order to join a monastery in Israel — that would later lead Helen Schucman to characterize Wapnick as "a very funny Christian."

Before going to Israel, Wapnick was introduced to Helen Schucman and Bill Thetford by a friend who was familiar with Wapnick's work linking psychology and mysticism. During their first evening together, someone mentioned a book that Helen Schucman had "written," and Wapnick first saw the seven black thesis binders that held the Course material in a corner of Thetford's apartment. But he did not look at them at that time. He went on to Israel and stayed for two months at a remote mountain monastery in the area of Galilee, selecting it as the endpoint to his spiritual search.

However, Wapnick twice dreamed of an unfamiliar "holy book" while in Israel, and upon his return to New York to tie up

the last ends of his life in America, he found himself unexpectedly eager to examine the manuscript he had been told about a
few months before. The following passage from *Absence from Felicity* succinctly reveals the would-be monk's sense of propriety:

> Helen's recollection was that I walked into the door and
> said, "Hello, here I am; where's the book?" While I knew I
> was anxious to see the material, I doubt if I would have to-
> tally forgotten my good manners. I would at least have said,
> "Hello, *how are you?*" And then, "Where's the book?" But
> obviously I could not wait to see "Helen's" manuscript.[1]

Thereafter, as Wapnick's written account continues, "it did not
take me very long to realize that *A Course in Miracles* was my
life's work, Helen and Bill were my spiritual family, and that I
was not to become a monk but to remain in New York with
them instead."[2]

Did the transmission of the Course through Helen Schucman
always seem credible to Wapnick? "I had tremendous faith in
Helen and trusted her implicitly," he declares. "I knew she didn't
have a dishonest bone in her body, and what she said had happened simply made sense." Wapnick also believed from the beginning that it was impossible for Schucman to have written the
Course material on her own. "In fact, when Helen and I were
editing the material she would sometimes get confused about
certain passages. We would read something aloud and she would
burst out laughing, saying 'I don't understand what this means!'
So the first Course teaching I ever did was to help Helen understand what it meant."

Unlike some other prominent Course students — including
Bill Thetford (see Chapter 2) — Wapnick has always been firm
in his belief that the source of the Course is the historical Jesus
Christ (whom he believes is not accurately represented in the
Bible). But why would Jesus choose such a peculiar method —
sending his message through the mind of a religiously ambivalent psychologist — to communicate with the modern world?

"Helen was very split," Wapnick concedes, "but part of her operated on a high spiritual level. On that level she could form a union with Jesus for the transmission of the Course. In a sense, you could say that Helen became a psychologist so that the Course could come through in the way it did — in a form appropriate to this psychological age.

"Helen was a Freudian who understood psychoanalysis very well," Wapnick adds. "I think that's why the Course so directly meets the needs of the modern Western mind. I believe Freud's work was extremely important to our culture's spiritual development. These days it seems that Jung is the darling and Freud is the bad guy, but despite his active resistance to religion, I think Freud's spiritual contribution was incredible. Even Jung said, 'I'm like Joshua standing on the shoulders of Moses.'"

Not Satisfied with a Mystery

Gloria Wapnick (née Malatino) was primed early for a radical spiritual path by an experience common to many: The religion of her childhood just didn't add up. "When I was growing up Catholic," she recalls, "I always had a problem understanding how a loving God could create a world where there's so much pain, suffering, and misery. The priests I asked could never give me a satisfactory answer; they'd just say it was a mystery. Even though I wanted to be a nun when I was very young, I eventually decided that if this was the best kind of world God could create, I really didn't need that kind of God. So I left the church, which dismayed my parents very much."

Although she looked into various paths in high school and college, Gloria never found any spiritual perspective that made "complete sense in terms of knowing the purpose of my life, what it was all about." She married, raised two children and divorced, but found herself still searching for a deeper meaning later in life. Referred by a friend to a psychic counselor (Pat Rodegast, the well-known channel of the Emmanuel teachings), Gloria went to see her "just out of curiosity" and was told that she would "find what I was looking for" at Wainwright House, a consciousness seminar center in Rye, New York. She registered for a weekend symposium there, and upon arriving found herself drawn to a workshop about *A Course in Miracles*.

"The night I arrived at the symposium," recalls Gloria, "I started reading the Course. When I first came upon the idea that God *didn't* create the world, it was as if a lightning bolt had struck me. It was so simple, so clear, yet I had never thought of it before because I was so angry at God."

Not long afterward Gloria would meet Ken at a conference. At a later meeting she admitted to him that there were two fears she couldn't let go of: heights and snakes. After listing some of the reasons that Gloria might be phobic about these phenomena, Ken said to her, "But that's not what you're actually afraid of. What you're really doing is running away from Jesus."

"When he said that something clicked," Gloria remembers. "I had to leave the table, and I cried most of the night. I knew I had to call Kenneth after that. He had opened something very deep inside me, and I knew I had to find out what it was."

Gloria was a history teacher and dean of students at a high school at the time she and Ken met in the late 70s. While Ken had already dispensed with his ambition to become a monk, he has said that he was "OK with the idea of celibacy" and that "Gloria knew something before I did"[3] about their developing relationship. Married in 1981, the Wapnicks started the Foundation for *A Course in Miracles* in 1982 and it was incorporated the following January. Their first teaching site in Ardsley, New York was in their home, a one-car garage converted into an office space, followed by a larger space within their second house outside of Peekskill. With three people on the Foundation staff by that time — who resided with the Wapnicks along with Gloria's parents and one of her sons — the one-acre property soon proved insufficient for FACIM's growing programs, and the Roscoe property was bought with a donation in 1988. Despite the moderate fees charged to students, FACIM has operated in the black in recent years, its revenues coming chiefly from program revenues and the sales of books and tapes. Plans for a new class and residential facility are under consideration.

What the Course is Not

Because the Course presents a contemporary synthesis of psychological and spiritual themes found across many traditions, it's not unusual to hear it described as being "just like" other paths — a characterization that the Wapnicks take pains to confront.

"We spend a lot of time helping people realize what the Course is not," Ken asserts. "It's not biblical; it's neither Judaism nor Christianity; it's not Christian Science; it's not New Age, Joel Goldsmith, or Edgar Cayce. The most common mistake that people make is to superimpose upon the Course their prior spiritual path. That's a natural mistake, but as long as you make it, you won't understand what the Course is saying."

And what does the Course say that distinguishes it from other paths?

"Fundamentally the Course says that only spirit is real and there's nothing else. It also says that God is not involved in the world of matter. Where it really goes beyond other traditions is in saying that we made up the world — as well as time and space — in an attempt to attack God."

In the words of the Course itself:

> The world was made as an attack on God. It symbolizes fear. And what is fear except love's absence? Thus the world was meant to be a place where God could enter not, and where His Son could be apart from Him.[4]

This message is so disturbing to some Course students, says Ken Wapnick, that "they alter the message, deciding that the Course means God didn't create the *horrors* in the world. But the Course is quite clear that the entire physical universe is not of God's making, but our own."

Adds Gloria, "This is the one concept to which people have

always had tremendous resistance. People find it very difficult to deal with because the direct implication of God not being responsible for this world is that we are. This means you have to take responsibility for your existence and everything about it — and who wants to do that?"

Indeed, most people find it difficult enough to take responsibility for their everyday behavior, much less the existential condition of the world at large. In the psychospiritual bestseller *The Road Less Traveled*, Christian psychiatrist M. Scott Peck suggested that the challenge of psychotherapy was not really getting people to see what's wrong with their lives, but getting them to do something about what they see. I ask Ken if this is similar to the challenge of responsibility the Course presents its students.

"I don't entirely agree with Peck," he replies. "I think most people are aware that *something* is wrong in their lives, but they don't know what it is — namely, their ongoing decision to remain separate from God. It takes a lot of work just to understand that. But once you get that far, you will automatically 'choose again,' as the Course puts it. Once you are clear about the choices before you — and that you are solely responsible for your life because it's *your* dream — you will make the right choice."

Is this "choosing again" comparable to the evangelical Christian notions of "getting saved" or being "born again?" Ken suggests that the choosing implied by the Course is properly seen as an ongoing process of growth rather than a salvational epiphany. "Once you choose differently," he explains, "you'll discover another choice to be made underneath that one, and another level underneath that one, and so on. This is a process of undoing the world we have miscreated. The ego invented time and space to put distance between the cause of the world — that is, our choice to believe in it — and its effect on us, so that we experience the pain of the world without realizing that we are the only cause of it."

The Wapnicks' view of the Course's challenge — that it is a lifelong discipline of assuming a daunting responsibility, challenging one's own fundamental perceptions, and learning how to surrender egocentricity to spiritual guidance — makes them especially concerned that people may perceive the Course as a pop spirituality that promises a solution to one's earthly problems through prayer or white-light meditation. This concern has made them skeptical at times of Course popularizers such as Marianne Williamson, whose third book *Illuminata* offers specific prayers about such everyday issues as money, sexuality, illness, and addictions.

"Many people who have read Marianne's books have come here for classes," observes Gloria, "and some of them end up asking if this is the same Course she talks about. People are getting the idea that the message of the Course is 'Pray to God and all your prayers will be answered,' and that's just not the point."

"The Course says the proper role of Jesus, or the Holy Spirit, is not to solve your problems for you," Ken advises, "but to be a loving presence in your mind that reminds you not to accept the world of time and matter as real. By joining with Jesus you correct your erroneous perception. That's very different from praying to Jesus to solve your problems in this world, or to have him tell you what to do."

Does that mean people who have come to the Course through Williamson or New Age connections are likely to find disillusionment in Roscoe? "I don't know if I'd call it disillusionment," Gloria muses, "but people do have to realize that the Course is not a magical, easy path to fulfillment. This is a serious undertaking that requires a lot of study and effort."

Part of the problem is that our whole society is accustomed to instant gratification, Gloria feels. "I often see people wanting a quick fix. People new to the Course tend to see Jesus or the Holy Spirit as a magic wand to solve their problems and get them everything they want. But when they realize that the Course asks for tremendously hard work — you have to pay constant attention to the workings of your mind, for one thing — they begin to fade away if they're not serious.

"Another thing the Course demands is that you try to let go

of grievances and work constantly to forgive," Gloria adds. "And forgiveness is the *last* thing most people want to do. The Course fundamentally challenges the ego, and that's very frightening. This is a simple path, but a very difficult one to take."

Since the Wapnicks do not perceive the Course as a system of psychological self-help in the popular sense, how do they think it works?

"Because Course students learn that they must accept responsibility for everything they think and do, eventually they become much less prone to rationalize their ego and their sense of victimization," suggests Ken. "This doesn't mean that their egos disappear. But students do begin to understand that their egos are to blame for their problems. They find hope in the realization that they don't have to change the whole world, or other people, in order to find peace."

"Before the Course I was prone to blame everyone else for everything that happened to me," admits Gloria. "We all tend to do that. After the Course, I realized that you have to take responsibility for your own life. You're not just a cork bobbing around on the ocean of life, being hurled around by the waves and the stormy weather."

Although it's clear that some students find a "softer" message in the Course than that which the Wapnicks convey — or follow only the parts that offer reassurance — there are countless stories of students responding to its teaching of exceptional responsibility with a notable resistance, sometimes to the point of committing violence against the book itself. I have heard accounts of the Course being thrown across rooms, tossed into rivers, even being soaked with lighter fluid and set afire. The record for destruction of ACIM is perhaps held by one student who complained that he was "probably making the Foundation for Inner Peace rich" by having destroyed at least seven copies of the Course in his ongoing study. Yet many of these same students buy new copies and return to their study, raising the question of what keeps them going. What is it that feels good about studying ACIM?

"What feels good is the sense of hope that the Course provides," Ken suggests. "Not a naive hope that God or the Holy Spirit will descend and take away your problems, but real hope that the possibility of happiness rests within yourself. Even if you haven't fully chosen that, you know that you can eventually change your mind by asking Jesus for help."

"The Course works if you apply it," Gloria asserts, "and if you ask for help and correction. The Course reminds you that Jesus and the Holy Spirit are always available within your mind. Many Course students have realized that *nothing* works in this world — no economic system, no political system, no religious system. These people realize that they want to awaken from the dream, and they recognize that the Course is what's going to help them awaken."

Ken adds that he believes the difficulty of the Course results from a conscious design evidenced not only by the psychological challenge it presents, but by its very language. "I think it's no accident that the sentence structure is difficult. If you like Shakespeare, you'll love the style, but it doesn't make it any easier to comprehend. Concepts aren't explained in a linear way, with definitions clearly given and principles built upon principles logically. Rather the Course's logic is circular, or what I would call *symphonic*. The way it's written you have to spend a long time unraveling it, struggling with it, even resisting it. The purpose of that process is to help you undo the ego's way of thinking. Some have reacted by saying all that struggle is really not necessary, but I believe that's the way the Course is meant to be experienced."

For new students, perhaps the most difficult challenge the Course presents is distinguishing between the voice of one's own ego and the voice of the Holy Spirit. Is there a way to tell for sure what kind of guidance one is listening to?

"The Course offers some means of distinguishing," Ken suggests, "one of them being that when you are following the Holy Spirit's guidance, you are 'wholly without fear.' But really the question is misplaced. The focus should not be on how you can tell which voice you're hearing, but on clearing out the obstacles to the voice of the Holy Spirit — namely, guilt and the ego's sense of specialness. The more you get rid of these interferences, the more you will hear the true voice of the Holy Spirit. The question of 'who's who?' will then arise less and less."

Gloria adds that Course students shouldn't expect the Holy Spirit to be a clearly discernible "voice" inside their heads, à la Helen Schucman. "The Holy Spirit can reach you in a dream, a phone call, something you overhear that 'clicks' for you. Because the Course does refer to a voice, sometimes people get confused and think they have to hear one in a literal sense."

The Course in the World

Ken's "purist" interpretation of ACIM means that he feels its principles should not be translated into specific moral or political stances — a position that is controversial both inside and outside the Course community. The Course has in fact been interpreted by some critics as a path of abdicating social responsibility (see Chapter 8). Yet Marianne Williamson, for one, spreads word of the Course while making no secret of her liberal politics. How do the Wapnicks respond to such divergent interpretations?

"The Course is strictly a mind-training system," Ken asserts. "It's certainly meant to be lived in the world, but I think people make the mistake of trying to apply it too literally to world issues. Since it says that there is literally no world, only a dream of one, the Course is not interested in trying to improve the dream. It wants only to change the mind of the dreamer. When that is accomplished, the dream will automatically change in one way or another. But it's the mind of the dreamer that is the focus of the Course."

While Ken opines that "Jesus is neither a Democrat nor a Republican," more recently incarnated Course principals have not been free of political affiliations. While not an activist by any means, Helen Schucman was a liberal Democrat. Overall it seems that the general politics of those currently involved with FACIM and FIP, the Course publisher, are liberal — although William Whitson of FIP, who spent a career in government service, says jokingly that he often feels like "a Democrat in the morning and a Republican by afternoon."

The Wapnicks both come from liberal political backgrounds, although Ken is slow to stake out a position on the issues of the day. Anyone who believes that long-term Course study will invariably induce political apathy, however, has not talked to Gloria Wapnick for ten minutes. During our first meeting, after I mentioned my early experience as a reporter covering environmental politics, she made a point of showing me the water-pollution safeguards that FACIM had installed to protect the health of Tennanah Lake. At our next meeting she discussed a letter she had written to Hillary Clinton in support of concerns raised by the activist organization Doctors Without Borders, about the health hazards to children of uranium-coated shells that had fallen on Iraq during the Persian Gulf War.

And both Ken and Gloria signed a two-part essay on the war in succeeding 1991 issues of FACIM's quarterly newsletter, *The Lighthouse*, reviewing the historical roots of Middle East territorial conflicts and criticizing the U.S. policy of withholding information about the war from its own citizens. They also questioned whether "the liberation of Kuwait [could] be justified by the destruction of Iraq and its people." Although the article's conclusion returned to Course principles — suggesting that "the Gulf War has given us all yet another chance to set aside our petty thoughts of separation, fragmentation, and condemnation, and to choose once again"[5] — the piece as a whole marked a departure for the newsletter, which usually concentrates on explication of Course principles without reference to worldly issues.

Gloria confirms that her Course study has fundamentally altered the nature of her politics. "Before the Course I believed I could actually make the world a better place by working for political and economic change. I had trained to go into the foreign service, thinking I could influence American foreign policy. After the Course I realized that I had been looking at the world as split between the forces of good and evil, when it was actually my split mind that needed healing. The Course teaches that if you condemn any part of humankind, you're actually condemning a part of yourself. . . .

"Remember the old saying, 'If you're not part of the solution, then you're part of the problem?'" Gloria muses. "What that means to me now is that if you join in the chaos of opposition then you're part of the problem whichever side you're on. I think it's possible to show people that there's another way of living in this world, a way that's different from the way we've been doing things."

Ken suggests that there may be a Course-like principle implied in the philosophy of progressive causes such as the civil rights movement. Recalling his participation in a sixties march in Mississippi led by the Reverend Martin Luther King, Jr., Ken says that even then he was "troubled to find just as much hatred among the marchers as among the whites who were resisting us. We were just certain that we were the good guys." But he took note of one of King's messages to the blacks in the march: "They can't break your back unless it's bent."

"He wanted them to change their mind about themselves," Ken explains. "The heart of that message is the same as that of the Course."

Still, both the Wapnicks feel strongly that the Course cannot properly be quoted to buttress anyone's political position on issues of the day. When I suggest that their frequent use of phrases like "joining with Jesus" might lead a casual observer to mistake the Wapnicks for Christian fundamentalists, Gloria is quick to establish their differences:

"I have a brother and sister who are born-again Christians, and we don't see things at all in the same way," she declares. "Their agenda is quite clear; they are right-wing Republicans who want to stop abortion, put prayer in the schools, and establish a theocratic state. The Course has no investment in any political aims, conservative or liberal. While fundamentalists oppose abortion because they believe that life begins at conception, the Course teaches that God created neither the world nor the body, and that there is no life outside of heaven."

When one considers the Course definition of heaven — as an "awareness of perfect oneness, and the knowledge that there is nothing else; nothing outside this oneness, and nothing else within"[6] — the gap between Course philosophy and the politically charged religiosity of the day becomes especially dramatic.

The Home Base of Course "Conservatism"

Within the rarefied world of Course politics, however, FACIM is the home base of a special kind of "conservatism." The growing culture of Coursedom passed a watershed of sorts when Sedona teacher Robert Perry published a commentary on "Liberalism and Conservatism in the Course Community" in the fourth issue of *Miracles Magazine*, acknowledging publicly the first significant schism to have become apparent in this nascent spiritual tradition.

"The conservative approach sees the Course as utterly unique, something that should be followed without mixing it with anything else," wrote Perry, also describing Course conservatism as "generally intellectual" and "heavily focused on study." Course liberals, he suggested, were "more willing to mix the Course with other things and to stress the idea that the Course is saying the same thing as other teachings." Then Perry noted the issue that has put Course liberals increasingly at odds with Ken Wapnick in recent years: their feeling that "there is no one true interpretation, that the Course means whatever it means through the eyes of each individual."[7] As one person put it to me, "If there are a million students of the Course, there are really a million Courses out there."

For the most part, the liberal interpreters of the Course have no problem with *what* Wapnick says about it; in fact many of them have studied at FACIM and acknowledge their gratitude for his insights. But since Perry's article — written before recent changes in copyright policies (described in Chapter 3) and the establishment of ITIP-ACIM — there has been increasing friction over what some teachers perceive as Wapnick's growing assumption of a role as the "official" interpreter of ACIM.

While Wapnick doesn't identify himself that way — "I've heard that some people say that," he remarks, "but people believe what they want to believe" — it is true that he generally refers to his explanations of the Course not as his personal interpretation but rather as "what the Course really says" or "what Jesus actually meant." Such language is not difficult to find among Course teachers of all stripes. But because of his association with the original manuscript of ACIM, Wapnick's consistent use of such authoritative language is more charged. It can be seen either as historically justified or as an overstepping of his function as just another teacher of the Course. As *Miracles Magazine* editor Paul Ferrini challenges, "How can there ever be an official teacher of the Course besides Jesus?"

If the evolution of every other spiritual tradition throughout history is any indication, this conservative/liberal schism and its attendant controversy over the relative authority of teachers will not soon be resolved. Robert Perry opined that "the main flaw of each side lies in excluding each other" and suggested that "by fusing together the truth within both, we can come to a more whole and transformative picture of what *A Course in Miracles* is."[8] Such unspecific idealism doesn't say much about how the differing approaches to ACIM may actually be resolved. How the Course community pursues such a "fusing together" of divergent perspectives — or fails to do so — will eventually demonstrate whether the Course teaching works as well politically as it seems to for many individuals.

Walking Their Talk?

Apart from Course politics, it is clear that Ken Wapnick commands high respect from most students who have come in contact with him or sampled his writings. Tom Leach of Hodgkiss,

Colorado, who spent two years on the FACIM staff and still returns to Roscoe regularly for classes, apparently speaks for
many when he says that "Ken and Gloria Wapnick really walk
their talk" in terms of exemplifying Course principles in their
everyday conduct.

Ken's natural reserve perhaps enhances the common impression, repeated to me a number of times by different sources, that
he "never gets angry." One woman student I met at FACIM remarked that she had seen Ken "be very firm in classes if he has
to be. I've even seen him tell people to shut up — but not in an
angry way." Wapnick says that he does get angry at times:
"Sure, I get annoyed. But I tend to be a patient man." Leach
notes that Gloria's style is "more upfront, more in your face,"
but still gives her high marks for integrity and fidelity to the
original intent of the Course.

Because of their unassuming demeanor and quiet lifestyle,
the Wapnicks might more likely be taken for small-town college
instructors than leading representatives of an esoteric spiritual
philosophy. For the most part they have avoided the assignation
of "guru" status by their students, but not always, as Ken Wapnick recalls in this published account:

> . . . a very sincere young man . . . approached me after a
> workshop, saying: "I know you must be a very holy person
> because you don't smoke cigarettes, don't drink coffee, and
> don't keep running to the bathroom." How he observed the
> final part of this trinity I still do not understand, but it
> would be wonderful if one's salvation were dependent only
> on satisfying these three criteria for spiritual development.[9]

It is clear, however, that Wapnick intends to exert a lasting influence on the legacy of the Course. Of his several books that
examine different aspects of ACIM, the most challenging is a
600-page volume entitled *Love Does Not Condemn: The World,
the Flesh, and the Devil According to Platonism, Christianity,
Gnosticism, and* A Course in Miracles. A formidable work of

scholarship in comparative religion, *Love Does Not Condemn* is nonetheless unlikely to become an academic reference in the near future, due both to the novelty of ACIM and its contemporary reputation, however inaccurate, as a pop New Age teaching.

When I ask Ken if he feels "ghettoized" as a scholarly author unrecognized by most of his peers in traditional religious studies, he says only that *Love Does Not Condemn* "was written for the future, when scholars and historians *will* want to know how the Course compares to other great teachings." In his tone one hears the quiet surety of a man who, like many other students of A *Course in Miracles,* looked far and wide for spiritual sustenance before finding what he sought from a totally unexpected source.

6
Where Psychology Meets the Perennial Philosophy:
Talking with Roger Walsh and Frances Vaughan

Roger Walsh was completing his psychiatric training in 1976 when he first saw *A Course in Miracles*, handed to him by his future marriage partner Frances Vaughan. "I opened it, saw the words *God* and *Holy Spirit*, then immediately shut the book and refused to have anything to do with it for two years," says Walsh. "But I kept meeting people I respected who respected the Course. The final straw was meeting Bill Thetford, who made a presentation at a meeting of the American Orthopsychiatric Association in 1978. I remember thinking, 'If this guy's interested, then I'm interested.' I started reading the Course again, and it took me about three months to get through my resistance to the language. Then it suddenly shifted from being obnoxious to being beautiful, and the teaching really opened up for me. My serious study of the Course has continued ever since."

Walsh, a professor of psychiatry, anthropology, and philosophy at the University of California at Irvine, and Vaughan, a therapist in private practice and past president of the Association for Transpersonal Psychology, represent a contingent of Course students that belies the skeptical view of it as a light-headed love doctrine (see Chapter 8). Since this contingent of intellectuals with high-powered academic degrees and psychological training included Helen Schucman and Bill Thetford, it is arguably more representative of ACIM's lineage than any other faction.

While Walsh and Vaughan are not primarily identified as Course teachers, they are reliable sources on two major aspects of ACIM's philosophical heritage: its continuity with psychotherapy and its commonality with certain core aspects of the world's great religious traditions, or what has been called the "perennial philosophy." Authors of fifteen books between them on such subjects as therapy, intuition, and shamanism, Walsh and Vaughan also edited three popular compilations of Course excerpts, now combined in an anthology edition entitled *Gifts from A Course in Miracles* (Tarcher/Putnam).

Growing up Episcopalian, Frances Vaughan says she was interested in comparative religion while an undergraduate at Stanford University. There she studied under Frederick Spiegelberg, who provided her first exposure to Eastern thought. She was a student of Buddhism with some experience in Zen meditation when she encountered the Course in 1975, receiving a photocopy of the original manuscript from Jerry Jampolsky. "I was going through a divorce in 1975," Vaughan recalls, "and the Course was tremendously helpful to me in dealing with guilt and anger."

Unlike many students who came to the Course after departing from their Christian upbringing, Vaughan found the Course philosophically similar to her Episcopalian training. "The core message that I got as an Episcopalian was that Jesus taught 'God is love.' The good news of the Gospel of the New Testament was that sins are forgiven. The rest of the message was 'Know the truth and the truth shall make you free.' That was it. And that's totally consistent with the Course."

Having sampled a number of spiritual paths before ACIM, Vaughan "liked the fact that you didn't have to join anything, belong to a group, or swear allegiance to a teacher" to undertake the Course discipline. "You simply had the material available and could study it on your own." Although she experienced some difficulty at first with its masculine tone, Vaughan says she "felt very much at home with the Course" before long.

Walsh, a native Australian for whom the Church of England constituted his earliest religious influence, says that he was "pretty much of an agnostic" by the time he arrived at Stanford University for his psychiatric training. "I was a hardcore neuroscientist oriented toward behavior-modification therapy and a related outlook on life."

A major turning point in Walsh's life occurred when he entered psychotherapy in 1974, "opening up a whole new world of inner feeling and imagery that I'd been totally out of touch with." Sampling a wide variety of trainings and workshops while pursuing psychiatric training and then his postdoctoral psychiatric research, Walsh found himself gravitating toward meditation practice and contemplative traditions — "although I didn't know exactly why, since I still regarded religion as the opiate of the masses."

Then came another turning point. "I experienced a blinding moment of insight," recalls Walsh, "when I realized that the contemplative core of the world's great spiritual traditions offered technologies for the induction of transcendent states of mind."

As Walsh points out in his book *The Spirit of Shamanism*, such "altered states of consciousness" (ASCs) were largely regarded as pathological disturbances by psychologists until the last few decades. Since then humanistic, transpersonal, and Jungian psychologies have accorded more respect to such ASCs as dreaming, meditation, and mystical experiences. As Walsh writes, "The net result is that Western psychology is now better positioned to understand and appreciate, rather than to pathologize and denigrate, religious experiences in general . . ."[1]

From this perspective, the early-seventies arrival of *A Course in Miracles* — with its unique blend of psychological and spiritual language plus an explicit discipline for "mind training" — could not have been more perfectly timed. But in Roger Walsh's view, what makes the Course so effective is not only its modernity but also some core characteristics that it shares with the world's most ancient and revered religious traditions.

"Higher Grades of Significance"

Common Boundary is a national magazine published in Bethesda, Maryland, that generally explores the meeting ground of psychotherapy and spirituality. Its advisory board includes both Walsh and Vaughan. In early 1989 *Common Boundary* featured a cover story by Roger Walsh about *A Course in Miracles*, a story that would later spark a hostile reaction by a prominent psychologist in the same magazine (see Chapter 8). Walsh's review of the Course was consistently glowing.

"One of the hallmarks of a profound teaching is that when you go through it again, you find what philosophers call 'higher grades of significance'," wrote Walsh. "This seems to happen each time I go through the Course. I'm now at the point where I feel it's on a par with any other material or discipline I've seen. . . . I'm inclined to think that this document may be a spiritual masterpiece."[2]

Walsh went on to delineate three contemporary advances in the understanding of comparative religion that help to clarify how the Course fits in with the world's major spiritual traditions. The first advance involves what is sometimes sardonically called the "spiritual supermarket" of the late 20th century — the unprecedented modern exposure, particularly in the West, to a worldwide variety of spiritual paths and perspectives. "A few hundred years ago, there were no tapes, not much in the way of books, and people were usually exposed to only one religion," observed Walsh. "Trying to bone up on another was not terribly popular and could land one on a funeral pyre."[3]

The second change was the discovery in 1945 of the Gnostic Gospels, or Nag Hammadi Library, revealing the existence of a number of early schools of Christian mystics who generally took a more metaphysical view of Christ and his teachings than the traditional school that came to dominate Western religious thought. Citing Elaine Pagels' popular work The *Gnostic Gospels*, Walsh summarized some major points of the Gnostic teachings that will sound familiar to any Course student:

The implications for Christianity are extraordinary. First, the [Gnostic] picture of Jesus is not of someone claiming to be forever unique or in any way ontologically distinct and forever set apart from the rest of humankind. Rather, he simply says he has arrived at a state that is latent within all of us. He speaks not of sin and guilt, but of endarkenment and illusion. He speaks of himself as having awakened and speaks of those who imbibe his words and practices as becoming like Him, one with Him: "He who will drink from my mouth will become as I am." So suddenly, for the first time, we have a picture of Christianity consistent with the mystical forms of other religions.[4]

The final advance is psychology's improving opinion of ASCs — from states of mind invariably considered delusional to states that may sometimes provide unique access to extraordinary insight and wisdom. As Walsh observed, "This means that the deepest spiritual wisdom may not be fully comprehensible to us unless we too train ourselves to experience appropriate states of mind"[5] — through such traditional spiritual technologies as meditation, yoga, contemplation, and devotional practices.

In fact, Walsh believes that the world's spiritual traditions were inspired in part by the altered-states experiences of the great teachers and prophets such as Jesus, Buddha, and Mohammed. If so, it's ironic that religion is often used today as a protection *against* extraordinary experiences. (Growing up Methodist in North Carolina, I was always bemused by the neighboring fundamentalists' proscriptions against social dancing — surely one of the milder inducements of altered states.)

In Walsh's view, then, authentic spiritual traditions are "those capable of inducing appropriate altered states, transcendence or higher development."[6] *A Course in Miracles*, he says, shares at least four similarities with older teachings:

- **How the teachings are revealed**
- **What the teachings say about the human condition**

- **What the teachings say about our potential**
- **What the teachings say about the means for realizing our potential**[7]

How the teachings are revealed. "I'm still terribly embarrassed to be associated with something channeled," confesses Walsh, "as were Bill Thetford and Helen Schucman. But as far as I can see, religions have usually been produced from very unrespectable sources. Jesus was condemned as a common criminal, Lao-Tzu wandered off into the desert as a total unknown, Confucius couldn't hold a job, and Mohammed was a suspect camel driver whom a lot of people waged war on."

Walsh admits that there's an "enormous amount of nonsense to be found in channeled material. The problem is that there's also some good stuff. It's much rarer, but it defies common-sense explanations. It seems pretty clear that some of the Bible was produced this way, as well as part of the Koran. In Judaism there have been scores of mystics who produced works by the process of inner dictation, and in Buddhism, many Indian and Tibetan texts were produced this way." Even in the West, Walsh adds, "the Greek oracle of Delphi — actually a series of priestesses who supposedly spoke on behalf of the god Apollo — stayed in business for nine hundred years."

Walsh is particularly impressed by the "voice" of the Course in comparison to other channeled teachers he has sampled. "If I try to sense the mind of Emmanuel, for instance, I feel a wonderful, compassionate presence, but there's still a feeling of individuality. By contrast, the mind behind the Course feels boundless."

What the teachings say about the human condition. Perhaps the most common feature of the great spiritual traditions is that they take a dim view of the human condition in its everyday, unspiritual state. "The teachings make it clear that things aren't good and there's an enormous amount of suffering going on," says Walsh. "They point to the sorrows and shortness of life; the inevitability of sickness, old age, and death; the ever-present

confrontation with meaning, purpose, and the questions of relationship and aloneness; and the uncertainty and fickleness of
fate." The first Noble Truth of the Buddha points to the inevitability of suffering in life, which Walsh cites alongside a passage from Psalms: "In the immensity of the universe we seem as
dust. Our lives are but toil and trouble; they are soon gone.
They come to an end like a sigh; like a dream. What person can
live and not see death?"

"*A Course in Miracles* agrees completely," remarks Walsh. "It
says this is an insane world of sorrow and death, and it is not
where you ultimately belong. Then why are we here? Both
ACIM and the contemplative core of the great traditions say
that the problem the world represents is really the state of our
minds. We're driven and dominated by unhealthy desires and
fears, obsessed by wanting to get more variations and intensities
of sensation and feelings. Plus, we're dominated by egocentric
concerns, driven by the twin powers of addiction and aversion.
From these spring the seven deadly sins of Christianity, the hin-
drances of Buddhism, the pain-bearing obstructions of yoga —
different names for similar afflictions."

Buddhism and the Course are very similar in their suggestions that our way of thinking literally creates the world we
see, says Walsh. The message of ACIM is that "you're so insane
you don't know you're insane. You're suffering from a shared,
unhappy, psychotic dream, and the Course offers an alternate
thought system you can substitute for that dream.

"This point about dreaming is very important," continues
Walsh, "because a lot of the deeper meaning of the great traditions is hidden unless you get the implications of this message:
that what we ordinarily take to be a fully wakened state is actually a dream." Walsh feels that the Course's explanation of our
waking hallucinations is among the best available in the world's
traditions:

Dreams show you that you have the power to make a world
as you would have it be, and that because you want it you

see it. And while you see it you do not doubt that it is real. Yet here is a world, clearly within your mind, that seems to be outside. . . . You seem to waken, and the dream is gone. . . . And what you seem to waken to is but another form of this same world you see in dreams. All your time is spent in dreaming. Your sleeping and your waking dreams have different forms, and that is all.[8]

What the teachings say about our potential. "We can get some sense of our true nature if we look at the opposite of our unenlightened condition as it usually is," comments Walsh. "Instead of finitude and limits, we find descriptions of infinity and boundless being. In place of time and change we find descriptions of the eternal and the changeless. In place of birth and death we have the unborn and the deathless. In place of angst and fear we have love, bliss, and joy."

Likewise, says Walsh, the great traditions suggest an enormous potential for the mind. "Enlightened mind is said to be free of the ravages of fear, greed, hatred, and anger. Christ called it the 'peace which passeth understanding'; for the Buddha it was *nirvana*, for the yogi it's the bliss of *samadhi*. As the Course says, 'A tranquil mind is not a little gift.'[9] The universal message here is that to the extent we quiet the raucous activity of our untrained minds, to that extent we will find our true self, a place of boundless peace and bliss. This is the Buddha's recognition of *anatta*, the awareness that the ego was an illusion all along. It's the goal of yoga, which means 'union of self with Self'. It's Taoism's alignment with the Tao, and for Christian mystics it was deification, Christ-consciousness, or oneness with God. In the Course's words, it's 'Let me remember I am one with God, at one with all my brothers and my Self, in everlasting holiness and peace.'[10]

"This all sounds like nice stuff," Walsh concludes. "The question is, how do we get there?"

What the teachings say about the means for realizing our potential. According to Walsh, authentic spiritual traditions offer not just a belief system but an explicit guide to training the mind so that one becomes open to higher states of being and awareness. Thus, all great paths offer what Walsh calls a "technology of transcendence." Looking across all these paths, Walsh finds five common elements of such technology:

> 1: *Ethical training*
> 2: *Attentional training*
> 3: *Emotional transformation*
> 4: *Motivational change*
> 5: *The cultivation of wisdom*

1: Ethical training. "The common thinking of religious morality is 'do this or God will get you,'" says Walsh. "This is not the perspective of the perennial wisdom, which views ethics as a means for training the mind. If we look closely we find that unethical behavior both *arises from* and *reinforces* painful and destructive mind states: anger, fear, greed, hatred, and jealousy. On the other hand, ethical behavior tends not to reinforce these mind states, hence reducing them and cultivating their opposites: generosity, love, joyfulness. So one becomes ethical not out of fear or guilt, but simply because one recognizes that this is what leads to greater well-being for oneself and others. Ethics is a skillful strategy."

2: Attentional training. "Our minds are a mess!" declares Walsh. "If you've ever tried meditation, you know the experience of sitting down to concentrate on following your breath, then realizing twenty minutes later that while there was certainly some breathing going on, *you* weren't around for it. The *Bhagavad-Gita* says, 'Restless man's mind is. So strongly shaken in the grip of the senses, gross and grown hard with stubborn desire for what is worldly, how shall we tame it? Truly I think the wind is no wilder.' Ramana Maharshi said, 'All scriptures without any exception proclaim that for attaining salvation mind should be subdued.' And then we have the Course saying, 'You are much too tolerant of mind wandering.'[11]"

Regardless of the path, Walsh suggests, the method of attentional training is basically the same: "a continuous bringing-back of attention to a predetermined object. The yogi returns again and again to the breath. The Course Workbook asks us to come back to our thought for the day. The aim is to constantly recollect the mind, returning it to what we have decided to focus on — and this gives power.

"In Buddhism there are 'four imponderables'," adds Walsh. "These are four things that you can't fathom, and they are: origination, or how the universe began; causation or karma, how things are caused; the scope of the mind of the Buddha; and finally, the power of the fully concentrated mind. Apparently a fully concentrated mind has awesome power at its disposal."

3: Emotional transformation. Walsh names two components to this element: the reduction of negative, "unskillful" emotions and the cultivation of positive, useful ones. As mentioned earlier, the perennial philosophy sees all unskillful emotions emanating from the obsessions of addiction and aversion.

"The Course has a variety of approaches to reducing our attachment to what it calls 'idols,' all the things we crave," says Walsh. "There is a whole series of Workbook lessons on this, including 'The world I see holds nothing that I want.'[12] It's not that we can't live with joy and love here in the world; the Course and other traditions make it clear that we can. But as long as we think that fulfilling our desires is what will make us happy, we're actually destined for unhappiness."

Anger and hatred are the two chief emotions rooted in aversion, says Walsh, and he cites a pungent Buddhist image for the assessment of anger's value: "They say we should regard anger as stale urine mixed with poison. The Course maintains that '[A]nger is *never* justified. Attack has *no* foundation.'[13] The Course's primary tool for reducing anger is forgiveness," adds Walsh, "and it provides an exquisitely detailed variety of approaches to forgiveness, more so than any other path I have found."

The second component of emotional transformation is the cultivation of positive or skillful emotions, believed to lead the spiritual aspirant toward states of unlimited love and compassion. "These states are what Buddhism calls the 'divine abodes,'" observes Walsh, "what Christianity calls *agape*, what the bhakti tradition calls divine love. In one lesson the Course likewise suggests 'God's will for me is perfect happiness.'[14]"

4: Motivational change. Walsh believes that the perennial philosophy encourages a number of shifts in one's deepest motivations, chief among them being the shift from wanting to acquire things, attention, or power, to pursuing inner development as the only lasting means of satisfaction. Another shift is simply from "getting" to "giving."

"Traditionally this has been called purification," reports Walsh. "Psychologists would recognize it as moving up Maslow's hierarchy of needs. For Kierkegaard it was epitomized in the saying, 'Purity of heart is to will one thing.' Jesus said, 'Seek ye first the kingdom of heaven and all else will be given to you.' What then is the highest motivation, the highest desire to focus on? In Mahayana Buddhism, we have the ideal of the *boddhisattva:* to awaken with the aim of using that awakening for the helping and healing of all beings. This may be the highest ideal the human mind has ever conceived, and in Buddhism it's believed to take place over many lifetimes in order to liberate all sentient beings."

A Course in Miracles is a bodhisattvic path as well, claims Walsh, "making it very clear that none of us are going to get out of this game until all of us get out of it. You can't clean up your mind only, because all minds are one and interconnected, according to the Course. It also makes clear that the work involved is in no way a sacrifice, because as one lesson says, 'All that I give is given to myself.'[15]

5: The cultivation of wisdom. Walsh identifies two kinds of wisdom that play a part in achieving our spiritual potential: *initial* and *final.* "Initial wisdom is what starts one on the path, trying meditation or reading the Course or whatever. One recognizes the suffering and unsatisfactoriness of the world and thinks, as Bill Thetford did, that there must be a better way. In Buddhism it's the recognition of *duhkha,* that unenlightened living does indeed lead to suffering.

"Final wisdom is a profound insight into the nature of mind, self, and reality," Walsh continues. "This is a direct, transcendental intuition, not of the mind or intellect. In the East it's called *prajna*, in the West *gnosis*, and in the Course *knowledge*. This wisdom is also known to be profoundly empowering and liberating. In Christianity it's 'the Kingdom of Heaven is within you'; in the Upanishads it's 'by understanding the Self, all this universe is known'; in Siddha Yoga it's 'God dwells within you as you.'

"This is enlightenment, *satori, moksha, wu,* liberation, salvation," Walsh comments— "different words for the same realization. The message of the great traditions as well as *A Course in Miracles* can thus be summarized very simply: Wake up!"

Is the Course a Psychotherapy?

Very simply, the purpose of psychotherapy is to remove the blocks to truth. Its aim is to aid the patient in abandoning his fixed delusional system, and to begin to reconsider the spurious cause and effect relationships on which it rests. No one in this world escapes fear, but everyone can reconsider its causes and learn to evaluate them correctly. God has given everyone a Teacher Whose wisdom and help far exceed whatever contribution an earthly therapist can provide. Yet there are times and situations in which an earthly patient-therapist relationship becomes the means through which He offers His greater gifts to both.[16]

The preceding passage is taken from a pamphlet entitled *Psychotherapy: Purpose, Process and Practice,* one of two brief addenda to the Course proper that Helen Schucman scribed in the years following the completion of the Text, Workbook, and Manual for Teachers (see Chapter 1). The existence of *Psychotherapy* strengthens the paradoxical association of the Course — unmistakably a spiritual discipline — with a healing methodology rooted in decidedly anti-religious theories of human behavior, including those of Sigmund Freud. In fact the mainstream of psychology has historically been devoted to fathoming the mysteries of our minds and behavior in strictly scientific terms, although practitioners of the "harder" sciences with longer histories have often looked askance on the entire psychological enterprise.

That's due in part to the fact that spirituality always seems to be lurking behind psychology's door, evanescent but undeniable as a shadow. Trace the semantic roots of the word *psychotherapy*, for instance, and you find the meaning of "soul healing." Freud's greatest student, Carl Jung, broke with his teacher over essentially spiritual questions. And it has been observed many times that the purely analytic mode of therapy leaves something to be desired in terms of changing human behavior and relationships for the better.

All too often the "patients" of psychoanalysis find that after years of treatment they are better able to recognize their neurotic and disheartening ways of living but still unable to change them. Real change, when it occurs, often follows an experience of "surrender" to a previously unrecognized source of wisdom — a wisdom that's internally realized and yet unmistakably distinct from one's previous, ordinary range of consciousness.

This recognition generally marks a transition from psychological self-exploration to the spiritual search. Only in recent decades has psychology begun to study this transitional arena, and then primarily in the progressive branch generally identified as "transpersonal" — where the study of the ego crosses over into the study of soul, spirit, and even more surpassing forms of consciousness. As Frances Vaughan comments in her book *The Inward Arc:*

> Traditionally, psychological growth and the spiritual quest have been perceived as separate and fundamentally antagonistic pursuits. Most Western psychology has tended to dismiss spiritual searching as escapist, delusional, or, at best, a psychological crutch. Spiritual disciplines, on the other

hand, have tended to regard psychology as an irrelevant distraction on the path of spiritual awakening. Here [in transpersonal psychology] these two apparently divergent approaches to the relief of human suffering are viewed as complementary and interdependent aspects of healing and the journey to wholeness.[17]

Co-editors of an anthology entitled *Paths Beyond Ego: The Transpersonal Vision* (J.P. Tarcher), Vaughan and Roger Walsh are both recognized as leading voices in what is sometimes called the "fourth force" of modern psychology (after Freudian psychoanalysis, behaviorism, and humanistic psychology). Partners in marriage as well as professional interests, they nonetheless have some disagreements on the finer points of the transpersonal outlook — one of them being whether *A Course in Miracles* constitutes a psychotherapy in itself.

"The Course is clearly designed not only to affect psychological healing," says Walsh, "but also spiritual maturation beyond the levels that most psychotherapies aim for. One might say its major emphasis is cognitive, in that the teaching comes to us in books and words, but it also has a strong relational component, a service component, a *bhakti* component — it has all these different strategies. Thus it's one of the most broad-range therapies available."

"I have a different view on this," counters Vaughan. "In Jung's sense that 'all religions are therapies for the soul,' I would say the Course qualifies as therapy. But I see psychotherapy as being based on the relationship between two people. In that light the Course is an effective self-development methodology, not a psychotherapy. Also, although the Course talks a lot about releasing the past, it doesn't give you a lot of 'how-to'; I think that's a piece of the work that we do in psychotherapy, dealing in specifics with a necessity that the Course discusses in general."

The hanging-on to guilt, its hugging-close and sheltering, its loving protection and alert defense,— all this is but the grim refusal to forgive. "God may not enter here" the sick repeat, over and over, while they mourn their loss and yet rejoice in it. Healing occurs as a patient begins to hear the dirge he sings, and questions its validity. Until he hears it, he cannot understand that it is he who sings it to himself. To hear it is the first step in recovery. To question it must then become his choice.[18]

While Vaughan's own style of therapy is derived from many influences, her description of it echoes the principles found in *Psychotherapy*. In place of the classic "transference" of psychoanalysis — a process in which the patient is allowed and even encouraged to develop a dependency on the therapist that is not unlike a child-to-parent relationship — Vaughan sees the process of therapy "as something that the client and I do together, a mutual exploration to see what is needed for healing in each particular case. It's important for me to meet a person heart to heart, and to be as fully present and transparent as possible. I don't do anything to the client, in terms of applying psychological tricks or techniques. I try to allow something to happen between us that allows people to change, grow, and heal."

> Ideally, psychotherapy is a series of holy encounters in which brothers meet to bless each other and to receive the peace of God. And this will one day come to pass for every "patient" on the face of this earth, for who except a patient could possibly have come here? The therapist is only a somewhat more specialized teacher of God. He learns through teaching, and the more advanced he is the more he teaches and the more he learns. But whatever stage he is in, there are patients who need him just that way. They cannot take more than he can give for now. Yet both will find sanity at last.[19]

Does Vaughan ever explicitly introduce the idea of "inner guidance" to clients, or explicitly recommend spiritual disciplines such as the Course? "I don't introduce spirituality unless people ask for it," says Vaughan, "or introduce it themselves. Mostly I try to listen; I do very little initiating as a therapist. When I write books or give lectures, that's when I'm taking the initiative. But in individual therapy I let the client lead, in terms of telling me what he or she needs. As far as the Course goes, I'll support someone's curiosity about it, in terms of answering their questions, but I wouldn't recommend it to anyone not already expressing an interest. As Bill Thetford used to say, this course is not for everyone."

> The patient need not think of truth as God in order to make progress in salvation. But he must begin to separate truth from illusion, recognizing that they are not the same, and becoming increasingly willing to see illusions as false and to accept the truth as true. His Teacher will take him on from there, as far as he is ready to go. Psychotherapy can only save him time. The Holy Spirit uses time as He thinks best, and He is never wrong. Psychotherapy under His direction is one of the means He uses to save time, and to prepare additional teachers for His work. There is no end to the help that He begins and He directs. By whatever route he chooses, all psychotherapy leads to God in the end. But that is up to Him. We are all His psychotherapists, for He would have us all be healed in Him.[20]

"One of the ideas from the Course I've found most useful in psychotherapy is 'Let all things be exactly as they are'[21]," remarks Vaughan. "Fritz Perls used to say that the greatest obstacle to change is wanting to change. As long as you're trying to get reality to match your pictures of how things are supposed to be, you're in a lot of trouble. The aim of psychotherapy is first of all to accept things as they are, and then, as the Serenity Prayer says, to accept the things you can't change and work to change the things that you can. One thing you can change is the sense of separation, realizing that you are not separate from God.

"But concepts of God vary enormously," continues Vaughan. "I don't try to impose a belief or tell people what's wrong. A spiritual teacher might say, 'This is how things are'; a psychotherapist asks, 'How are things for you?' It's by joining with the client that I may enable her to see things differently, change what she can and accept what she cannot change. The work proceeds in the direction of self-forgiveness. When clients begin to heal their own feelings of guilt, then they're able to become more compassionate, loving, and forgiving of others."

No one who learns to forgive can fail to remember God. Forgiveness, then, is all that need be taught, because it is all that need be learned. All blocks to the remembrance of God are forms of unforgiveness, and nothing else. This is never apparent to the patient, and only rarely so to the therapist. The world has marshalled all its forces against this one awareness, for in it lies the ending of the world and all it stands for.[22]

Since *A Course in Miracles* makes an uncompromising connection between forgiveness and a radical shift in perception, should it perhaps not be taken on unless one has therapeutic experience?

"I wouldn't say that anyone should not work with the Course," replies Vaughan, "but I certainly think psychotherapy helps. It's often said that it's better to have a strong ego before undertaking any spiritual practice, that you have to be somebody before you can learn to be nobody. And it's advantageous to have completed the developmental tasks of growing up, so that you don't get tempted by a 'spiritual bypass' that might gloss over unresolved psychological issues."

Roger Walsh adds that research in psychotherapy has shown that "people who do best are the people who need it least. Anecdotally speaking, this seems to be the same in spiritual practice. The more skills and maturity you bring to it, the more you're likely to gain, although that seems somewhat unfair.

"But how people progress is very difficult to predict," Walsh muses. "Bill Thetford always said that he was amazed how many people got so much out of the Course, when his initial assumption was that it was too intellectual to have mass appeal. He was astounded to find relatively uneducated people thriving on it, sometimes doing better than students with a stronger intellectual or psychological background."

Frances Vaughan concludes that the Course works for many because, regardless of its language or difficulty, "it does help people reduce fear, guilt, and anger, and increase their experience of peace, love and joy. I've never met anyone in any culture who didn't want to be able to give and receive more love. The Course is simply one effective way of helping people do that."

No one is healed alone. This is the joyous song salvation sings to all who hear its Voice. This statement cannot be too often remembered by all who see themselves as therapists. Their patients can but be seen as the bringers of forgiveness, for it is they who come to demonstrate their sinlessness to eyes that still believe that sin is there to look upon. Yet will the proof of sinlessness, seen in the patient and accepted in the therapist, offer the mind of both a covenant in which they meet and join and are as one.[23]

7
Why the Course is Not Christian – Or Is It?

The heavily Christianized language of *A Course in Miracles*, which makes frequent references to God the Father, His Son, and the Holy Spirit, has been a source of substantial confusion about its message and orientation. Casual readers and surface-skimming critics have mistaken the Course for a contemporary restatement of traditional Christian theology. And there's no doubt that some novice students have happily taken it to church only to find that it receives less than a warm reception from their ministers or church elders.

That's because the superficial resemblance of Course language to biblical prose rapidly disintegrates as soon as one comes across certain statements proposing complete reversals of contemporary Christian thought. Add in that the voice making such radical propositions claims to be that of Jesus Christ himself, and there's a wrenching surprise in store for any traditional Christian who decides to give this thick blue book, usually printed on familiarly thin "bible" paper, a serious look-see.

Compare, for instance, the message of a legendary Bible verse memorized by generations of Sunday school students to ACIM's treatment of the same subject:

For God so loved the world that he gave his only begotten
Son, that whoever believes in him shall not perish but have
eternal life.
John 3:16

You will not find peace until you have removed the nails
from the hands of God's Son, and taken the last thorn from
his forehead. The Love of God surrounds His Son whom
the god of crucifixion condemns. Teach not that I died in
vain. Teach rather that I did not die by demonstrating that
I live in you. For the undoing of the crucifixion of God's
Son is the work of the redemption, in which everyone has
a part of equal value. God does not judge His guiltless Son.
Having given Himself to him, how could it be otherwise?
ACIM: T-11.VI.7:1-7

These claims by the Jesus of the Course that he "did not die"
and that everyone has an equal part in "undoing" the crucifixion
are just two of many startling theological departures that ACIM
takes from biblical orthodoxy. In the words of the Reverend Jon
Mundy, "There are lots of points on which the Course doesn't
work in a traditional Christian context. The Course says there's
no hell and no devil. The whole concept of the Atonement is different. The whole thing about the cross and the Resurrection is
different. It just doesn't work as traditional Christianity."

But that didn't prevent Mundy from giving it a try. From the
time he encountered the Course in 1975 until he resigned from
his Methodist pulpit in 1989, Mundy attempted to share the
new teaching of the Course with his congregation. "That was a
long time to hang in there," he recalls, "and I was very actively
teaching the Course from the pulpit. I didn't make any bones
about where my information was coming from; I was very clear
about it." But what brought an end to Mundy's experiment presenting the Course in a Christian church was not his own realization that the two perspectives were incompatible. "What
happened was that some fundamentalists moved into my church

and realized that I was not speaking their language. And that was the end of it."

To evangelical Christian critics of *A Course in Miracles* — two of whom will be quoted later in this chapter — such a turn of events doubtlessly sounds just and satisfying. In the future it is likely that fundamentalists will have many more opportunities to dislodge an encroaching Course from the pews and pulpits of mainline churches. But any evangelical crusade against Course followers homesteading on Christian territory will have to acknowledge an unexpected ally. Because the "top gun" of the Course movement — as one evangelical critic calls Kenneth Wapnick, Ph.D. — doesn't think ACIM belongs in church either.

Remarks from a Gentlemanly Debate

In 1989 Wapnick sat down with Father W. Norris Clarke, a Jesuit priest and philosopher, to have a long and polite discussion about the doctrinal differences between the Course and biblical Christianity. Clarke, whom Wapnick credits with "an open-minded and non-judgmental approach to non-Catholic teachings,"[1] spent thirty-one years as a professor of philosophy at Fordham University before his retirement in 1985, founding and editing the *International Philosophical Quarterly* for two and a half decades. Clarke, a friend of Wapnick's for many years, also appeared in the 1987 film documentary *The Story of A Course in Miracles*, elucidating a few of the major contrasts between the Course and the Bible.

The 1989 dialogue was videotaped for distribution by the Foundation for *A Course in Miracles*, but a technical hitch prevented its reproduction and Wapnick published the transcript as a 100-page FACIM book in 1995. *A Course in Miracles and Christianity: A Dialogue* stands as an intriguing debate between a gentle Catholic elder — who sounds bemused by the sheer differentness of a radical new teaching — and an articulate heretic, equally gracious in tone, who nonetheless displays the confidence one might expect in a "top gun."

In the introduction to *Dialogue,* Wapnick outlines four major thematic contrasts between the Bible and *A Course in Miracles:*

1) *A Course in Miracles* teaches that God did not create the physical universe, which includes all matter, form, and the body; the Bible states that He did.

2) The God of *A Course in Miracles* does not even know about the sin of separation (since to know about it would make it real), let alone react to it; the God of the Bible perceives sin directly . . . and His responses to it are vigorous, dramatic, and at times punitive, to say the very least.

3) *A Course in Miracles'* Jesus is equal to everyone else, a part of God's one Son or Christ; the Bible's Jesus is seen as special, apart, and therefore ontologically different from everyone else, being God's only begotten Son, the second person of the Trinity.

4) The Jesus of *A Course in Miracles* is not sent by God to suffer and die on the cross in a sacrificial act of atonement for sin, but rather teaches that there is no sin by demonstrating that nothing happened to him in reality, for sin has no effect on the Love of God; the Jesus of the Bible agonizes, suffers, and dies for the sins of the world in an act that brings vicarious salvation to humanity, thereby establishing sin and death as real, and moreover clearly reflecting that God has been affected by Adam's sin and must respond to its actual presence in the world by sacrificing His beloved Son.[2]

Shortly concluding that there is "no way" to reconcile biblical and Course theology, Wapnick concedes that "it is a continual source of amazement . . . for one to observe how frequently this reconciliation is attempted."[3] Thus, far from attempting to hitchhike the Course onto the established institutions and broad reach of Christianity, Wapnick makes it clear that he, for one, is trying to make sure the Course blazes its own trail.

Dialogue presents discussion between Clarke and Wapnick on a number of specific issues, including the origin of the world, the nature of Jesus, the meaning of the Eucharist, and differences between the Course and Christianity on everyday challenges of living in the world. Two of these issues are summarized here.

One is the problem of evil, about which the Course has been criticized elsewhere. In his collection of lectures entitled *Further Along the Road Less Traveled*, noted Christian psychotherapist M. Scott Peck cited the Course as "a very good book, filled with a lot of first-rate psychiatric wisdom" while also dunning it as a spiritual "half-truth" that fails to deal with the problem of evil.[4] (Now in retirement, Peck declined to elaborate on these comments for this book.)

In *Dialogue*, Clarke and Wapnick elucidate the biblical and Course approaches to evil thusly:

CLARKE: Let us be perfectly honest. The problem of evil is indeed one filled with mystery for our limited human minds, and not one possible for us to crack with our own limited vision of world history and what God is planning for beyond death. But Christian faith can shed considerable light on it, I think. First, the moral evils of the world, deriving from the free evil moral decisions of human beings and their consequences, such as hatred, selfishness, exploiting of others, etc., are our own responsibility and not due to God at all, who only permits this so as not to override our freedom and remove our possibilities of doing moral good, too. Freely given love and service by human beings is such a lofty good that God is willing to run the risk of our free choice of evil instead of good. . . .

There is also the further mystery, which human experience bears out, I think, to all of us who have lived long enough, that somehow the full depth and richness of human character is simply not reached by embodied spirits like us unless by passing through the challenge, purification, and transformation of suffering. Herein lies the mystery of the Cross and the passion of Jesus himself . . .

WAPNICK: . . . In terms of creation, there cannot be both good and evil in the Course's view of reality, because there is only one God. The phenomenon of opposites exists only in the illusory world of perception and matter, which God did not create. And as *A Course in Miracles* says in the Introduction to the text, "The opposite of love is fear, but what is all-encompassing can have no opposite." And so the Course's non-dualistic God of creation is only Love, which means that evil does not exist because there can be nothing but the Love of God.

However, evil, which in *A Course in Miracles* is equated with the belief in sin and separation from our source — God — most definitely does exist in the dualistic, post-separation world of dreams. But since all this occurs only within the collective and individual dreams of the world, sin and evil cannot and do not truly exist, because only a misthought in a dreaming mind believes it can will in opposition to the Will of God, and bring into existence a world of multiplicity. Therefore within his fevered dream of sin, the Son actually believes that he has destroyed the oneness of Reality, which he judges to be an evil act deserving only punishment.[5]

Thus while Clarke and Wapnick agree that evil *happens* in the everyday world, their perspectives offer different views as to its ultimate *nature*. And what is to be done about evil? Depending on how conservative or liberal one's brand of Christianity is, a sinner may be forgiven or punished by God for his free choice of evil. But the sinner certainly runs the risk of punishment, including an afterlife in hell, if he remains unrepentant. Per the Course, the discipline of accepting and extending forgiveness is what everyone must undertake in order to awaken from the

dream in which evil (not to mention time, space, and matter) —
seems so real. (It should also be noted that in the view of the
Course, the only hell is the one the unforgiving ego constantly
creates for itself: a nightmare of separation from God, albeit a
nightmare spiced with just enough pleasure and temporal love
to keep most people addicted to it.)

On another point, *Dialogue's* discussion of the Eucharist reveals a dramatic difference between the Course and Christianity
(particularly Roman Catholicism) on the significance of symbol-
ism and ritual:

> CLARKE: According to this doctrine, traditional from the
> earliest days of the Christian Church, the Eucharistic lit-
> urgy is the reenactment in symbolic form of the original
> redemptive sacrifice of Jesus, in imitation of Jesus' own ini-
> tial enactment at the Last Supper, which he asked his fol-
> lowers to keep doing in memory of him. This is done when
> the ordained priest, speaking in the name of Christ the
> High Priest, eternally living now as risen and present at
> every Mass, pronounces the "words of consecration" in
> imitation of Jesus, which really and truly transform the in-
> ner reality of the bread and wine into the body and blood
> of Jesus, but veiled in mystery under the remaining ap-
> pearances of bread and wine. . . . Then at the Communion
> service following, the believers partake of the body and
> blood of the sacrificed and now risen Christ under the ap-
> pearances of bread and wine, in obedience again to Jesus'
> command, "Unless you eat my body and drink my blood
> you shall not have life in you . . ." *(John 6:53) . . .*

> WAPNICK: From the point of view of *A Course in Miracles*,
> seeking outside oneself for salvation is a principal charac-
> teristic of specialness . . . The special love relationship is
> one in which we believe someone or some object outside
> ourselves has something we lack: the capacity to make us
> happy and peaceful, or the capacity to save us. And so we

seek to take these special persons or objects in and make their holiness or power our own, thereby completing our inherent incompleteness with something outside us and therefore truly not our own. In this sense, a special relationship would hold whether one is considering a love object, food, alcohol, or the body of Jesus. Thus, listening to the voice of specialness, we would believe that we lack the holiness and innocence of Christ, our true Self, but Jesus has what is missing in us. Therefore, if we are to have it, we must get it from him by partaking in the sacrament of the Eucharist, a process that only reinforces this lack, but does not undo or heal it.

. . . Jesus is no different from us, but rather he urges us to choose like him, joining with his *mind*, and not his body. So from the Course's point of view, it would make no sense for Jesus to share his illusory body with us in communion.[6]

It should be added that the Course takes a similar position in regard to *all* rituals, whether they be Christian, Buddhist, Islamic, or New Age in character: "Your claim to miracles does not lie in your illusions about yourself. It does not depend on any magical powers you have ascribed to yourself, nor on any of the rituals you have devised. It is inherent in the truth of what you are."[7] Thus *A Course in Miracles* stakes out a position that differs from common religious belief: that no ritual or spiritual practice has any meaning in itself, its value depending entirely on whether it helps the practitioner change his or her mind about reality.

Despite the many doctrinal differences they inventory, Father Clarke and Ken Wapnick end their *Dialogue* on a note of religious brotherhood:

CLARKE: As Jesus said, I came that you might have peace; I came to give you my peace.

WAPNICK: The Jesus of *A Course in Miracles* would echo that too, certainly.

CLARKE: So we differ on much, but also agree on much. Let me give one last quotation from Charles Morgan, the novelist: "There is no surprise more magical than the surprise of being loved; it is God's finger on man's shoulder."

WAPNICK: That's wonderful. If I could add something relevant to that: *A Course in Miracles* would say that there is no greater joy in this world than the joy of knowing that one is forgiven, and that forgiveness can only come through experiencing the Love of God through Jesus or the Holy Spirit.[8]

If this genial discussion between a kindly priest and a spiritual psychologist truly summed up the schism between the Course and contemporary Christianity, the debate would be a decorous one indeed. But *A Course in Miracles* has drawn the attention of some Christian critics decidedly less liberal than Father Clarke. And whenever the Course has drawn *their* attention, its top gun has drawn some fire.

Unmasking "the Jesus of the Course"

The Spiritual Counterfeits Project (SCP) is the sort of organization that's hard to imagine materializing anywhere besides its politically contentious home base of Berkeley, California. In what might be called an expression of the "counter-counterculture," SCP is composed largely of evangelical Christians who share a background of familiarity or firsthand experience with Eastern religions or New Age spirituality and have returned to the Bible as the touchstone of truth.

SCP sounded the first warning about ACIM to its constituency with a critique by Frances Adeney in its newsletter of June/July 1981, noting some of the "inroads into the Christian Church" that the Course was making — including the appearance of Jerry Jampolsky on evangelist Robert Schuller's *Hour of Power* television show. "Schucman's new, do-it-yourself spirituality is actually not new at all," commented Adeney. "The Hindus have been saying for centuries that the world is illusion, that all is one and that escape from pain is realized by denying its reality. . . . The 'voice' that speaks in those volumes may or may not be the voice of Helen Schucman," concluded Adeney. "It is definitely not the voice of Jesus Christ."[9]

But SCP didn't really bear down on the Course until seven years later, when an SCP *Journal* entitled "Spiritism: The Medium and the Message" devoted most of its pages to several substantial articles about ACIM by SCP researcher Dean C. Halverson. His work included a lengthy interview with Ken Wapnick, an interpretive essay entitled "Seeing YourSelf as Sinless," and a chart comparing passages from the Course with Bible verses (see pp. 154–155).

Halverson's research into the Course was meticulous, and included a sort of collaboration with Wapnick that began well before their interview. Several years prior to writing his articles for the *Journal*, Halverson had sent Wapnick a manuscript critical of the Course, which Wapnick felt was "way off base" in its representation of the principles of ACIM. He replied at length, suggesting several points on which he thought Halverson "could legitimately criticize the Course from a fundamental Christian perspective. After that, Dean responded with a very nice letter asking further questions," recalls Wapnick.

Halverson, who told me he filled two notebooks with Course excerpts before drafting the manuscript he sent to Wapnick, later attended a workshop led by Ken and Gloria and interviewed them during a lunch break. When he discovered later that his tape recorder had malfunctioned, he asked Ken for a repeat interview, which was granted and appeared in the *Journal*. The printed interview was cordial, and Halverson seemed chiefly intent on drawing Wapnick out on the principles of the Course. At one point, however, he challenged Wapnick on his selective quoting of the Bible in one of his books, *Forgiveness and Jesus*, which bears the subtitle *The Meeting Place of* A Course in Miracles *and Christianity*. The following exchange occurred in response to Halverson's charge that Wapnick was avoiding Bible passages that did not fit his mapping of that "meeting place":

WAPNICK: Absolutely right. In my book I was selective. I picked and chose. Anything consistent with the Course, I took as valid, and anything that wasn't, I took as invalid. . . . Some parts of the Bible have the Holy Spirit as their source. Other parts are from the ego. Any passage that speaks of punishment or hell, I understood as being from the ego. Any passage that speaks of forgiveness and love, the unreality of the body, etc., I took as an expression of the Holy Spirit. I did not take the Bible as being totally true or totally false. I said here are some things that I feel are valid, here are some that are not valid.

HALVERSON: You reinterpreted it?

WAPNICK: Yes. There's no question. That is what I did.[10]

Replying to Halverson's articles, a letter by Wapnick in the succeeding edition of the *Journal* applauded Halverson's "sincere attempts at fairness in presenting material which you so strongly disagree with."[11] Despite their disagreements, Wapnick and Halverson seemed to enjoy a high degree of mutual respect; the Christian writer described the Course editor to me as "a very gracious person. He and I hit it off pretty well." Wapnick remembered Halverson in person as a "very nice, serious, gentle guy — not what I expected of the Spiritual Counterfeits Project."

But Halverson's challenge to the Course itself was less gentle. In the conclusion to "Seeing YourSelf as Sinless," Halverson suggested that the Course's view of reality, sin, and redemption is dangerously flawed:

Sin, according to the Course, is the false belief in separateness, which is unreal. It is this false belief that gives rise to the physical world. It is also this false belief that gives rise to personhood. For to be a person is to be an individual,

CHARTING THE COURSE
compiled by Dean C. Halverson

The Course	The Bible

GOD AND THE UNIVERSE

The world you see is an illusion of a world. God did not create it, for what He creates must be as eternal as Himself. *C-4.I:1-2*

In the beginning God created the heavens and the earth. *Genesis 1:1*

JESUS

There is nothing about me [Jesus] that you cannot attain. *T-1.II.3:10*

At the name of Jesus every knee should bow. . . . and every tongue confess that Jesus Christ is Lord. *Phillippians 2:10-11*

THE CHRIST

Christ waits for your acceptance of Him as yourself. . . . *T-11.IV.7:3*

Is [Jesus] the Christ? O yes, along with you. *C-5.5:1-2*

Jesus answered: "Watch out that no one deceives you. For many will come in my name, claiming, 'I am the Christ,' and will deceive many." Matthew 24:4-5

[John the Baptist] did not fail to confess, but confessed freely, "I am not the Christ." *John 1:20*

THE ATONEMENT

I [Jesus] was not "punished" because *you* were bad. The wholly benign lesson the Atonement teaches is lost if it is tainted with this kind of distortion in any form. *T-3.I.2:10-11*

For what I [Paul] received I pass on to you as of first importance: that Christ died for our sins according to the Scriptures. *1 Corinthians 15-3*

THE SOURCE OF SALVATION

My holiness is my salvation. *Workbook Lesson #39*
My salvation comes from me. It cannot come from anywhere else. *W-pI.70.7:3-4*

Salvation is found in no one else [but Jesus Christ], for there is no other name under heaven . . . by which we must be saved. *Acts 4:10-12; cf. John 3:14-19, 14:6*

THE MESSAGE OF THE HOLY SPIRIT

The Holy Spirit dispels [guilt] simply through the calm recognition that it has never been. *T-13.I.11:4*

When [the Holy Spirit] comes, he will convict the world of guilt in regard to sin. *John 16:8-9*

HUMANITY'S SPIRITUAL IDENTITY

The recognition of God is the recognition of yourself. There is no separation of God and His creation. *T-8.V2.7-8*

You are part of Him Who is all power and glory, and are therefore as unlimited as He is. *T-8.II.7:7*

They exchanged the truth of God for a lie, and worshipped and served created things rather than the Creator. *Romans 1:25*

In the pride of your heart you say, "I am a god. . . ." But you are a man and not a god. *Ezekiel 28:2*

SIN

All our sins are washed away by realizing they were but mistakes. *W-pI.98.2:6*

. . . all your sins have been forgiven because they carried no effects at all. And so they were but dreams. *C-5.4:1-2*

No one is punished for sins, and the Sons of God are not sinners. *T-6.I.16:4*

If we claim to be without sin, we deceive ourselves and the truth is not in us. If we confess our sins, he is faithful and just and will forgive us our sins and purify us from all unrighteousness. If we claim we have not sinned, we make him out to be a liar, and his word has no place in our lives. *John 1:8-10 cf. Romans 3:23; 6:23; Ephesians 4:18*

CONDEMNATION

You have condemned yourself, but condemnation is not of God. Therefore it is not true. *T-8.VII.15.4-5*

The wrath of God is being revealed against all the godlessness and wickedness of men who suppress the truth by their wickedness. *Romans 1:12*

THE END TIMES

The Second Coming means nothing more than the end of the ego's rule and the healing of the mind. *T-4.IV10:2*

The Final Judgment on the world contains no condemnation. *W-pII.10.2:1*

When the Lord Jesus is revealed from heaven in blazing fire with his powerful agents [then] he will punish those who do not know God and do not obey the gospel of our Lord Jesus. *2 Thesians 1:7-8*

Copyright 1987 by Spiritual Counterfeits Project. Excerpted from Vol. 7, No. 1 of the SCP Journal by permission of SCP and Dean C. Halverson.

separate and distinct from others and from God. By affirming separateness as illusory, the Course abolishes the value
of both the physical world and personhood. By declaring
all personhood to be unreal, the God of the Course com-
mits the severest form of judgment. . . .

The God of the Bible, however, offers genuine good
news: not that salvation is a restored union with an impersonal Mind but that salvation is a restored *communion*
with a personal God. It is only because God is personal and
distinct that our existence as distinct persons has value and
meaning. . . .

The God of the Bible solved the problem of sin not by
annihilation but by reconciliation, not by obliterating separateness but by restoring a relationship. In the Course,
the problem is perceptual, the solution impersonal. In the
Bible, the problem is relational, the solution interpersonal.
Scripture, thus, affirms the value of personhood. Biblical
reconciliation seeks to restore and preserve the worth of
the person.[12]

Halverson's final judgment on ACIM was that its source was
neither Jesus Christ nor Helen Schucman:

The good news of the Course, upon closer inspection, turns
bitter. But that should come as no surprise. For the Jesus of
the Course is not the Jesus of the Bible, but an angel of
death and darkness masquerading as an angel of life and
light *(2 Cor. 11:14).*[13]

A Personal Encounter

Two years after his work on the Course was published by SCP, I
contacted Dean Halverson while researching my first investiga-
tory article on ACIM. By that time he was employed by International Students, Inc., a Christian evangelical organization in
Colorado Springs, where he remains today. While I acknowledged

to Halverson at the outset that I was both a student of the Course and a journalist surveying it as a social phenomenon, I was careful not to challenge his assertion that ACIM is essentially an elaborate satanic strategy of deception. My sole intent for that interview was to update Halverson's published comments, and my best tool seemed to be the cool professionalism of the reporter, who suspends personal reactions in order to procure the maximum information without getting snagged in sticky arguments.

Halverson was on to me, however. When I thanked him for his time and cooperation, he asked, "You mean that's all?"

I replied that yes, I'd reached the end of my questions and needed no further information at the present time. In a tone that was somehow both contentious and companionable, Halverson challenged: "You mean we aren't going to *get into it?*"

So we got into it, and the much more personal discussion of the ensuing two hours was at turns truly exploratory and maddeningly circular. Halverson — who preferred that I not identify him as a "fundamentalist" because of the word's "anti-intellectual connotations in the popular media" — returned again and again to the Bible as his standard against which all ideas and beliefs must be judged. I once accused him of tautological thinking:

"You keep saying that the Bible is true because it's true."

"No," he countered, "it's true because it fits reality."

Because I could claim no significant biblical scholarship, I had no effective counter-argument save the observation that the Bible has inspired a vast array of interpretations and practices that, taken together, obviously do not reflect a whole and seamless picture of reality. Halverson himself agreed with SCP's characterization of Christian Science, the Church of Latter-Day Saints, and Jehovah's Witnesses as "mainline cults" that distort the Gospel. These distortions arose, Halverson contended, from Christians who misinterpreted the Word. I replied that I had the feeling other kinds of Christians might say the same about his perspective, leaving the innocent observer with the question *Which Christian am I to believe?*

For me the most revealing part of our discussion came as we were discussing the ethicality of *A Course in Miracles.* Surprisingly, Halverson admitted that he thought a Course student and a Bible student might come to similarly ethical decisions about moral dilemmas in the short term, but that the Course student would be misled in the long run — because, returning to the passage from Corinthians he had paraphrased in print, "the Bible tells us that Satan will present himself disguised as an angel of light." I countered with the Course's suggestion that there are only two emotions — love and fear — and that one of them is useless and illusory.

"Are you willing to consider the possibility," I suggested, "that ultimately 'there is nothing to fear'?[14]

Halverson's reply was a quite serious warning about the agent of evil he believes to be loose in our world. "Are you willing to consider," he said, "that there most certainly is?"

"The Course is Self-Defeating and Contradictory"

While researching this book I contacted Dean Halverson again to ask if he or anyone else had updated his work on the Course. Halverson referred me to Donald Dicks, who has a ministry in Georgia called the Atlanta Christian Apologetics Project. (The word *apologetics* is a theological term meaning "defense of the faith.") A forensic toxicologist by profession who holds three master's degrees in religion and philosophy, Dicks attends a Presbyterian church but identifies himself as a Southern Baptist. He has not published any criticism of the Course but has spoken about it at the First Baptist Church of Atlanta, at Christian conferences about cultism, and before other conservative evangelical groups. While he doesn't find the Course to be widely known in evangelical circles, he says it has "definitely made inroads into liberal Christianity — which I regard as an oxymoron, by the way." Dicks hopes to write a book on ACIM someday, which suggests that he anticipates its influence will spread farther.

Describing his critique of the Course as "more philosophical and less biblically oriented" than Halverson's work," Dicks identifies "four pillars" upon which rests ACIM's claim to truth: *intuitive knowledge* (referring to ACIM's origin in channeling); *monism* (or nonduality); *the idea of a corrupt Bible and Church*; and *an esoteric interpretation of the Bible*.

"All we have to go on is the word of Helen Schucman," says Dicks. "She said the Course was the voice of Jesus. But who is this Jesus? It's supposedly the Jesus of the Bible, but that would mean the Bible is corrupt. That's an idea that comes from liberal theology, which assumes an anti-supernatural stance as it starts critiquing the Bible."

How does Dicks know the Bible is infallible? "It can be shown not to be corrupt by looking at textual criticism, and by looking objectively at the manuscripts we have. . . . The Bible has been demonstrated to be the Word of God by fulfilled prophecy, and by the reliability of testimony and eyewitness accounts."

By contrast, says Dicks, "the Course is self-defeating and contradictory. It's neither consistent nor logical, even if Ken Wapnick says it is." (Dicks has studied Wapnick's work as well as the Course itself; it was Dicks who contacted the Foundation for Inner Peace asking to be referred to the "top gun" of Course teaching.) As an example of the Course's inconsistencies and contradictions, Dicks offers the idea that "the Course sees the physical realm as illusory, yet we read the Course with our physical eyes, and we're supposed to believe it. This whole idea of the physical realm being illusory — which you have in Hinduism and Christian Science as well — just doesn't do you any good. Isn't the illusion of pain as real as pain itself?"

In an echo of Halverson's critique of ACIM's "impersonal" God, Dicks adds that "the God of ACIM doesn't know what's going on in the Son of God's dream, which is to say everything we experience. Compare that to the biblical God, who knows the very number of hairs on our head, who loves us so much that he sent his only-begotten Son to die for our sins, who cares about everything we care about. There's an immense contrast here. The God of ACIM is heartless."

Dicks also feels that the Course is simply not a very good read. "The Bible is much easier. There's a narrative, there's something going on. The Course is more ethereal and harder to follow, especially in the way it redefines well-known terms. It leaves you scratching your head, asking 'What in the world is this talking about?'" (On that point at least, many students of the Course would agree.)

Dicks, who attended a six-week study group on the Course, also feels that the teaching induces its students to resist challenge and questioning."It's like you have to ask permission to critique the Course," complains Dicks. "It's a very defensive book in that it says that the ego, which is a bad thing, *analyzes* whereas the Holy Spirit *accepts*."[15] Dicks says that he saw this principle demonstrated in his Course study group, where his repeated challenges to the group leader were turned back: "I was told by the instructor that all questions emerge from the ego. Once when I said that I needed some time to express an idea, he said, 'Well, only the ego needs time.' And he had been talking for five ninety-minute sessions!"

Finally, Dicks feels that the Course leads people astray by advising them to go within and listen for the voice of the Holy Spirit. "That means there's no ultimate authority," he points out. "So I could interpret the Course any way I want to. It's that same New Age thing about creating your own reality; I don't see any difference. And I don't see how you could live this stuff out in our world. It's just not livable. Historical orthodox Christianity *is* livable, and it's true."

When I ask Dicks how the Course has become so popular given the substantial flaws he sees within it, he allows that "there has to be something good in all these alternative religions, whether the totality of any religion is true or not." When I ask if he would then agree with Halverson that a Course student, while being misled in the long run, might do all right over the short term, he pauses before asking with a chuckle, "How short?"

A Universal Experience?

There's a story that the noted depth psychologist Carl Jung once surveyed the diverse field of research and therapy that his pioneering work had spawned and said, "Thank God I am Jung and not a Jungian." One has to wonder if Jesus Christ might say something to the same effect were he to reappear today and survey the vast collection of beliefs, practices, and undeniable distortions that have arisen from his original teaching and now coexist under the very broad umbrella of "Christianity" — many of these approaches claiming to be the one true interpretation of his creed.

"*Christian* is one of the fuzziest words in existence," opines Course teacher Robert Perry, pointing out that "even the Course uses the words 'real Christian'[16] to characterize someone thinking along its lines." Of course there is considerable disagreement not only about proper interpretations of the message and example of Jesus Christ but also about the validity and historicity of many parts of the Bible as well. Richard Smoley, a scholar of Western spiritual traditions who is both a student and a critic of the Course (see Chapter 8) asserts that "few of the fundamentalist teachings have much to do with the Christianity of the New Testament, based as they often are on distorted translations of the original. I've read parts of the Bible in Greek and Hebrew, and every time I've found myself exclaiming, 'My God! Does it really say *that?*'"

Interpretive variations and doctrinal schisms have arisen in every major spiritual tradition as soon as — and sometimes before — the originator or first prophet of a tradition passes away. As this book has shown, significant differences in interpretation of *A Course in Miracles* already exist, and the teaching is hardly two decades old. Robert Perry observes that "the Course's attitude toward Christianity and the Bible is multi-faceted," noting that Ken Wapnick's position on the Course's discontinuity with Christianity is regarded as extreme by some other Course experts.

But the Course itself suggests that all theological differences have a limited significance:

All terms are potentially controversial, and those who seek controversy will find it. Yet those who seek clarification will find it as well. They must, however, be willing to overlook controversy, recognizing that it is a defense against truth in the form of a delaying maneuver. Theological considerations as such are necessarily controversial, since they depend on belief and can therefore be accepted or rejected. A universal theology is impossible, but a universal experience is not only possible but necessary. It is this experience toward which the course is directed.[17]

What might be the nature of the "universal experience" toward which Course students are directed? Jon Mundy says that when the time came for him to choose between church orthodoxy and Course teaching, he chose the Course because, for him and many others he knows, "It *works*. It transforms people's lives. You really do begin to look at things differently. You begin to see that what's important is honesty, patience, and forgiveness, and you let all the other stuff go."

In my brief experiences of comparing notes with evangelical Christian critics of the Course like Dean Halverson and Donald Dicks, it was difficult for me to comprehend exactly how their literal, conservative interpretations of the Bible will lead them to their spiritual destination. But in their willingness to share ideas and conscientiously examine a spiritual perspective that they have concluded is useless and even dangerous, I detect the same qualities Jon Mundy credits the Course with teaching: honesty, patience, and even a willingness to forgive.

When such qualities of relationship can be shared and strengthened even in the midst of passionate disagreements, the distance to everyone's spiritual destination may be immeasurably diminished. Perhaps this is what *A Course in Miracles* is getting at when it suggests that the journey to God is "a journey without distance to a goal that has never changed."[18]

8
Critiques of the Course

"I hate *A Course in Miracles*, and I'm coming out to do some-thing about it."[1] These contentious words were spoken by the most prominent critic of the Course to date, and they symbolize a conundrum in the sparsely populated field of Course critiques.

While the evangelical Christian critics cited in the previous chapter might be suspected of bringing foregone conclusions to their study, they clearly did their homework and judged the Course from a largely accurate understanding of what it says. They are also open to spirited discussion of their findings. Strangely enough, equally virulent criticism of the Course has issued from a decidedly opposite camp of anti-authoritarian thinkers. Yet these critics have apparently conducted far less thorough analyses and are unwilling to discuss their published conclusions.

Meanwhile some prominent theologians and popular philoso-phers who might be expected to provide thoughtful evaluations of such a rapidly growing spirituality have nothing at all to say about it. For the most cogent non-theoretical assessment of the problems associated with Course study, one has to turn to long-term students who have discovered its difficulties and pitfalls first-hand.

In this chapter I will attempt to assess this puzzling arena of non-Christian criticism of A *Course in Miracles*, concluding with some criticism of my own based on ten years experience as a student and nearly as many years surveying the Course phenomenon as a journalist. It's my hope that this summary will provide a starting point for future exhaustive analyses of the Course teaching by scholars in comparative religion and philosophy who are not identified with the Course. For while it's clear that ACIM readily triggers some hostile first impressions, all of these impressions taken together fall far short of a thorough critique.

At the time of this writing, some of the best-known experts in the aforementioned fields are unwilling to issue an opinion about A *Course in Miracles* for the record. People I contacted who either did not reply or declined to be interviewed about the Course included Harvey Cox of Harvard University, Martin E. Marty of the University of Chicago, Scott Peck (see previous chapter), *Care of the Soul* author Thomas Moore, Wade Clark Roof of the University of California at Santa Barbara, Huston Smith of UC-Berkeley, and Princeton University professor Elaine Pagels, author of *The Gnostic Gospels* and *The Origins of Satan*.

In her letter declining participation, Pagels revealed that "I have certainly looked at A *Course in Miracles* and found some interesting elements in it, but it is far from the center of my interests." Smith, author of *The Illustrated World's Religions*, replied that "though I respect what I have seen of the Course, I haven't worked with it, so I am not qualified to comment."

But some critics who *have* taken a stand on the Course clearly do not feel it necessary to have worked with the teaching to draw dramatic conclusions about it. The best-known among them is the noted archetypal psychologist James Hillman — the man who hates A *Course in Miracles*.

The Course as "Omnipotent Fantasy"

In early 1989 *Common Boundary* magazine published an essay by Roger Walsh summarizing the Course philosophy (see Chapter 6)— an essay that drew the attention of Hillman, author of a score of books including the recent best-seller *The Soul's Code* (Random House). His philosophy inspired the best-selling works of his student Thomas Moore, and Hillman himself is widely respected as one of the most original and provocative interpreters of the Jungian legacy of depth psychology.

In a reply to Walsh's essay published in the September-October 1989 issue of *Common Boundary* entitled "A Course in Miracles: Spiritual Path or Omnipotent Fantasy?" Hillman made his feelings about the Course known in no uncertain terms. It should be noted that the article originated not as a written piece but as a conversation with *Common Boundary* contributing editor Barbara Goodrich-Dunn, and consisted entirely of Hillman's reactions to statements by Roger Walsh. As subsequent inquiries have revealed, it is uncertain whether Hillman has ever examined the Course first-hand.

Describing himself as "shocked and enraged" that *Common Boundary* "would publish an article that has no common boundary with psychology," Hillman charged that Walsh's presentation of Course ideas contained "old-fashioned, self-deluding Christianity" adding that "the roots of fascism exist within [the Course] philosophy. . . . Everybody would like to make the world as he or she would like it. But trying to get the power to make the world that way is a form of insanity. This is also what Mussolini and Hitler had: an omnipotent fantasy."[2]

Hillman also maintained that the Course promotes the extinction of strong emotions and passionate convictions. Noting that Walsh had suggested that the Course, like other spiritual traditions, advocates the relinquishing of fear, anger, jealousy, and hatred, Hillman then issued a defense of each of these emotions:

Fear is absolutely essential to staying alive. If my fear were extinguished, I had better not go out and cross the street because I'd get run over immediately. If jealousy were extinguished, I would lose all coupling and mating emotions which exist in animals and birds. Jealousy belongs with feelings of closeness. If I were to lose my anger I would lose my social sense. I would have no sense of justice, of abuse, of political terror, because I wouldn't be angry any more. I wouldn't notice. If I were to lose hatred, I would lose culture because culture is not only based on love, but on hatred, too. . . . So if the Course is going to extinguish those emotions, what have we got left? Hallmark feelings? Safe, mediocre, passive emotions? Sanitized pain relievers?[3]

Partly as a result of discouraging strong feelings, concluded Hillman, "the Course keeps us from being political. It keeps us from protesting because the mess 'out there' is merely a cognitive illusion. . . . *A Course in Miracles* is Republican right-wing politics in the guise of spiritual reformation. It's not even good conservatism. It's reactionary."[4]

While a lively round of letters followed in the succeeding issue of *Common Boundary*, the response from Roger Walsh printed alongside Hillman's article was brief. "Unfortunately, the critique by James Hillman is not informed and seriously misrepresents the Course," wrote Walsh. "The positions he attributes to it are not only incorrect in most cases, but in many cases are diametrically opposite to what it says."[5]

Hillman's scholarship on the Course, directly challenged by Walsh, is difficult to assess because Hillman has consistently refused to document his study. Replying to a 1990 letter in which I requested a telephone interview and asked for specific Course text references to illustrate some of his assertions, Hillman sent a note saying, "I don't want to do this. I've said what I wanted to say and have nothing to add." Barbara Goodrich-Dunn told me at the time that she did not know the extent of Hillman's Course study, but did say she knew he was "not displeased about the controversy" their article generated.

"I know that Hillman is very concerned about the lack of critical thinking in a lot of New Age psychology," explained Goodrich-Dunn. When I relayed that remark to Roger Walsh, he remarked, "Well, I certainly have no disagreement with him about that."

While researching this book I wrote to James Hillman requesting a follow-up to his critique of the Course. Noting that his 1989 remarks remained the most prominent hostile review of ACIM in print, I asked him again to substantiate his major criticisms — either with quotes from the Course itself or with other evidence he had gathered before or since his published statements. I specifically inquired if he could cite instances of the Course being used to promote fascistic ideas or programs; if he knew of a significant number of Course students who are passive and apolitical; and if he could identify any prominent or influential right-wing Republicans who espouse the Course teaching.

Hillman's written response was succinct: "I have no answers to your questions and do not have the interest to pursue them. You may make of that fact what you will."

The Course as "Masked Authoritarianism"

A more focused critique of *A Course in Miracles* appeared in a widely reviewed 1993 book entitled *The Guru Papers: Masks of Authoritarian Power*, by Diana Alstad and Joel Kramer. Alstad, an instructor in humanities and women's studies with a doctorate from Yale, and Kramer, a yoga adept and former instructor at Esalen Institute, wrote their book to expose the "authoritarian structure" they feel is "interwoven and disguised in most arenas of human interaction, including religion, morality, power, institutions, the family, intimacy, and even sexual relations and personal problems, such as addiction."[6]

For the most part *The Guru Papers* eschews criticism of particular institutions, movements, or individuals, instead providing a more general analysis of such topics as "The Seductions of Surrender," "Fundamentalism and the Need for Certainty," and "Love and Control." Two exceptions to their "essentially structural" critique include a five-page commentary on the Reverend Jim Jones and the mass suicide at Jonestown — and ten pages on *A Course in Miracles*.

Kramer and Alstad focused on the Course "because it purports to be non-authoritarian, while claiming to be channeled by no less an authority than the spirit of Jesus Christ. . . . We single it out because it is a classic example of programming thought to renunciate beliefs."[7] Most of the ensuing critique focuses on the Workbook of the Course, which in Kramer and Alstad's view pursues a kind of brainwashing proceeding along three routes:

1. promulgating detachment from the world by denying its reality;
2. decreeing forgiveness and the letting go of grievances to be the only route to love and salvation;
3. promising immortality and the elimination of all negativity through identifying only with what is delineated as the god aspect within oneself.[8]

The authors also note that the avowed purpose of the Workbook is to "eventually bring forth one's 'Internal Teacher' which in turn, without any external authorities, will lead one to truth. . . . This claim is worth examining because under the guise of presenting objective truth that any seeker can find, what is actually going on is the age-old ploy of authoritarian doctrination: A worldview is presented by an unchallengeable authority as the truth to be found. . . . Nothing could be more authoritarian, for who could argue against a disembodied spirit with the credentials of a traditional God?"[9]

An obvious answer is Helen Schucman, the Course channel who argued with the alleged voice of a disembodied spirit in her head until the end of her days (see chapters 1 and 2). Kramer and Alstad's charge about the authoritarianism of the Course is further weakened by two facts. First, most authoritarian systems rely on an organization or embodied figure of authority rather than an implicit one. Second, many Course students do in fact argue with its voice even as they study the message.

Many contemporary students — including such leading proponents as Jerry Jampolsky, Marianne Williamson, Ken Wapnick, and Judy Skutch — come from Jewish backgrounds and thus were not particularly inclined to regard the voice of Jesus as a divine or unimpeachable authority in the first place. Possibly a majority of students are veterans of other spiritual disciplines — including more traditional and overtly authoritarian structures — who report that what they like about the Course is its "take it or leave it" accessibility. Still others with agnostic orientations tell stories like that of Roger Walsh (see Chapter 6), who shut his copy of the Course as soon as he encountered its claim of spiritual authorship, and did not reopen it for two years — until consistently positive reviews by respected peers convinced him to take another look. As Ken Wapnick relates, "I've heard countless stories of the Course sitting on people's bookshelves for several years before they happen to read something in it that suddenly makes sense."

Thus Kramer and Alstad's critique incorporates little knowledge of what Course students are really like, or what they have to say about how the teaching actually affects them. Even when Kramer and Alstad rely on a student's own words to draw an interpretation of the Course's effects, their methodology and conclusions are decidedly questionable.

"He Feels Better"

To illustrate their contention that "those willing to be programmed get programmed," Kramer and Alstad assert that it is necessary to examine not only the Course's Workbook exercises "but also the nature of the mind that is willing and able to do them daily for an extended time."[10]

> As an example we will paraphrase and quote an enthusiast and teacher of the Course. We use this person's words only to represent a position which we (and he, too) believe is similar to that of many others. Consequently, we do not think the identity of the person matters. He initially states that before doing the Course, he was very disappointed in

life because he saw that ideals important to him would not or could not be achieved in this world. "The more I faced the 'real world,' the less real I felt." He had "a divided sense of self that didn't measure up to anything"; and his "fragmented idealism" was "contaminated by conflicting ambitions."

Here is a person who wanted the world to fit into what were most probably ideals of purity, where non-violence, compassion, selflessness, and love would reign supreme. It is not surprising this man would gravitate toward a world-view that presented these four items as in fact reigning supreme, this being done by denying the reality of the world where they do not reign supreme. This same person went on to say,

After years of thrashing about in a senseless world that seemed to oppose my highest aspirations, I have simply forgiven that world . . . I'm no longer concerned with defining what the "real world" is — perhaps, as the Course asserts, there is no world at all, but I do know I have gained a personal sense of authenticity.

He then concluded that he now feels better than he ever felt before.[11]

The danger of this kind of feeling better, Kramer and Alstad explain, is the "great illusion . . . that through denial one can transcend what one is afraid of, whether it be death or isolation. . . . What all renunciate worldviews such as *A Course in Miracles* really create are internally divided people who need an external authority to help keep control of their unwanted parts."[12]

Kramer and Alstad did not acknowledge or footnote their source, making it difficult for readers to follow up their research or challenge their conclusions. Reading their critique as a journalist, I decided that I would try to contact the quoted student myself. Beginning to read his excerpted statements a second time, I realized that this wouldn't take much footwork — because the increasingly familiar language of this "programmed" student was my own.

In fact, the quotes Kramer and Alstad excerpted originally appeared in my first personal essay about *A Course in Miracles*, published in 1988 by *The Sun: A Magazine of Ideas*. In order to offer my own interpretation of what I wrote — about which I can be reasonably authoritative — it is necessary to reproduce the entire passage edited by Kramer and Alstad. Italics indicate material they deleted or did not include:

> After years of thrashing about in a senseless world that seemed to oppose my highest aspirations, I have simply forgiven that world *by realizing that it was largely defined and limited by my own pessimism*. I'm no longer concerned with defining what the "real world" is — perhaps, as the Course asserts, there is no world at all — but I do know that I have regained a personal sense of authenticity. *I know that I am here to learn and, through writing, to teach whatever I can discover, record, and synthesize. No other definition of myself is needed.*[13]

This essay, written during recovery from a prolonged illness during which I encountered and completed my initial study of *A Course in Miracles*, represented a sort of personal "coming out." In it I was exploring how what I had recently learned might be usefully extended to a world from which I had felt sequestered for several years by an intense struggle of physical suffering, psychological self-confrontation, and spiritual crisis.

By learning how to relinquish long-time habits of pessimism and cynicism, I felt that I was "loosing the world," as the Course puts it, from my demands and judgments.[14] I no longer expected the *world* to fit ideals of "non-violence, compassion, selflessness, and love," as Kramer and Alstad suggest; rather I had come to realize that fulfilling and communicating such worthy ideals were *my* responsibility. To pursue them I needed to rely on a greater sense of guidance than my habitual ego-self. *A Course in*

Miracles was invaluable in helping me discover and contact such a sense of guidance.

While examining *The Guru Papers* I became curious as to why anti-authoritarian writers like Kramer and Alstad would take the liberty of interpreting my writing without contacting me to discuss their perspective in a fair and egalitarian manner. (Reaching me would have been easy enough; my address was published with *The Sun* essay, and responses from readers were explicitly invited.) I also wanted to discuss with Kramer and Alstad my reactions to their work before writing this book.

In my letter requesting their cooperation, I advised Kramer and Alstad that they would have the opportunity to preview what I wrote about them in manuscript, correct any factual inaccuracies, and discuss any points on which they might feel misrepresented before publication. (This has been my standard policy as a magazine journalist for the past decade, and was followed with everyone in this book who consented to an interview.)

In a written response Diana Alstad stated that "we are truly sorry if you feel misrepresented." She did not explain why she and Kramer opted not to discuss my Course experience with me before interpreting it for publication. She also declined to be interviewed, stating that "we are not interested in involving ourselves in a dialogue about the value of *A Course in Miracles.*" This refusal to engage in discussion about the Course is ironic, to say the least, since Kramer and Alstad remark in *The Guru Papers* that they "have a surety and confidence in what we are saying. But confidence need not be authoritarian in itself if one is truly open to being shown wrong. The essence of ideological authoritarianism is unchallengeability, not confidence."[15]

"Another World-Denying, Escapist Spiritual Philosophy"

Another round of Course criticism was sparked by the 1995 publication in *The Sun* of an interview I conducted with Kenneth and Gloria Wapnick (the source material for Chapter 5 of this book). Although the interview was assigned and accepted by editor Sy Safransky (who has studied the Course), the issue following its publication featured a letter from *The Sun's* copy editor Seth Mirsky, revealing that he had objected to publication of the article.

"It pains me to see *The Sun* promoting a spiritual philosophy so antithetical to what I value about this magazine," wrote Mirsky, including "[*The Sun's*] refusal to buy any spiritual bill of goods, however facilely packaged." Mirsky claimed that if one "looks beyond the defensive protestations of Kenneth Wapnick . . . one finds in the Course what could fairly be described as a variety of Christian fundamentalism . . . [an] evident hostility to free thought and critical reason [and] a hatred of the world. . . .

"In this time of accelerating ecological destruction," Mirsky concluded, "with multiple wars raging around the world and the triumph of meanness and selfishness in our national political culture, *A Course in Miracles* presents us with just what we surely do not need: another world-denying, escapist spiritual philosophy — comfort for the comfortable, affliction for the afflicted."[16]

When I requested an interview to explore these criticisms, however, Mirsky declined to participate. "I do not claim any special expertise on the Course," Mirsky wrote in a letter refusing the interview, admitting that all he knew about ACIM was what he had read in the interview and a few hundred words of excerpts published alongside.

A bonafide mystery of the Course is exactly how it inspires such virulent attacks from critics who have apparently spent little if any time examining it first-hand or talking with students about its effects. A clue lies in the historical perception of spiritual paths that are regarded, accurately or not, as "renunciate" in nature.

"One has to understand that these charges about apoliticism and world-hating have been made against spiritual traditions of all sorts," remarks Roger Walsh. "There has long been a fear among some people — perhaps Karl Marx is the best known example — that spiritual seeking merely perpetuates social pathology and inequality, and may occasion a permanent withdrawal from the concerns of the world. However, many spiritual seekers withdraw for a while and then return to share what they have learned in order to help the world. This is what historian Arnold Toynbee called 'the cycle of withdrawal and return.' He discovered that it was a characteristic feature of the lives of those people who contributed most profoundly to human well-being."

Marc Polonsky, a Course student with a long history of political activism, points out that politics and the search for inner peace are not necessarily antithetical. "I don't understand the logic of thinking that if we feel at peace inside and are not moved to hatred and blame, then we won't feel like doing anything constructive in the world. Over fifteen years I've been arrested, I've organized, I've written letters, I've even walked across the country for my beliefs. In the midst of this, the Course was a soothing, centering balm for my mind and soul.

"I think if someone wants to be passive," concludes Polonsky, "they'll find an excuse to be passive, and if one is moved to make a difference in the world, one will find ample reinforcement for this impulse wherever one looks."

Although my own experience may not be typical, I would add that the Course actually enabled a greater degree of political involvement on my part — not because it carries any political message in itself, but because Course study enabled me to become less neurotic and self-absorbed, and therefore able to commit more time, energy, and money to concerns beyond my personal survival and well-being. I also find that the Course's central doctrine of forgiveness has profound political implications, even if no such implications are spelled out in the teaching itself. (For a critical opinion of the apoliticism of the Course by a student, see Ted Grabowski's personal statement in Chapter 9.)

Finally, a survey of the published hostile criticism of *A Course in Miracles* would be incomplete without mentioning a full frontal attack by the author and professional skeptic Martin Gardner in the Fall 1992 issue of *The Skeptical Inquirer*, published by the Committee for the Scientific Investigation of Claims of the Paranormal.

Gardner's essay on "Marianne Williamson and 'A Course in Miracles'" is riddled with factual inaccuracies, including a repetition of erroneous information about Helen Schucman sourced to Michael Murphy (see Chapter 2), an assertion that Ken Wapnick "struggles to harmonize the Course with Christian doctrine," and the quaintly sexist description of Marianne Williamson as a "frail brunette" — perhaps the only time in hundreds of pages of media reviews that Williamson has ever been described as anything short of dynamic. Gardner relies heavily on the tabloid *New York Post* for his juiciest charges against Williamson, concluding that she is "self-absorbed and relishing her glitzy fame." Near the end of his article, Gardner stretches the language of skeptical inquiry to its rhetorical limits by asking, "Will the sexy little guru rediscover love, sweet love? And will her followers, along with other disciples of the Course, ever succeed in plugging the holes in their heads?"[17]

Not Exactly Easy Reading

A frequent criticism of the Course by its own students and others who have attempted to examine it is that its patriarchal, Christian, and just plain difficult language puts up a formidable barrier to study. Rick Fields, a prominent writer in American Buddhism and the editor of *Yoga Journal*, probably speaks for untold thousands when he says that "the Christian language was just too much for my taste."

Course student and psychotherapist Frances Vaughan says that the consistently masculine tone of the teaching "was not something I liked about the Course at first, and I would translate terms like *Son of God* to *Child of God* as I read it. I'd also substitute *enlightenment* for *salvation,* and so on. What worked for me was to take what fit, and let pass the things that didn't." Over time, however, Vaughan says that her technical difficulties with the Course terminology diminished to the point of irrelevance.

Institute of Noetic Sciences (IONS) president Willis Harman found his early study of the Course slowed by an indefinable resistance. "I tried to study the books every day, but after the first six months it dawned on me that I hadn't finished a single page of the text. Every time I started reading, I'd end up at the refrigerator looking for something to eat, or getting drowsy and falling asleep. When I realized that something strange was going on there, I began to take it much more seriously."

Charles T. Tart, Ph.D. is a senior research fellow at IONS and a retired psychology professor from the University of California at Davis who edited the landmark book *Altered States of Consciousness*, a rare best-seller among scientific anthologies. He remembers that the Course presented special difficulties for a mind trained in the scientific approach to reality.

"The Course really came in at a right angle to most of my professional work," Tart remarks. "I could find a lot of stuff in there that fit my understanding of how we 'live in illusion' — that is, how we use psychological defense mechanisms that distort our perceptions and create trouble for us. But basically the Course goes right for the heart, and the heart is not a standard part of scientific discipline. So it was tough for me."

Echoing Ken Wapnick's frequent assertions that *A Course in Miracles* should not be mistaken for an easy path to personal fulfillment or spiritual enlightenment, Course publisher Judy Skutch says, "I don't think serious students find it easy at all. We're all involved in a worldly thought system that is a direct antithesis to the Course. Some people come to it looking for a reinforcement of their feelings for peace, love, and light, and that's what they'll find. But their eyes may glaze over when they come to the Course definition of the ego as a murderer. There are many paths that will tell you of your perfection in spirit, and that you are loved. The Course does that too, but it may not be the best place to go for it."

The most cogent published summary of the difficulties engendered by Course study appeared in the Fall 1987 issue of *Gnosis*, a "journal of the Western inner traditions," a quarterly magazine based in San Francisco. Writer Richard Smoley, who went on to become editor of *Gnosis*, announced in his essay "Pitfalls of *A Course in Miracles*" that he had worked with the Course for a number of years, finding it to be "an effective tool for spiritual growth. It seems to be especially useful for intellectuals who feel the need to deepen qualities of love and compassion. . . . Yet, like all spiritual paths, the Course has its pitfalls."[18]

One of these, says Smoley, paradoxically derives from a Course virtue: its encouragement to students that they listen for the voice of the Holy Spirit within. "The independence permitted by this approach is wonderful for developing a sense of responsibility for oneself,"[19] allows Smoley. But he points out that the destructive voice of ego can easily be mistaken for authentic spiritual guidance, thus leading the Course student astray. Smoley comments:

> Normally if this happens, some kind of balance is restored by the response of others. But the Course emphasizes very strongly that we are not to judge others: "In order to judge anything rightly, one would have to be fully aware of an inconceivably wide range of things, past, present, and to come. . . . Who is in a position to do this? Who except in grandiose fantasies would claim this for himself?" *(ACIM: M-10.3:3-7)* Thus, any criticism offered by somebody else can be immediately turned against him or her: "You're judging me!" — which, among Miracles students, often closes the book on the issue, though rarely satisfactorily. In my experience, this has caused legitimate questions and problems to fester into something really quite bad, whereas they might have been settled easily if one student had permitted himself to listen to the other's "judgment."[20]

Partly for this reason, Smoley feels that *A Course in Miracles* is actually poorly suited to group study. As he writes, "A group or organization that is trying to live by the Course's teachings may arrive at a decision by consensus. Yet a member chosen to carry it out may do exactly the opposite, on the grounds that the Holy Spirit directed him otherwise later on. And who's to say he's wrong?"[21]

Smoley's concerns about the misidentification of divine guidance seem valid. One doesn't have to visit Course study groups or electronic discussion forums for long to hear the Holy Spirit cited frequently as the internal broker of every conceivable decision, intuition, or lucky break, from deciding to divorce or pull up stakes to finding a wished-for parking space. There is generally less discussion over whether it's truly the Holy Spirit at work in all these occasions; short-term benefits are often taken for proof of divine guidance.

Ken Wapnick observes that one of the key misperceptions that arises in Course students is "the idea that it's the easiest thing in the world to hear the Holy Spirit — that a little light meditation is all that's required to get the Holy Spirit to tell you what to do. But the reason the Course as a whole exists is to help us clear out the interference that blocks the Holy Spirit. That interference is huge, and it's not a simple matter to get rid of it. The ego won't dissolve immediately simply because you begin to think you want it to dissolve."

Richard Smoley also suggests that Workbook lessons such as #97, "I am spirit," and #199, "I am not a body. I am free." can encourage Course students to lose "a firm grounding in the physical. . . . Often one does sense in Miracles students a lack of a firm foundation, an ethereal or dreamy quality that can be pleasant to be around but may also represent a spiritual dead end."[22] Wapnick identifies this quality as a tendency among novices. "It's true that many students new to the Course have a tendency to get dreamy and spaced-out. A friend of mine calls them the 'bliss ninnies'. . .

"I find that I often have to tell people, *Don't forget to be normal*," continues Wapnick. "Students can end up thinking that they shouldn't lock their doors at night because the Course tells them to trust, they should cancel their insurance because the Course says not to plan the future, and they should feel guilty for sneezing because the Course says, 'Sickness is a defense against the truth.'[23] So I have to remind them to be normal. Of course, be sympathetic to someone who's sick. Don't preach to them about their illness being a defense.

"What people tend to do is deny where they are," Wapnick explains, "or they try to *reinterpret* their current behavior along the intellectual lines of the Course rather than *change* themselves according to inner guidance. The Course doesn't ask us to deny our feelings and experiences — in fact, it does just the opposite. It says we should look clearly at our feelings in order 'to bring them to the truth.' You can't do the second without the first, without being fully aware of what you feel."

The tendency to deny one's flaws and contradictions and evade uncomfortable truths is arguably a universal expression of the human condition and is by no means unique to Course students. But it is clear that some students exploit the Course's ideas about forgiveness and the illusory nature of the world as novel mechanisms of denial. When confronted with one's mistakes, it becomes all too easy to say that "everything's an illusion anyway" or "we've all been forgiven." Neither of these excuses would carry much weight outside Course circles. But as Richard Smoley has pointed out, the culture inside study groups can become rarefied to the extent that such protestations can effectively short-circuit discussion and confrontation. The result is that truth and genuine understanding may be sacrificed to a false harmony and cloying religiosity.

But to the extent that Course students resort to denial and evasion, they are also evading explicit directives of the Course itself, such as:

Honesty does not apply only to what you say. The term actually means consistency. There is nothing you say that contradicts what you think or do; no thought opposes any other thought; no act belies your word; and no word lacks agreement with another. Such are the truly honest. At no level are they in conflict with themselves. Therefore it is

impossible for them to be in conflict with anyone or anything. . . . Conflict is the inevitable result of self-deception,
and self-deception is dishonesty.[24]

Every thought you would keep hidden shuts communication off, because you would have it so. It is impossible to
recognize perfect communication while breaking communication holds value to you. Ask yourself honestly, "Would
I want to have perfect communication, and am I wholly
willing to let everything that interferes with it go forever?" If the answer is no, then the Holy Spirit's readiness
to give it to you is not enough to make it yours, for you
are not ready to share it with Him. . . .

You will not be able to accept perfect communication as
long as you would hide it from yourself. For what you
would hide *is* hidden from you.[25]

The Problem of Ultimacy

The Course presents a more profound problem than its potential
for exploitation, however. ACIM's fundamental challenge to the
reality of all that we see, hear, and feel in our ordinary state of
consciousness can have a disorienting effect on some students, an
effect that may not be soon resolved. A woman who said she had
been studying the Course for more than a year posted the following impassioned message to an ACIM online discussion group:

If we are supposed to view the world differently, if what we
see is not real, how do we go about our everyday activities?
Do we quit our jobs and sit and contemplate? Do we actively fill every free moment with passages and practices of
the course?

Why are there babies dying every day from poverty and
violence? Are we supposed to see this as not real?. . . .
What about children who don't understand anything on a
higher level? Do we dismiss them from salvation? Do we

teach them at age 2 that everything they are seeing is not real? That they must change their perceptions?. . . I truly am confused and in my quest for salvation, by turning to God, have sought out these questions and have gotten no answers. It's almost impossible to pretend that we are not who we are. Try as I may, I still have to work to pay bills, yet I find it hard some days to get up in the morning, to prepare myself for the day knowing that all the things I am doing in the eyes of the Lord are not real and, moreover, meaningless. . . . I really feel like this is an obsession that leads to depression, especially when so much time is invested in understanding the concepts of ACIM.

To this message one on-line correspondent answered, "I'm with you. I threw my ACIM books out." But another responded, "I know that I, too, went through a phase of passivity and a sense of detachment for a while, but this passes with working with the Course."

To understand why and how ACIM can throw its students for a loop — even to the extent that some abandon it — it's necessary to contemplate the difference between ordinary churchgoing religion and esoteric mystical paths such as the Course. According to San Francisco State University philosophy professor Jacob Needleman, author of the 1970 classic *The New Religions* and more recent titles such as *Lost Christianity, The Heart of Philosophy* and *Money and the Meaning of Life*, the world's great religious traditions have always consisted of an outer shell of moral teachings and prescribed beliefs, and an inner core of more demanding transformative practices. As Needleman told me in a 1989 interview:

Christianity, Judaism, and Islamic belief all provide people with moral precepts: ways of living meant to be obeyed by the masses. Any such way of living is based on a particular vision of human nature and society, and is intended to give balance and steadiness to our experience. It's not intended to *transform* us, to give us *nirvana* or God-realization. But if kept authentically, it can bring a few people who are seeking more to "the path" in relatively good shape. Their psyches are not torn apart or so terribly neurotic. This is the point of the exoteric function of the great religions — what Islam calls the *shariat*, its laws, customs, and traditions. It's a very important part of balancing human life, and at their best these rules provide guidelines for handling our various energies with compassion for one another.

Within the *shariat* is the *tarikat*: the way or the path. In Islam, this esoteric function is embodied by the Sufis. Many great teachers have said that the esoteric work is only for those who have been through the exoteric, and have achieved the necessary balance. It's true that the message of the great esoteric traditions is that only an inner change can genuinely infuse outer actions with truth, love, and power. But most of these transformative techniques were intended for people who had lived in balance with a tradition. What we're getting recently in the West is a lot of information about inner practice, available to people who haven't really had an *outer* practice.[26]

What can happen to people who encounter a transformative inner practice if they haven't had much of an outer one? Says Needleman, "If a spiritual practice is too intense, it 'blows your mind' and becomes overly fascinating, or leads you into fantasy. You could compare the esoteric core of a religion to a very pure, high-octane fuel. Put it into an old Volkswagen, and the car will go like hell for a mile before it blows apart."[27]

This vivid image may explain a lot about the disorienting effect of the Course on its students (and perhaps even its combustible effect on some critics). What is startling about the Course in view of Needleman's analysis is that it appears to be a transformative inner practice that has come to us *without* an accompanying outer practice — that is, no commandments for moral behavior and no simple, direct judgments about various challenges of daily life.

Thus one of the greatest difficulties of *A Course in Miracles* might be called the problem of ultimacy — the fact that it operates as an ultimate teaching about the nature of consciousness and reality in a world where so many people need simpler, more direct answers to their everyday problems. In my own experience, the Course is not sufficient as a "troubleshooting" guide to everyday life. No one should mistake it for a substitute for psychotherapy, peer counseling, or simple human communion in times of distress. Particularly in the early stages of study, the Course can be quite confusing or even distressing if one attempts to apply its teaching too literally to chronic or everyday problems.

The changes in consciousness that the Course can effect may be quite profound, but they come about in a subtle and gradual manner. Those people for whom the Course eventually works as a transformative path — truly connecting them to an internal agency of reliable, ego-surpassing wisdom — may indeed transcend the need for more specific forms of personal or moral guidance. This is the advanced state of instinctive morality that St. Augustine was probably referring to when he issued the mystical directive "Love and do what you will."

But all paths to such states are fraught with dangers and opportunities for delusion. Thus, anyone who undertakes a path like *A Course in Miracles* would be well advised to stay in touch with respected and caring peers who do not share the path, its assumptions, and its lingo. Reliable outsiders can provide invaluable "reality checks" to the esoteric seeker along his or her way — and sophisticated skeptics can provide some necessary tests of one's spiritual learning.

Of course, ACIM is not the only esoteric path available to seekers in the modern "spiritual supermarket." However dangerous it may be for people to take up an inner practice when they haven't had an outer one, it would appear that the growing social phenomenon of "inner seeking" is unlikely to reverse itself. As a *Newsweek* poll revealed in 1994, 58% of Americans say they feel the need to experience spiritual growth, and 33%

report having had a religious or mystical experience.[28] A more exhaustive 1987 survey conducted by *Better Homes and Gardens* revealed that 62% had begun or intensified personal spiritual study not long before the poll, compared to 23% who said they had become closer to a religious organization.[29]

Perhaps more people are lately drawn to esoteric spiritualities because the outer paths of the great religious traditions have been slow to adapt their exoteric guidance to the needs of a rapidly-changing world, as witnessed by the stresses and strains to which the Catholic Church is now subject. Or perhaps it's because the world's established religions have drifted too far from their inner, transformative core — a predicament that Jacob Needleman diagnosed two and a half decades ago when he wrote *The New Religions*. In discussing the central crisis of Western religion, he said:

> It is as though millions of people suffering from a painful disease were to gather together to hear someone read a textbook of medical treatment in which the means necessary to cure their disease were carefully spelled out. It is as though they were all to take great comfort in that book and what they heard, going through their lives knowing that their disease could be cured, quoting passages to their friends, preaching the wonders of this great book, and returning to their congregation from time to time to hear more of the inspiring diagnosis and treatment read to them. Meanwhile, of course, the disease worsens and they eventually die of it, smiling in grateful hope as on their deathbed someone reads to them yet another passage from the text. Perhaps for some a troubling thought crosses their minds as their eyes close for the last time: "Haven't I forgotten something? Something important? Haven't I forgotten actually to undergo treatment?"[30]

Even as Needleman wrote those words, a new "textbook" spelling out a spiritual cure to what ails us was being composed, and would shortly become available to the world. As this chapter has shown, we still lack any exhaustive, reasonably impartial assessments of the quality of this new guide to transformation, although positive anecdotal reports (some of which appear in the next chapter) continue to mount. The extent to which *A Course in Miracles* proves to be an effective esoteric therapy for the existential illness of humanity — whose painful symptoms include unhappiness, profound suffering, enmity, and oppression — remains to be seen.

PART III:

Living with the Course

9
The Voices of Students

In this chapter some students of *A Course in Miracles* speak for themselves. Since my research suggests that Course students cannot be typified, the selection of voices presented here is a representation of their diversity rather than any "norm." These short essays were drawn from a variety of sources, including postings to on-line discussion groups, original interviews, and some solicited essays. From beginners to veterans, from those who have made the Course the focus of their lives to those who accept only a part of its teaching, these fourteen voices all attest in different ways to the remarkable influence of a teaching that is scarcely twenty years old.

A Different Dragnet

The following essay is written by a detective and ten-year veteran of the Los Angeles Police Department who took up the Course shortly before posting the following message to an on-line discussion group. He says that although the Course is "not the first spiritual path I have attempted to stumble through, it certainly seems to be the most timely for me."

Due to my profession, I mostly see the world in the light of hate, anger, greed and fear. In the wake of the O.J. Simpson case, and the fact that I work in south central L.A., these views of the world have come to a head for me.

I was beginning to feel that I was no different from the people I was trying to put in prison. I nearly quit a few weeks ago. Then I began reading the Course in a bookstore. As I was thumbing through it, an amazing realization hit me: I *am* no different from the people I was trying to put in prison. Perhaps becoming a police officer was my way of dealing with what was inside of me . . . what *is* inside of me. I can't lie and say that all of a sudden I see the people I prosecute as holy, loving children of God. I would have to see myself as that first. But I do see that it is my perception of people and the world that creates the pain, the anger, fear, greed, and hate I have been living in for such a long time.

As a detective I have worked on the worst crimes you could imagine. I know it will be very difficult to forgive child molestors, and to think of them as holy and loving. However, I do see that the Course seems to say that the evil I see in these crimes and people is merely my own view of the world. I truly believe this. The world I see is of my own creation. The violence and hate I see is not from a loving God. This realization is only a spark needed to follow this path.

I know this will be a life's worth of learning, and I expect it will not be easy. Anger is easy, peace is difficult. Hate is easy, love is difficult. The most difficult for me to deal with has always been fear. I think if I can conquer my own fears, I can do anything.

A Mistaken Attack

Kathi J. Kemper, M.D. practices pediatrics in Seattle, Washington and is the author of The Holistic Pediatrician *(HarperCollins). The following is her account of a "peak experience" applying the lessons of the Course.*

I was attending a convention in Philadelphia. After the evening speaker I returned to my hotel room to freshen up before another round of discussions. As I stood in the bathroom combing my hair, I noticed a large man dressed in army fatigues standing in the bathtub. As I whirled around, he grabbed my arm and started to close the door. My mind seemed to split in two and everything seemed to happen very slowly. I could hear myself screaming and knew the terror of imminent attack. But another part of my mind clicked onto the Course: "You are my brother. This is a mistake. You can't attack me. There can be nothing but love between us."

These thoughts were repeated over and over in my mind very clearly, even though I could hear my own screaming as if from a distance. We were looking in each other's eyes during this time. Before the door was shut all the way, he stopped and said, "There must be some mistake. I think I have the wrong room." He let go of my arm and fled the building.

For me this experience is a powerful affirmation of the truth of love and how we are all connected to that truth even when we seem to be thinking, saying, doing, or even screaming very different things. The stranger seemed to be attacking me; I seemed to be screaming; yet on some deeper level, we were acknowledging our oneness, and recognizing that everything else we think, do, or say is a mistake.

I often think of this experience when I am confronted with the question, "What would you do if faced with a gunman threatening you or a loved one?" Obviously this is where people think the rubber meets the road and that we'd either shoot the person, defend ourselves, or let someone be shot. I don't know what the right behavior is for anyone; nor do I know what I will "do" if I'm ever faced with that situation again. I only pray that some part of my mind will remain sane enough to remember the truth of our oneness.

Giving and Receiving

Charlie Cowan was the original founder of the Northwest Foundation for A Course in Miracles. *Cowan currently lives in San Diego and teaches a weekly class on the Course at a Unity church.*

I've been an ardent student of the Course since 1986; my loving and loved wife, Shirley, shares my devotion to the Course and its principles. Eight years ago we divested ourselves of everything — jobs, business, house, cars — and devoted ourselves fulltime to the Course. We traveled the western US talking to Course students, then settled down about three years ago as resident managers of a mobile-home park.

I can't speak for anyone else, of course. But as for me, I have invested everything I ever thought I owned in the Course and its principles. One of those principles is: Giving and receiving are, in fact, the same thing; you cannot but receive what you give. Since I am a terrifically selfish individual, I had to give *all* to the principles I teach in order to learn.

As for what I received in return:

1. Recovery from alcoholism
2. Loving and loved wife, Shirley
3. Friends with whom I can share a laugh and a tear at any time, for any reason
4. Happiness
5. Peace of mind
6. Personal receipt of miracles in my life and those around me
7. Restoration of my relationship with God
8. Realization of a loving relationship with my family of birth
9. Forgiveness of my temporal father
10. Forgiveness of myself
11. Reunion with my daughter and son

And what did all this cost me?

1. My guilt
2. My fear
3. My pain
4. My loneliness

Not bad for an old drunk, don't you think? Fair trade in my book. By the way, I have invested a total of $0.00 in the books, since they were a gift, and I once bought a tape for $0.50 at a flea market. But I didn't like it much. I prefer to listen to the Voice of Peace inside.

Marrying the Course

Tom Davies of Orem, Utah has a religious background in Mormonism and a professional history in the neurosciences, a discipline that once convinced him that the brain was the source of all thought and behavior. He says now that he recognizes the "power of the mind to invent the illusion of a physical world." A student of the Course since 1986, Davies recently founded Love and Forgiveness *magazine.*

The Course has been a thorn in the side of my wife since I began studying it ten years ago. Initially I tried to push it on her; she honestly tried to understand it, but without success. Then she became resentful of the time and money I was spending on Course-related projects, such as a weekly study group in our home and a newsletter I published.

Before my involvement with the Course we didn't talk much with each other. She did her thing and I did mine. Gradually, as my understanding of the Course increased, I realized the extent to which our relationship was a special one: I was using my wife to satisfy my needs and vice versa. When I realized this, I decided I wanted to change that special relationship to a holy relationship. I could do this only if I was willing to love her unconditionally — to see her as guiltless regardless of what she might do. Because we are committed to each other, this shift in perception has been relatively easy.

As my perception changed, our ability to communicate improved. We started talking more about our feelings. I learned to understand her legitimate concerns about the Course (and other things), and she has learned to accept (within reason) my involvement in the Course. More than anything, each of us is certain of our love for each other and that we would not intentionally hurt one another.

I hardly ever get angry at my wife anymore, because I now

understand and accept her as she is. When I do occasionally get angry, I recognize that I have chosen fear rather than love, and I attempt to change my perception of whatever it was that caused the anger.

Based on my experience, divorce is not the only or primary option when a couple disagrees about the Course (or anything else). When two people love and respect each other, differences can be overlooked. However, when two people start to lose that love and respect for each other, differences suddenly become important. It is not the similarities or differences that make for a successful relationship, but the love that is shared in that relationship.

Seeing the Light

Ann (last name not provided) *in Virginia:*

I was an atheist until about two and a half years ago, shortly before I stumbled across — or was led to — the Course. Up to that time I could not accept any role for God in my life, nor did I have any firm belief in "life after death." But my study of the Course has inspired many experiences leading to a complete reversal of my former beliefs.

Occasionally during meditation I have called to and communicated "psychically" with loved ones who have passed on. I believe that these are actual communications and not just my imagination, because the content of these communications is very specific and often very surprising to me. The messages I have received have often totally contradicted firmly held beliefs I have had about situations.

Emboldened by these experiences, I once called on the spirit of Helen Schucman herself, and I asked open-endedly for her advice on how to study the Course. I did indeed receive advice, and it was the most useful advice I have ever received from anyone. Though I phrased my question open-endedly, I was expecting — and hoping for — some advice that would help me with a specific career problem. Instead I was told to simply relax and focus on "the Light" for as long as I could. The Light was extremely bright inside my mind and I was filled with a great sense of well-being. I had never known a feeling like this before and I have known it on few occasions since. During this time I was still hoping for specific advice about my career, waiting to hear "words." But no words came at all. Still, the feeling was so wonderful that I was content to allow it to flow through me for as long as I could.

After about twenty minutes distracting thoughts began to enter and the Light faded, so I let it go. I felt happy, confident, and peaceful. After a minute or so a strange thing started happening: I heard a quiet, confident voice that was my own, yet much more authoritative than my mental voice normally is. The voice gave me unpleasant advice about some important relationships I was involved with. Then it described three past lives I had been in, and how they tied in with some issues I was facing in this life. At this time I did not believe in reincarnation. Most of this information came to me right away, but more filtered in over the next eighteen hours or so.

None of this advice related directly to the career problem that had been on my mind, and I certainly wasn't seeking the advice that I received. If a friend had offered these words of wisdom to me without my request, I would have been deeply offended. Secrets I had been keeping even from myself were exposed by this knowing voice, and I was really quite embarrassed! But in time I chose to follow the advice I received.

Looking back, I can see that taking the advice marked a major, positive turning point in my life. Still, after having heard this wise voice, I wondered whether it was really Helen Schucman who had helped me. Later I read in Ken Wapnick's *Absence from Felicity* that when Helen was asked for advice, her answer to people was that she would not ask Jesus for help on their behalf, but she would pray *with* them. On reading this it struck me that I had been helped the same way, being instructed to hold on to my awareness of the Light. The answers I received afterward were not from Helen, but were the result of her spiritual joining with my mind. I was able to access her clarity in order to strengthen my own. For as the Course instructs, all minds are joined.

Not Seeing the Light

Michael Gann, age 45, is a graduate student in psychology at the University of Southern California. He prefaced this message with a quote from Douglas Adams' Hitchhiker's Guide to the Galaxy: *"In the beginning the universe was created. This has made a lot of people angry and been widely regarded as a bad move."*

In 1987 I was a member of the American Stock Exchange acting as a floorbroker in the index options pit. During the crash I lost a considerable number of clients and approximately half of my income. For several weeks after the crash I went through a period of depression about my losses and a marriage that was essentially over. One day I realized that although I had considerable losses, I still earned many times more money than I had ever dreamed I would. What struck me most was how foolish I felt about investing so much of myself in earning money. I concluded that there had to be more to life than this and that my feelings of emptiness were about more than mere money.

When I was young, I was peripherally involved in Theosophy and astrology, and later attended weekly channeling sessions, but found them a bit hokey. Although there was an intuitive appeal about some of the channeled messages, I knew it was not for me. I read many different New Age books before coming across *A Course in Miracles*. In the first class I attended, I immediately felt that the Course was speaking to me, although the class seemed to lack something. One evening a fellow student told of a workshop he had attended given by Ken Wapnick, and what he reported about Ken's teaching attracted me. I made plans to attend a FACIM workshop the next weekend, and my first weekend at the Foundation was a defining moment in my study of the Course. Ken's explanation of the Course cut through me like a knife.

The most useful idea of ACIM for me is that although we

may take sidetracks along the way, we all go home together. The dream metaphor — that the Son is asleep, dreaming of exile — is perhaps the most comforting, reassuring idea I have ever encountered.

Sometimes, perhaps most times, I think it's incredibly difficult to practice the Course. Although it requires very little, that much can seem like a tremendous sacrifice. When I moved to Los Angeles, I started attending a group that had met for many years. It wasn't long after I started telling them what I thought the Course really says that half the group dropped out. Two years later I still meet with them, but now I prepare discussions and bring in more of Ken and Gloria Wapnick's work. Now the group no longer beams white light at people, even though they still pray for sick members. Once in Santa Monica I walked out of a group that spent the entire evening praying for someone's recently deceased dog. There are many more stories about groups that hold rituals and beam white light, but they all speak to the same error: Our fear is such that we need to make the Course and the world pretty, and deny our projections.

Beyond Magic

Michael Brewer, age 37, is an American living in Switzerland with his Swiss-born wife and daughter. He says that his spiritual life began with the practice of affirmations in his early twenties — affirmations that paid off in material circumstances but still left him unsatisfied because his "desires were a bottomless pit." His affirmations began to follow the Course philosophy in 1983, but he still found himself struggling with the issue of control, "doing some things God's way and some things my way." He undertook the Course Workbook for the third time when he felt he was finally ready to surrender control completely.

As soon as I did this, my house of cards came tumbling down. Relationships crumbled, jobs fell apart, money ceased to flow, cars broke down, traffic tickets gathered around me like flies. Frantically I waved my magic wand of affirmations, but it no longer worked. The Course says that the vision of one world costs you the vision of the other. Now I was confronted with the gaping void I'd spent all these years stuffing. I saw that I'd been affirming and manifesting as fast as I could to keep one step ahead of a guilty secret I'd hidden from everyone, even myself. I'd perceived a number of events and situations of my childhood as abusive. I had interpreted this to mean that God was punishing me and that I'd never be able to trust this God to give me what I needed.

So my ego had taken charge of grabbing those things for me, and like a willful child I had grabbed at attention, money, and love. In my decision to usurp God lay my personal fall from grace. I was an angel who'd tumbled screaming from heaven; the realization that I'd done all this to myself was met with days of anguish and tears.

But then trumpets sounded. My ego, that child wailing in wet diapers, was picked up and held, and looked into a wise compassionate face whose eyes brimmed with unconditional love. I remembered who I was, the beloved Son of God, and tears of joy rained down that day. Since I let go of lists of affirmations, my life has taken me to places I'd never expected to go. I've learned through the Course to move over and let God do the driving. To be honest, I still tend to give advice about His driving, tell Him where to go, even occasionally grab the wheel. I think I'm happiest when I catch myself getting ready to grab the wheel, and stop. I feel happy in my life most of the time, though it's not the loud, cymbal-crashing happiness I used to look for. Rather it's a sweet voice in a scented breeze, telling me there is no lack within me and reminding me that life is much easier in the passenger's seat. This change of perception is what the Course calls a miracle, and miracles are what await us beyond magic.

Course Psychology, Yes; Course Metaphysics, No

Ted Grabowski is a 40-year-old attorney in northern California with a daughter in college. With positive memories of his Catholic upbringing, Grabowski nonetheless came under the spell of "science and philosophical materialism" in his early adulthood, coming to believe "that everything could be explained with physics and brain science." He earned degrees in psychology and philosophy before entering the practice of law.

Carl Jung once said that for the first 35 years of our lives we develop the ego, then spend the rest of our lives getting rid of it. So it was with me. It was not until I had reached that magical age that the Course would come into my life and have a wonderful transformative effect. Of all the books I read while getting my psychology degree, there was only one psychology book that seemed to touch me in an enduring way: Gerald Jampolsky's *Love is Letting Go of Fear.* I consistently found peace in applying its teachings. At the time I did not know about the Course or that Jampolsky was a student of the Course. Not long after, I picked up Marianne Williamson's *A Return to Love* and was overwhelmed by the love and peace I found there. I returned to the bookstore to get a copy of the Course, but they were out of it. Instead I bought a copy of Ken Wapnick's *Forgiveness and Jesus;* when I saw the gentle painting of Jesus on the cover, I started to cry. I had been away from Jesus and God for so long that the joy of coming home was overwhelming.

Thus I became a serious Course student, reading the text, doing the lessons, reading commentaries, and listening to tapes. I was transformed by the psychospiritual principles of the Course, particularly the teaching that there are only two emotions, love and fear. I softened and experienced peace more often, coming to understand in a very real way that anger is never justified. I learned to listen for the still small voice for God.

My discovery of the Course excited my interest in spirituality in general. I attended lectures by New Testament scholars and began to read widely in transpersonal psychology and comparative religion. In my study of the Course there was one teaching I found particularly inconsistent with the teachings of the historic Jesus. Why did the Course say that the world was made as an attack upon God? Although many believe that Jesus is the source of the Course, this did not sound like something Jesus would say. I tried to reconcile this statement with Christianity and the teachings of mystics of other spiritual traditions, without success.

I went on to study the history of Gnosticism and learn about the Hindu teachings known as the Advaita Vedanta. I would later learn that Helen Schucman's mother had been a student of Christian Science, and that Bill Thetford was raised in a Christian Science home. I believe there is compelling evidence that Helen was exposed to the major principles of Christian Science[1] — a religion that contains key ideas from Hinduism. I believe that the Course combines a psychology consistent with the teachings of the historic Jesus with a form of Hindu and Platonic metaphysics which is not.

A puzzle piece was missing until I read Ken Wilber's *Sex, Ecology and Spirituality* (Shambhala) wherein he describes a three-step process toward enlightenment. First, one detaches from the belief in the limited false "I" of the ego. Next, the mystic reidentifies with God — the One — which is love. Finally there is a descent back into the multiplicity, meaning the recognition of God's love in creation and God's many creatures. God's many creatures are not to be seen as illusory attacks upon God but as manifestations of a God of love.

A fundamentalist view of the Course as inerrant and sufficient prevents many students from realizing that the Course fails to complete the third step of nondual enlightenment so beautifully and consistently described by the great mystics. The experience of the history of spiritual thought is that a "freezing of action" frequently occurs when one stops at the first two stages. Without taking the final step many Course students cannot answer the following questions without first consulting the Holy Spirit: *Should I plant a tree? Should we find a cure for cancer and AIDS? Should I feed the hungry and clothe the homeless?*

For someone who has studied the life and teachings of Jesus, there are just too many things that do not ring true about the metaphysics of the Jesus of the Course. Jesus was a Jew who taught a love for life and creation. Many Course students believe that the Jesus of the Course teaches that all form in the universe — including the giant redwoods, flowers, and our pets — were made by the separated Sonship as an attack upon God. Jesus spoke in parables so that even children could understand them. Also Jesus served and healed, and calls us to serve and heal. The Jesus of the Course does not ask us to serve or act — but only to heal our minds. While the best gifts are those that are given with a selfless intent, a sandwich given to a homeless person by an egotistical and unhealed giver, unguided by the Holy Spirit, is still a beautiful and loving gift — a *mitzvah*.

While I still find inspiration in the many psychological insights contained in the Course, I am now convinced that the Course's metaphysics results from a judgment of the entire phenomenal world as unworthy of God —a failure to love God unconditionally. So now I still read the Course for its insights on the psychology of love, forgiveness, projection, and guilt. But I find my metaphysical truth in the lives and teachings of the great mystics who did not go within and stay there — or judge the world or God's many creatures into the oblivion of unreality.

A Fundamental Change

Allen Watson is a partner with Robert Perry in the Circle of Atonement teaching center in Sedona, Arizona (see Chapter 3). He has worked as a computer systems manager and written a column for a computing magazine. Watson describes himself as a former "born-again Christian" who went on to sample a variety of esoteric teachers and practices, including est, various channeled teachings, Eastern religions, and the American guru Da Free John.

I read the Course Text in about one month. I could not put it down. The moment I started reading, I knew I had found something tailor-made for me. All of the spiritual truth I had treasured in Christianity that seemed overlooked by most Christians was there. All the familiar symbols, but reinterpreted beautifully. All the scope and breadth of the Eastern religions, much of the insights from psychology — all there. I read day and night. I laughed aloud as I read, sometimes with total joy, transported by the solid awareness that there is no Will but God's, and never has been. I had at least one full-blown mystical experience, a sort of "cosmic consciousness" experience.

However, I was deeply troubled by the way the Course disagreed with the Bible in so many respects, things like the sacrificial, atoning death of Jesus Christ; the reality of sin; and not a small thing to me, the inerrancy of the Bible. The rest of the Course appealed to me so strongly, seeming to say what I had been struggling to understand for my entire life, that I decided to disregard the parts I didn't like and just take what I did like. My enthusiasm slowed down a little, however.

I set the Text aside for the next year or two and did the Workbook for the first time. It took me about two and a half years. My indiscipline was glaring; I was still experimenting with other things. Eventually I was confronted with a decision about whether or not to become a formal "friend" of Master Da Free John (the initial step to becoming a devotee of the guru). What came through very clearly in that difficult period was that I already had a guru: Jesus. And his path for me was the Course.

I began reading the Text again and discovered, much to my surprise, that somebody had been tampering with my thought system. I was no longer attached to fundamentalist doctrines. I was willing to consider that they might be wrong, and the more I read, the more I realized that the parts of the Course I liked could not be true unless the parts I was having trouble with were true also. "This course will be believed entirely or not at all."[2] My fundamentalist basics, which I had believed would be part of me forever, just fell away.

Consulting Unlikely Companions

Mike Gole has been an ordained minister for over thirty years. He currently pastors an Assembly of God church in southern California.

Marianne Williamson's *A Return to Love* entered my life unwanted; one of my book club memberships sent it to me by mistake. It was one of those divine mistakes that play so subtly into nudging one's life path in a new direction. Although the book sat on my shelf unread for a year, there came a time when love seemed far away in my life, and the words *A Return to Love* caught my eye. I read the book cover to cover in a day and wanted more. The *more* I was seeking I found in *A Course in Miracles*.

As a student and teacher of the Bible in a fundamental, evangelical church, I found the Course felt like reading a letter from an old friend. I experienced much of the joy and confusion that I did when I first started reading the Bible and started seeking out the truths hidden there. Many questions that had gone unanswered for years started to vanish as I read the Course, though they were quickly replaced by many new questions. An important difference was the way the Course teaches its students to deal with unanswered questions: the way of peace, a nonthreatening approach to letting God be the teacher.

The Course asks us to set aside all of our beliefs for a few moments to allow God to teach us something for the day. Such a simple shift in my own thinking allowed me to enter into a whole new experience of learning. After all, if I didn't like what I was reading or practicing for those few moments, I could go back to believing exactly the way I did before. There was no fear that if I read something disagreeable, I would be forever cut off from God. The Course gave me the grace and freedom to set aside its teaching; it was a wonderful freedom that no other teaching had offered.

Now that I was free from my past and the pull of my ego, the Workbook lessons took on a life of their own. I found myself spending as much as two to three hours daily integrating the lessons into my life, and the most amazing transformation took place. Far from being frustrated by taking so much time to work on lessons and read the Text, I discovered that time was irrelevant to getting certain daily tasks done. Activities that used to take several hours were completed in just a few minutes. Going to the grocery store and housecleaning were accomplished effortlessly, in record time. And activities related to my ministry were seen with such clarity that it became a joy to see God work them out with such grace and peace.

The most striking example of this has been my experience with the Course teaching of forgiveness. My years of church service have been marred by seeing members attack each other; splits and disputes seem common to every ministry. Even with a primary message of love from the Gospels, church members have suffered many hurts from the inability to forgive.

I, too, had suffered all my life with unforgiveness and bitterness against those who had opposed my ministry or gossiped behind my back. As I read the Text and worked through the first fifty Workbook lessons, I became convinced that forgiveness was the only escape from this insanity. So I started to experiment with forgiveness with a person who had caused a division in my current ministry.

The Course teaches us that when we forgive our brothers, we are also forgiving ourselves. If I see my brother with no sin, I will see myself that way too. It was a subtle shift in thinking for me, but it is such shifts in thinking that the Course identifies as "miracles." And what a miracle there was in store for me: A few months after the person I was inwardly forgiving had left the church, he suddenly appeared in the parking lot after one of the services. We'd had no contact since his departure. As I walked toward him I was filled with love and joy for him; all of the feelings of attack and hate were gone and I saw him in his innocence. Without a word I walked up and embraced him. We just stood there holding each other; it was a wonderful healing.

The only difficulty I've had with the Course was in trying to harmonize it with the Bible, as the Course uses many biblical terms in startlingly different ways from Christian orthodoxy. For me it has become much easier to see the two teachings as companions that stand on their own merits. I believe both have been given to us by God, and they both give us His light. There is no better summary of what I've learned from the Course than Workbook lesson #50: "I am sustained by the Love of God."

Meditating at Twentysomething

At 27, Seattle resident Jennifer Wallenfels is younger than most Course students. A graduate of Evergreen State College specializing in arts and music, Wallenfels was working as a secretary when she wrote the following statement. Noting that she might not have become a Course student were it not for Marianne Williamson's A Return to Love, *Wallenfels now feels that Williamson's work addresses a "beginner's level" and that she has since moved on to Ken Wapnick's "graduate studies."*

ACIM teaches me that inner peace is my only goal. What a relief! I've spent so much of my life struggling to be something. Now I know I don't need to struggle to create some wonderful person — I only need to uncover it. That's incredibly difficult, but it seems better than struggling against the world. Even when I'm ignoring what ACIM says, and trying all my old ego tricks, I still know in the back of my mind that there's another way to look at the world. It's good to know that the truth will always be there for me when I'm ready to come to it. Before finding the Course I didn't have a sense of having something to come back to. It's an anchor for me in that way.

The last time I dropped off my study, I got really angry! I don't know how many times I did that workbook lesson "My thoughts do not mean anything.[3]" At one point I revisited that lesson and suddenly thought, *What do you mean, my thoughts do not mean anything?! They damn well mean something!* They mean my continued imprisonment, I know. I'm not sure why that had never really impacted me until that moment.

It constantly amazes me how I can read, realize, and understand these concepts, but so easily slip back into my old ways of thinking minutes or even seconds later. I have to reread and re-remind myself constantly of these things, even though I know how absolutely true they are.

One issue that I'm dealing with right now is that I've realized I'd rather read *about* the Course than read the Course itself. Similarly I'd rather read about the Course than meditate. The reason is obvious: I'm afraid of what I will find if I look inside.

I have always been one to resist discipline, then feel guilty about it. But if I don't discipline myself to meditate I never will, and part of me says *You're wasting time, you're delaying your peace.* Another part says *Accept where you're at, don't push, and don't feel guilty.* Both are true, I guess.

My moments of greatest peace have always sneaked up on me, so to speak. I suppose that's when my ego doesn't have its defenses up, but they seem to come out in full force when I sit down to meditate. So sometimes I wonder if it matters anyway. At any rate I'm trying to learn to accept where I'm at, moment to moment, regardless of how "spiritual" that is.

Forgiving Hitler

Michael Berkes, Ph.D., speaks over a dozen languages and has consulted on several translations of the Course. He is also pursuing a Hungarian translation. Trained as a merchant banker in London, in recent years he has worked as a consultant to international financial institutions. Berkes currently lives in northern California.

I was born in the British Protectorate of Palestine in the late twenties to two pioneers who met and married there. My parents were broke and disillusioned when we moved back to their native Transylvania in 1936. My first memory upon arrival is the sacking of a synagogue, watching the holy scrolls dragged out and trampled by Fascist hoodlums, who then put the torch to it all and a few Jewish businesses for good measure.

Having come from a kibbutz, I couldn't fathom why my schoolmates would not resist the beatings that we got while going to and from school. They would cover their heads, more to prevent their hats from being knocked off (a sin to the orthodox) than to ward off the blows. I hated everything about my new home, and I was especially angry at my father for abandoning my native land for this cold and inimical hellhole.

When the Nazi persecution began in earnest, my parents found a kindly priest who was willing to give us papers certifying that we were "cradle-born Catholics," providing that we took instruction and asked to be converted. This added a layer of guilt and confusion to my troubled soul while I lived through slave labor and the Allied bombings. After the war I found out what had happened to almost all of my extended family beyond my parents and myself: they were slaughtered in the death camps. My beloved grandmother, who was of German descent, was shot by an SS officer because she could not walk fast enough toward the cattle cars headed for the camps.

When we were liberated and learned all this, I found that I was unable to deal with the pain, unable to grieve, and unwilling to return to Israel. All I could do was swear that the curse of being a Jew would not be passed on to my children. For the next thirty years I lived the lie of being a Gentile. I tried to repay the kind priest and lessen my guilt by becoming a practicing Catholic, but that only served to increase my inner confusion and deep guilt.

When I came across the Course and learned that "forgiveness is the key to happiness," I balked, argued, and resisted for a long time. How could I forgive the murder of my grandmother and many other relatives by the lowlife who seemed to have crawled out of the viscera of abomination? Even closer to home, how could I forgive my father for tearing me out of my free and happy surroundings in the kibbutz, and subjecting me to vicious racism? Finally, how could I forgive myself for turning my back on my native land and the religion of my forefathers, pretending for thirty years to be something I was not?

It took me untold hours of working with the Course to admit a slight chance of forgiving myself. I had to repeat the struggle to forgive my father. Oddly it was easier to look upon the perpetrators of the Holocaust once I had worked through forgiveness of myself, my parents, relatives, and friends. I started by forgiving the "little Nazis" and then the bigger ones, until I finally got all the way to Hitler. I remember a propaganda film showing him at his Eagle's Nest in Bavaria, playing with the two German shepherd dogs he obviously loved very much. This led me to the thought that he must have been terribly abused as a child to have become an adult who could only trust dogs with his love. Then I thought of the Course, asking me to see the face of Christ in front of the one I need to forgive, in order to overcome my grievances. I did that, and it worked.

I cannot say that forgiveness on that scale is finished and done with for me. I have to return to basics every time I find myself blaming an evil "them" for the problems of the world. But with the realization that I have "unforgiven" again, the work of "reforgiving" becomes easier and quicker.

There is a prayer in the Course that I think of often:

I give you to the Holy Spirit as part of myself.
I know that you will be released, unless I want to use you
    to imprison myself.
In the name of my freedom I choose your release, because
    I recognize that we will be released together.[4]

I say to myself that we can be released *only* together. Whenever I am fixated on something that someone did to me, or have trouble letting go of anything, I make use of that invocation, seeing the other person being released along with myself. This has worked miracles for me.

Extremes of Experience

Stephen Horrillo, 34, of Fort Lauderdale, Florida, was in a severe motorcycle accident at age sixteen. During emergency treatment he clinically died and was revived three times; thereafter he became addicted to painkillers and wore a leg cast for five years. Dropping out of premed after two years partly because of drug addiction, Horrillo got into the business of selling solar water heaters; his boss paid him commissions in cocaine. When he was 29, Horrillo's grandfather shot and killed his father. With his father dead, his grandfather in jail and his mother distraught, Horrillo "got so deep into drugs I had two doctors and still needed to forge prescriptions to maintain my habit." Arrested twice for prescription forgery,

Horillo was advised by a probation officer to start a Twelve Step recovery program. When he began to desire "something beyond AA," he soon found the Course through the Unity Church. Horrillo had been a student for three years at the time of this writing.

In recovery from addiction, I was warned to avoid people, places, and things that were a threat to my sobriety. So I promptly got rid of my drug-addict friends, stayed out of bars, and did my best not to get hungry, angry, tired, or lonely — or "HALT" as they call it in AA.

After a few years of sobriety I felt less threatened by going out to clubs or by people who drank, but then my poison became negative people, especially "victim type" women. I was uncontrollably attracted to them, and there were an abundance of them in Twelve Step meetings. My title then became "rescuer," and I still have hefty credit-card balances left over from that stage. For a while I needed to practice avoidance, the way I had done with bars and people who drink.

Mainly due to the Course, dysfunctional women are now neither a threat nor an attraction to me. Through the Course I was able to look beyond all the dramas in my life and begin to see the world from a place of neutrality. I learned how to live from my center, not my outer layers of personality, and it seems that those living from their center are attracted to me as well. It's like the idea that "the Christ in me beholds the Christ in you." If I'm approached by some beautiful, vulnerable woman with tears in her eyes asking for my help, I'm able to ask the Holy Spirit how to help rather than helping myself to her.

But I get tested on this from time to time, so I know I'm not fully healed. I am still at the point where I need to identify some people as unhealthy, but I know that even the need for that sort of assessment will eventually fade away.

I'm coming to the acceptance that the nightmare is finally over; I have really been enjoying my life for the past two years. I can even look back on the past and see it differently. And I'm to the point where I feel I can afford to give back what has been given to me, so I'm exploring what I can do to be of service.

Saved by the SOBs

Carol Howe is a full-time Course instructor in Florida whose teaching and learning experience began in 1977. She recalls Judy Skutch telling her that Bill Thetford "needed to be socialized" and charged her with that duty. Indeed, when Howe lived in Denver Thetford would come to visit with her family, helping with carpooling and other daily activities of family life that he had never known. Still, Howe says that Thetford would sit in on her Course workshops anonymously, preferring not to reveal his history and identity to strangers. Howe also taught with Jerry Jampolsky and managed his speaking schedule before his partnership with Diane Cirincione. In the following statement Howe answers the question "How does the Course work?"

I think the Course works exactly like it professes to work, which is that it brings into conscious awareness the literal feeling of madness that drives us all. It brings fear and terror to the surface so that you can become aware of the consequences of the choices you've made so far, and learn to make different choices. My direct experience is that the Course brings up things that are not so much unconscious as invisible, because the spotlight of attention has not been on them: fear, guilt, and the unloving forces that tend to drive our lives.

What the Course has to say about the unreality of the world is difficult to grasp, but that idea is where you eventually come to, not where you start. You start with people being in pain, driven by their feelings of unworthiness. The Course leads you by the hand through that sort of self-discovery, and it does this primarily through relationships.

The idea is that the SOBs out there will save you, because you learn to notice what comes up for you in their presence. Instead of running away, you realize that difficult people are *triggering*, not *causing*, your own feelings of guilt, fear, and unforgiveness. Then you have a chance to deal with what has come up in a responsible way.

The Course puts comforting arms around you while it says,

"Now we're going to look at the ways you've lived and what you've valued in order to point out that it hasn't really served you." It's both kindly and intense in that way, and it's true that things can get worse at first rather than better. If you say "I want to be free" and really mean it, then all the negative ideas and feelings that you're still attached to will come up right in your face — but for your release, not for punishment. *A Course in Miracles* is a tremendously powerful tool, and I have seen it deliver exactly what it says it will deliver when you do what it says to do.

10
The Presence of the Course

I n *The Gnostic Gospels* Princeton University theologian Elaine
Pagels lists some of the beliefs of Christianity that are widely
accepted yet nonetheless "astonishing" on their face:

> The creed requires, for example, that Christians confess
> that God is perfectly good, and still, he created a world that
> includes pain, injustice, and death; that Jesus of Nazareth
> was born of a virgin mother; and that, after being executed
> by order of the Roman procurator, Pontius Pilate, he arose
> from his grave "on the third day."[1]

The beliefs of the early Gnostics, while more in line with central
elements of the "perennial philosophy," probably had no more
face validity than those beliefs we now regard as Christian orthodoxy. A central assumption of Pagels' book is that what came
to be accepted as religious truth by most of the Western world
had less to do with inherent validity than with politics and
power struggles. As she concludes, "It is the winners who write
history — their way."[2]

Historical controversies aside, it is worth questioning why
anyone ever adopts the astonishing beliefs that can be found in
any religion — from the Western notion that the sacrificial

death of a divine figure somehow pays for all the evil deeds of humankind, to the Eastern notion that the everyday world we see, hear, touch, taste, and feel is fundamentally illusory. In a world where most of the material and medical advancements of civilization are owed to science, not religion, why do so many people turn to belief systems that are plainly *irrational* in the sense that they transcend the bounds of what can be logically deduced or scientifically proven? In short, why do people choose to believe any of these crazy mystical ideas?

One answer of course is that people raised in strong religious traditions simply never learn to question the creed that shapes their whole view of reality. But an answer that is more revealing of our culture's recent spiritual renaissance — and that certainly has more to do with the growing popularity of *A Course in Miracles* — stems from the inadequacy of rational materialism as a way of explaining our existence and providing personal guidance.

For however much science ultimately promises to dispel every last shred of mystery about nature and our lives on this earth, the fact remains that our lives are steeped in mystery at every moment. We do not know exactly what or who we are, why we feel what we feel from moment to moment, or why we behave in the ways we do. (Even when we learn that a specific gene may "determine" our proclivity to a particular disease or character trait, the questions remain: *How?* and *Why?*) In a sense everyone is a mystic who has ever been mystified — and when it comes to answering the "big questions" of life, I suspect that most people are mystified throughout their lives.

A spiritual *awakening* can be seen as the recognition and acceptance of the mystery we live within. At their best, spiritual *beliefs* provide a meaningful roadmap through life's mystery. Finally, an authentic spiritual *discipline* is the means by which one learns to activate the potentials latent within the mystery of human consciousness. There are no statistically valid measures by which to plumb the potentials of mind, heart, and spirit, and no laboratory-approved safety regimens by which to utilize them. Everyone who ventures upon a spiritual path does so at personal risk. And while there are universal elements to all spiritual journeying, each individual's path is uniquely personal.

This chapter presents some concluding commentary on the reportage about *A Course in Miracles* presented so far in this book, and about spiritual exploration in general. To further define my point of view and bias, I will share a brief travelogue of my own spiritual path — which usually looks to me like a faintly marked trail between the devil and the deep blue sea.

A Change of Course

My family was never very religious, and we stopped going to church regularly when I was about twelve. That was fine with me, as Sunday school hadn't held any appeal to me for a while. Ever since I had memorized John 3:16 in order to earn a wall plaque with the verse written on it in gilt lettering, I'd had the feeling that there was something amiss with churchgoing religion. I had first thought that Sunday school was the place one could ask the big questions of existence that weren't handled in regular school. But I soon learned that questions like *Where does the universe begin?* and *If God loves us and is in charge of everything, why does He let people get sick and die?* were answered either with befuddlement or with stern reminders to read more of the Bible until the urge to ask those big questions went away. By adolescence I had become largely agnostic, mostly in reaction to the fundamentalist and commercialized strains of Christianity — including the "Praise The Lord" ministry of Jim and Tammy Bakker — that pervaded my hometown of Charlotte, North Carolina.

When I moved to California in my early twenties, I had set my sights on a career in investigative journalism with a special interest in environmental politics. But I didn't last long in the field, as I became increasingly troubled by my chosen profession's tunnel-vision grasp of reality. While my editors and mentors encouraged me to look for people's baser motives, they were not at all interested in the investigation of deeper motivations. For them it was sufficient to document the greed of a crooked politician; I wanted to know what made him greedy.

Also it took only a few years in investigative journalism to see that an entire career could be spent attempting to dislodge a few corrupt politicians from power, which looked like a zero-sum game to me. I wanted to have a distinctly positive effect on the world, not just eliminate a few of its negatives. Slowed by these professional doubts and distracted by personal anxieties, I backed off from journalism and simply tried to make a living for the next ten years working as a self-employed typographer, always intending to use any extra time to continue my writing career.

But I proved to be a break-even businessman at best, and by my early thirties I still didn't know what I wanted to write about. I was beginning to worry that I would never put together a fruitful life when I fell seriously ill with a mysterious, debilitating malady that was still a few years away from being medically identified as "chronic fatigue syndrome" (CFS).

That was when my rational grasp of the world began to suffer the slings and arrows of a prolonged "altered state" experience — lasting seven years from the sudden onset of CFS to the point at which I could consider myself completely recovered. My spiritual conversion came at the cost of great suffering and a hard-fought resistance every step of the way. Yet in retrospect I see that conversion as an *uncovering* of the spirituality that was always within me, rather than the wholesale adoption of a previously alien perspective.

Although my health crisis did not involve any kind of substance abuse, I look back on my experience with CFS as one of recovery from psychological addiction to guilt, cynicism, fearfulness, and suspicion — all of which I had long believed to be the most realistic, practical attitudes for dealing with a cruel world. The idea that one could see the world or govern one's own consciousness in any other way was completely foreign to me until I encountered *A Course in Miracles*. Like many other

Course students, I have my own story of how an odd turn of events paved the way to that encounter.

In the first few months of my illness I was angry with my body's failure to perform as expected anymore, and I pursued purely medical solutions to a literally dizzying array of symptoms — frequent migraine headaches, traveling muscle pains, severe and continuous gastrointestinal distress, mental confusion, and overwhelming fatigue. But as increasingly vivid, poignant, and unforgettable dreams surfaced in my prolonged sleeping sessions, I slowly began to entertain psychological (and even deeper) roots to my condition, and I began reading widely in the fields of psychology and consciousness. For the first and last time in my life I also entered psychotherapy, which consisted mainly of spilling out long-withheld emotional troubles to a very caring and attentive counselor.

Shortly after beginning therapy I came across a mention of *A Course in Miracles* in a book called *Higher Creativity* (J. P. Tarcher) by Willis Harman, in which the healing power of affirmations was discussed. Increasingly willing to try anything that might restore my health, I had tried meditating with a few affirmations, but always ended up feeling silly for trying to change the way I thought or felt — much less my physical condition — simply by repeating positive ideas to myself.

However, a point that Harman made suddenly struck home for me: that an habitually unhealthy state of mind could be perpetuated by the semiconscious repetition of *negative* ideas to oneself. When I closely reviewed my habitual state of mind in the few years prior to the onset of CFS (looking to my personal journals as a "smoking gun"), the prominent role of such negative self-brainwashing was undeniable. I was profoundly shaken by the realization. Harman described the Course as a thorough "mind-training" in an opposite way of thinking, and I was intrigued.

I was also suspicious because the Course cost $40 in hardcover (for three separate volumes). Not knowing its length or density, that sounded like a rip-off to me. On the next trip to my medical doctor I resolved to stop at the metaphysical bookshop across the street and peruse the Course long enough to form an opinion about it. (At that point, forming a quick and decisive opinion about things was still one of my major coping strategies.)

When I got to the bookstore, the first thing I saw was two entire shelves of the three-in-one paperback edition of *A Course in Miracles* priced at $25. Startled, I asked the store owner how long he had carried the books. "I just shelved them," he replied. "The paperback was released recently and it came in this morning." For the first of countless times in my experience as a Course student, a soft *click* sounded in my head and I bought my first paperback copy.

Considering my immediate and visceral distaste for its Christian language, it is amazing how rapidly and intensively I undertook the Course Workbook and the daily reading of its Text. I was reading several other books at the time, and for a short while the Course seemed unremarkable in comparison, apart from its peculiar syntax.

But within weeks my dreams began to feature the blue book with regularity, and the daily Workbook lessons suddenly shifted from a curious chore to a compelling necessity. Somehow the crushing oppression of my illness and apparently failed life was lifting, at least inwardly. Something new was happening in my consciousness, and I wasn't sure what it was. At times this uncertainty provoked more than a little anxiety.

It was after one episode of such anxiety that I decided to tell my therapist of my new undertaking; I had otherwise kept the Course a secret from friends and helpers. I was also beginning to wonder where my course of therapy was heading, as I had vented most of my intimate anxieties over a couple of months and my counselor seemed to offer little more than patient listening and occasional words of kind encouragement. After I expressed my misgiving about the passivity of therapy and confessed my new esoteric adventure — wondering if my therapist might intervene or at least issue a warning about getting involved in strange religions — there were two surprises in store for me.

First, my counselor shared his observation that my illness had apparently forced me to confront myself to a greater degree than most of his clients who had been seeing him for much longer. "I spend most of my time trying to get people to face the kind of things you've come here and told me about," he said. Then he added, "If you can handle the Course, you probably don't need me anyway." *Click.* Indeed, I soon left therapy with my counselor's blessings.

While I would not recommend *A Course in Miracles* as a cure for any specific disease, I do credit my study of the Course as the central factor in my complete recovery from CFS. I used a wide variety of medical and psychological approaches, all of which played their part in resolving a diabolically creative disorder that, in its severest phase, could aptly be described as everything going wrong at once. But the Course helped me make sense of the process of healing, in ways too numerous and complex to describe here. The Course also strengthened my sense of intuition about which avenues of healing to pursue at different times.

CFS eventually cost me my livelihood, my financial resources, my closest relationships, and what I had formerly regarded as my "self-esteem." But in the process of a long and difficult recovery guided by the decidedly *irrational* influence of the Course, I gained a full-time profession in writing, a close and loving marriage, better physical health than I had known before the onset of CFS, and finally, a powerful sense of inner calling to replace my old schemes of personal success.

In retrospect I wouldn't have my spiritual path follow any other route. But there were countless times when I seemed stuck in dead ends or unable to negotiate the next perilous hairpin turn. I honestly do not know what got me through it all except a growing sense of strength from a mysterious source that is somehow both within me and from beyond me — a source of strength that I can only call spiritual.

"To be fatigued is to be dis-spirited," suggests the Course, "but to be inspired is to be in the spirit. To be egocentric is to be dis-spirited, but to be Self-centered in the right sense is to be inspired or in spirit. The truly inspired are enlightened and cannot abide in darkness."[3]

Of Cults and Nuts

I initially completed the Text and Workbook of the Course relatively rapidly, within eighteen months. Except for a six-week discussion group I attended early in my study, my first experience with the Course was solitary. Thus I was a little surprised later on to learn the extent of the social phenomenon that ACIM has spawned. I am still of the opinion that the Course is primarily a self-study curriculum, and I tend to agree with fellow student Richard Smoley that the Course's inherent weaknesses can be inadvertently magnified by groups who devote themselves to it.

That said, the problems that show up in Course groups are essentially no different from the problems that show up in other religious or tightly knit social organizations. Insular or mushy thinking, socially reinforced self-deception, presumptions of superiority, and cultish obeisance to questionable leaders are certainly not unique to Course groups; all these elements can be found in political parties, the military, government bureaucracies, and successful corporations.

By and large the Course community has avoided the development of cultish cliques; in the eyes of many Course veterans, the Endeavor Academy in Wisconsin is the major exception to the rule. Yet even among ex-residents who have made their serious concerns about Endeavor public knowledge, one finds a genuine respect for the passion of that unique community and its controversial leader, the Master Teacher.

From my own study of alternative religious groups over the years, I find that Americans in general — and the mainstream press in particular — have little understanding of the power and appeal of religious devotion, especially when it is focused on alternative paths or teachers. We tend to regard such devotion outside the religious mainstream as a bizarre, invariably destructive aberration in a culture that's supposed to be devoted to individual freedom above all. But in a society where many individuals find themselves morally adrift in their unhappy freedom, we are likely to see a further proliferation of so-called cults that offer their members a deeply sought social identity, reliable rules of conduct, and an up-close focus for their spiritual passion.

What may help us to better integrate such pockets of religious devotion into society is to view them a bit less fearfully than we have so far. The press is prone to speak of cults as if they invariably represent a cancer within the social organism. I would suggest that they are more helpfully seen as a bad flu — that is, something we'd like to avoid that can have potentially debilitating or even fatal consequences, but that also may be periodically inevitable. Two of the techniques of holistic health may be usefully applied to this sort of flu: if we look more deeply into its root causes and don't over-medicate the symptoms, it may actually run its course more quickly, with a greater gain in our social immunity after it passes.

Of course a great deal depends upon how cults are defined; sometimes any phenomenon that's new or esoteric can have the "cult" tag hung upon it. Several times over my years of researching the Course I've encountered people who have said, "Oh, the Course in Miracles — isn't that a cult thing?" No doubt such free-floating impressions are due in part to ill-informed critiques of ACIM that have found their way into print and public notice. On the other hand it's likely that some of the Course's bad rep could be sourced to people's encounters with over-enthusiastic students slinging the Miracles lingo or an immature teacher glibly advertising ACIM as the latest spiritual snake-oil remedy. After surveying the field for a decade, however, it's my conclusion that the general population of Course students and instructors is no nuttier than humanity in general — and a significant proportion of Course followers have apparently achieved a remarkable reformation of their lives and characters.

Enlightenment Versus Delusion

Exactly how *A Course in Miracles* achieves this transformative effect is beyond the investigative scope of this book, and in fact no one seems to have a comprehensive explanation. Even some of the most veteran students can only say, "It just works for me." I can't add much to that. I do know that I have experienced the Course as a remarkable discipline of confronting my worst internal enemies — what the preface to the Course calls "blocks to the awareness of love's presence"[4] — and learning how to let them be replaced by less judgmental, more caring, and more truly objective attitudes. The Course is difficult only to the extent that self-confrontation is difficult. The resistance that many students experience along the way attests to the Course's consistency in facilitating a discipline of self-examination and surrender.

In terms of spiritual growth, exactly what one surrenders to is the crux of the matter. Anyone who has experienced a breakdown of their habitual personality and fundamental frame of reference is vulnerable to "conversion" to new spiritual or psychological orientations that may be much healthier — or tragically more destructive — than their old egocentrism. In their earliest stages the processes of enlightenment and delusion can be nearly indistinguishable. Both involve becoming "as a child" while the mind and heart open to substantially new feelings, perceptions, and world-defining concepts.

After this initial opening, however, maturing spiritual aspirants will become *more* sensible, if less rigid and narrow-minded. Their perceptions are less likely to be skewed by unresolved emotional disturbances, and they have a greater range of intuitive resources to draw upon. Conversely, a sure sign of progressive delusion among spiritual aspirants is an increasing illogic and vagueness — particularly a tendency to excuse in-

consistencies of belief and behavior with references to one's supposedly superior advancement of consciousness. The general attitude goes like this: "If you were as enlightened as I, everything
I do would make sense to you."

A lot of counterfeit enlightenment has been passed off as authentic wisdom in this way, either by alleged spiritual masters
or their devotees. (For instance, if we were all as enlightened as
the late Bhagwan Rajneesh, wouldn't it have been perfectly clear
to everyone why he needed ninety-one Rolls-Royces?) Little
if any such weirdness would get by the Course's exacting re-
quirements for its graduates, or "teachers of God"; in its Manual
for Teachers, ACIM lists their identifying characteristics as
trust, honesty, tolerance, gentleness, joy, defenselessness, generosity, patience, faithfulness, and open-mindedness. Cumula-
tively taken, these qualities don't leave much room for greed,
hubris, or obfuscation.

The advanced spiritual seeker will be able to explain himself
or herself in simple, direct terms and admit to any unresolved
contradictions in belief and behavior, embodying a sincere hu-
mility in place of presumed superiority. Gandhi, for instance,
once observed that he had faced three great enemies in his
struggle to bring about change. The first was the British government, on which he could claim some significant effect; the second was the Indian people, whom he found considerably more
intractable; and the third great opponent — the one whom he
despaired of ever changing for the better — he identified as
himself.

Also, it has long been observed that great spiritual teachers
can both enjoy and learn from the company of the "simplest" or
most untrained people they encounter. They do not need to talk
down to anyone or assert their own advancement. In Zen Buddhism the ultimate goal of meditation is to achieve the unfet-
tered, nonjudgmental simplicity of "beginner's mind." Similarly
A Course in Miracles asserts that "complexity is of the ego, and
is nothing more than the ego's attempt to obscure the obvious."[5]

Four Suggestions for Spiritual Pathfinding

The most salient question for new spiritual seekers, as so many modern Westerners are now becoming, is what safeguards they can employ to avoid veering off on paths of delusion, or at least avoid remaining on them past the point of their limited educational value (for sometimes it is undeniably valuable to experience disillusionment). Based on my experience as a researcher of many alternative spiritual viewpoints, I have four general guidelines to suggest. My explanation of each will use the Course for illustration.

1. *Let your path "come to you."* Philosopher Jacob Needleman once suggested that "an authentic spiritual path makes itself known, but does not attempt to persuade."[6] A great advantage of the modern spiritual supermarket is that a worldwide variety of spiritual paths and perspectives is now available to most people at their nearest bookstore or on the worldwide electronic network accessible by home computer. No longer does anyone have to accept the religious background of their family or native culture as the only proper spiritual path, particularly in the West. Thus it seems wise to survey as many paths as possible when attempting to find an appropriate discipline for self-transformation. After time and careful consideration the "intuitive fit" of a particular discipline should become obvious.

Among its students *A Course in Miracles* is legendary for "finding" them in unexpected ways, and for offering a strong intuitive appeal even when it seems bizarre or frightening. On the other hand untold numbers of people find no appeal in it whatsoever, and it does not purport to be the best or only true path to spiritual growth. Although some scattered teachers may proselytize it, neither the original publisher nor the major Course teaching academies have been evangelical.

2. *Make sure that your chosen path offers challenge without imprisonment.* A disadvantage of the modern spiritual supermarket is that it offers people the opportunity to become spiritual dilettantes, identifying themselves with one or more transforma-

tive disciplines without ever actually undertaking any of them. Whether one chooses to focus on yoga, Zen, the Course, or Christianity, it's important to actually *follow* the discipline(s) the path offers, and endure the inherent discomfort (and lifelong challenge) that a real spiritual discipline entails.

However, an important sign of an authentic path is that it will implicitly give you "permission" to quit, with no strings attached, whenever it no longer seems appropriate or productive. The Course is remarkable for its capacity to keep serious students engaged in its discipline even when it proves quite difficult — and to bring students back even after they have decided it was just too hard to continue. That it does this without recourse to external authority or social enforcement attests to a potent mystical quality embedded within the Course discipline.

But if one does decide to leave the training behind at any stage, the Course itself exacts no penalties nor demands excommunication; after all, it's just a book. (By the same token, Course students who feel that a study group or teacher *is* using the teaching to create a sense of enforcement or entrapment should question the validity of the situation.)

3. *Look for results, not romance, from your chosen path.* A sign of spiritual dilettantism is that it will produce only superficial changes of style in people's character and behavior. This is a frequent failing of various New Age fancies, in which people find it easier — and far more romantic — to become a channel for the wisdom of the distant Pleiadians than to actually become wiser on their own.

Although one should grant oneself a "grace period" with a new spiritual discipline — during which personal problems may seem to get worse rather than better — after five years a dedicated commitment to a spiritual path should produce definite, observable improvements in one's character and consciousness. Such improvements are not to be confused with circumstantial or material benefits, which can neither be ruled out nor expected to accompany inner changes.

Questions one can use to determine whether a spiritual path is really "paying off" include:

Have I become more at peace within myself and in my relationships since undertaking this discipline?

Do I blame less and have more compassion about my own difficulties and those of others?

Do I experience more joy, empathy, and revelatory insight?

Is my social and political conscience more informed and effective, regardless of how my forms of activism may have changed?

And finally: *Do I sometimes tap transcendent states of consciousness through the natural means of my own trained and focused awareness?*

As this book has shown, many Course students will attest to the efficacy of their chosen discipline in bringing them very positive answers to these questions.

4. *With experience, expect your spiritual practice to become "ordinary."* The Dalai Lama of Tibetan Buddhism, one of the world's most respected spiritual and political leaders, often refers to himself as merely "an ordinary monk." This should not be taken as a sign of false modesty, but in fact a sign of advanced spiritual achievement, for it signifies a seeker who has learned to shed the temptations of what Tibetan teacher Chogyam Trungpa identified as "spiritual materialism."

There is no denying that *A Course in Miracles* can seem quite exotic to beginning students, and the first year or two of its study may feel like a prolonged "altered state" experience that seems to set the student off from other people and everyday reality. If study is sustained for a longer period, however, the Course points its students toward the ordinariness of spiritual mastery by its lack of emphasis on ritual and other religious trappings — a rare orientation among the world's major religions — and by emphasizing the spiritual equality of everyone, including Christ, within the "Sonship" of God.

That is not to say that veteran Course students never entertain inflated ideas of themselves and their path. But if one adheres faithfully to the Course discipline, it has a way of bringing one's hypocrisy and inflation up for conscious review on a regular basis. Over time, learning to "catch" one's own arrogance before it is translated into overbearing behavior becomes second nature — as do constructive and compassionate ways of thinking and behaving.

Sometimes I have been greatly startled to recall a typical moment of my "old" consciousness before I undertook the Course, and to notice the contrast between my self-awareness then and now. While I have a ways to go to be entirely free of anger, cynicism, and selfishness, the degree to which I have been liberated from such self-defensive attitudes is remarkable. I believe it is a far greater degree of growth than I would have achieved through normal maturation without benefit of the Course. And yet my "new" consciousness does not strike me as an exalted state or a great personal achievement. Indeed, it seems like a normal way of life until I happen to recall how ordinary — but comparatively miserable — my pre-Course personality and beliefs felt to me.

The Uniqueness of the Course

In his book *Love Does Not Condemn*, Ken Wapnick summarizes the major philosophical strains running through the massive mystical document he helped edit into its final form:

> Thus, we can see . . . how the Course is an amalgam of different approaches, yet a successful integration of them: It is *Neoplatonic* in terms of describing the downward progression (or projection) from the One; *Gnostic* in its clarity on the world not coming from the Divine at all, exposing the ego's trickery in back of it; and *Christian*, not only in its language, but through its recognizing a benevolent presence

of God experienced in the world — the memory of His love (the Holy Spirit) in the split mind — not to mention the central place accorded to Jesus.[7]

In a less scholarly vein I would add that the Course is decidedly *contemporary* in its exacting analysis of ego psychology, and uniquely *American* in its populist accessibility as a do-it-yourself, take-it-or-leave-it spiritual curriculum. While major elements of the Course can be recognized in other spiritual perspectives and in modern psychology as well, the diverse yet well-integrated wholeness of the Course has not been preceded nor replicated. Nor is its "forward momentum" matched by any other spiritual discipline or psychological perspective I have encountered.

What I mean by this is that the Course gives the serious student a dramatic sense of accelerated growth that is not limited to the particular insights and information of the teaching itself. For instance, most of my research into other psychologies and spiritual paths — constituting the work that I refer to as "the journalism of consciousness" — came after my initial study of *A Course in Miracles* and was in fact enabled by the sense of inspired curiosity that the Course awoke in me. While I still often consult the Course as a kind of spiritual touchstone, in no way do I feel constrained to limit my investigations to the concepts or point of view it sets forth. In this way, too, I find that the Course promulgates a democratic open-mindedness that can fairly be called both modern and American.

Finally, perhaps the one quality of the Course I find most remarkable is its uncanny provision of a "presence" that I can only describe as wise companionship. Even though it is just a book, I often find myself regarding my copy of the Course as almost a living thing that might at any moment speak to me — no doubt with the same calm authority that its Voice once silently requested of Helen Schucman, "Please take notes."

Considering how aggravating the Course can be at times — I now use my second copy because I damaged the first one by throwing it against the wall so many times — this sense of companionship is all the more uncanny. Yet it is merely the fulfillment of a promise that *A Course in Miracles* explicitly extends at the close of its Workbook of daily lessons.

> This course is a beginning, not an end. Your Friend goes with you. You are not alone. No one who calls on Him can call in vain. Whatever troubles you, be certain that He has the answer, and will gladly give it to you, if you simply turn to Him and ask it of Him. He will not withhold all answers that you need for anything that seems to trouble you. He knows the way to solve all problems, and resolve all doubts. His certainty is yours. You need but ask it of Him, and it will be given you. . . .
>
> You do not walk alone. God's angels hover near and all about. His Love surrounds you, and of this be sure; that I will never leave you comfortless.[8]

Appendix

Selected Resources

A Course in Miracles
The hardcover Viking edition of the complete Course is generally available in US bookstores for $29.95. Viking has also released the following companion media:

The Gifts of God, Helen Schucman's volume of poetry created through the same process of inner dictation as the Course

Supplements to A Course in Miracles, a combined edition of the original *Psychotherapy: Purpose, Process ,and Practice* and *The Song of Prayer: Prayer, Forgiveness, Healing*, also scribed by Helen Schucman from the original Voice

A Course in Miracles: What It Says, an audiotape by Kenneth Wapnick, Ph.D.

Readings from A Course in Miracles, an audiotape by William Thetford

Concordance of A Course in Miracles

Although Viking has not released a paperback version at this writing, some bookstores may still be carrying the $25.00 softcover edition of the Course published by the Foundation for Inner Peace. Scholarship Policy: The Foundation for Inner Peace has always made copies of the Course available free to anyone who writes citing financial hardship and stating that they wish to have a copy for their personal use. This policy will be followed as long as the Foundation continues to have copies on hand.

The Original Course Publisher

FOUNDATION FOR INNER PEACE
    P.O. Box 598
    Mill Valley, CA 94942-0598
    Phone: (415) 388-2060   Fax: (415) 388-9010
    E-mail: info@acim.org
    Web page: http://www.acim.org

Major ACIM Teaching Centers

See Chapter 5 for a profile of the following "teaching organization" of the Foundation for Inner Peace:

FOUNDATION FOR A COURSE IN MIRACLES and
Institute for Teaching Inner Peace Through A Course in Miracles
(Kenneth & Gloria Wapnick)
    1275 Tennanah Lake Road
    Roscoe, NY 12776-5905
    Phone: (607) 498-4116   Fax: (607) 498-5325
    Web page: http://www.facim.org

See Chapter 3 for profiles of the following organizations.

MIRACLE DISTRIBUTION CENTER (Beverly Hutchinson McNeff)
    1141 E. Ash Avenue
    Fullerton, CA 92831
    Phone: (714) 738-8380   Fax: (714) 441-0618
    Orders: (800) 359-ACIM
    E-mail: info@miraclecenter.org
    Web page: http://www.miraclecenter.org

FOUNDATION FOR LIFE ACTION   (Tara Singh)
    P.O. Box 481228
    Los Angeles, CA 90048
    Phone: (213) 933-5591

INTERFAITH FELLOWSHIP   (Rev. Jon Mundy and Rev. Diane Berke)
    P.O. Box 250
    Washingtonville, NY 10992
    Phone: (914) 496-9089
    E-mail: interfaith@interfaithfellowship.org
    Web page: http://www.interfaithfellowship.org

THE CIRCLE OF ATONEMENT   (Robert Perry & Allen Watson)
    P.O. Box 4238
    West Sedona, AZ 86340
    Phone: (520) 282-0790   Fax: (520) 282-0523
    E-mail: alwatson@sedona.net
    Web page: http://www.sedona.net/nen/circleofa

CALIFORNIA MIRACLES CENTER   (Rev. Tony Ponticello)
    2269 Market Street
    San Francisco, CA 94114
    Phone: (415) 621-2556   Fax: (415) 255-9322
    E-mail: miracles@earthlink.net
    Web page: http://www.miracles-course.org

ENDEAVOR ACADEMY   (Ted Poppe, Administrator)
    P.O. Box 206
    Lake Delton, WI 53940
    Phone: (608) 253-6898   Fax: (608) 253-2892
    E-mail: endacademy@baraboo.com
    Web page: http://www.baraboo.com/bus/endeavor/academy.html

HEARTWAYS PRESS   (Paul Ferrini)
(*Miracles Magazine* back issues, books by Paul Ferrini, and workshops)
    P.O. Box 181
    So. Deerfield, MA 01373
    Phone: (413) 665-0555   Fax: (413) 665-4565

Additional ACIM-Related Resources Online

Web pages

"Renaissance America"   (Marianne Williamson)
    http://www.marianne.com

"About A Course in Miracles"   (Mark Lavender)
    http://www.unc.edu/ lavender

Miracle Studies — United Kingdom
    http://www.netlink.co.uk/users/miracles

Miracle Studies — Australia
    http://hsfo.health.latrobe.edu.au/ACIM/Miracle.Studies

"MindBodySpirit" ACIM page — South Africa
    http://www.pix.za/mbs/spirit/acim.htm

Discussion Groups

    Available on major online services including America OnLine,
Compuserve, and Prodigy; check their directories or New Age
and Religion forums. On Internet newsgroups, search for
"talk.religion.course-miracles". To subscribe to a free e-mail
discussion group, send the message "subcribe acim" to:
listserv@artsit.unimelb.edu.au

    Send the message "subscribe acimwkbk" to the same address
to receive free commentaries on ACIM Workbook lessons.

Course-Related Service Organizations

CENTER FOR ATTITUDINAL HEALING (world headquarters)
    33 Buchanan Drive
    Sausalito, CA 94965
    Phone: (415) 331-6161   Fax: (415) 331-4545
    Email: home123@aol.com

JOSEPH PLAN FOUNDATION
    P.O. Box 481228
    Los Angeles, CA 90048
    Phone: (213) 933-5591

NATIONAL EMOTIONAL LITERACY PROJECT FOR PRISONS
(Robin Casarjian)
    Box 194, Back Bay
    Boston, MA 02117

VISIONS FOR PRISONS   (Dan Millstein)
    P.O. Box 1631
    Costa Mesa, CA 92628
    Phone: (714) 556-8000   Fax: (714) 241-1301

Christian Apologetics Organizations

The following groups are critical of the Course and other alternative or New Age spiritual perspectives that diverge from a fundamental Christian viewpoint.

SPIRITUAL COUNTERFEITS PROJECT
    P.O. Box 4308
    Berkeley, CA 94704
    Phone: (510) 540-0300
Quarterly SCP Journal is available by subscription for $25 annually.

ATLANTA CHRISTIAN APOLOGETICS PROJECT   (Donald Dicks)
    P.O. Box 450068
    Atlanta, GA 31145

CHRISTIAN RESEARCH INSTITUTE INTERNATIONAL
    P.O. Box 500
    San Juan Capistrano, CA 92693-0500

Continuing Research

If you have comments or information that might be relevant to future editions of this book, you can write the author directly.

D. Patrick Miller
1678 Shattuck Ave. #319
Berkeley, CA 94709
E-mail: fearlessbook@earthlink.net

Notes

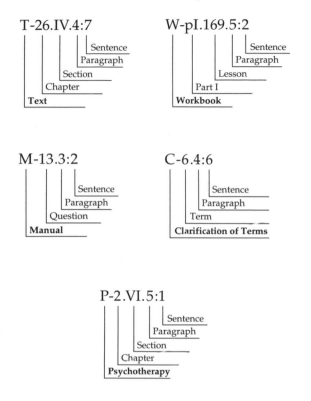

in = Introduction
ep = Epilogue

With the exception of Course Workbook lessons cited simply by number, in the following notes the citation of quotes from *A Course in Miracles* (ACIM) follows the standard system illustrated above. (Ellipses correspond to breaks in the quoted material.) This system keys all quotes to the Second Edition only (including the current Viking edition), in which every sentence is numbered. The First Edition did not feature sentence numbering.

Introduction

1. James Hillman with Barbara Dunn, "A Course in Miracles: Spiritual Path or Omnipotent Fantasy?", *Common Boundary*, Sept/Oct 1989.
2. Quoted by D. Patrick Miller in "A Course in Miracles: A Balanced View," *Free Spirit*, Dec 1990/Jan 1991.
3. Willis Harman in the Foreword to *Journey Without Distance*, by Robert Skutch (Berkeley, CA: Celestial Arts, 1984).
4. Jon Mundy, *Awaken to Your Own Call* (New York: Crossroad Publishing Co., 1994).
5. ACIM: T-6.I.15:2–6 . . . 16:1
6. ACIM: M-2.1:2

Chapter 1

1. Ken Wapnick has said that Helen Schucman made at least "eight and a half" starts on her autobiography. Unless noted otherwise, the quotes in this book come from a 70-page typewritten version provided to me by Judith Skutch Whitson. In that manuscript Schucman refers to Bill Thetford as "John" to protect his identity; I have restored the correct name in all instances.
2. Helen Schucman, an unpublished autobiography.
3. Ibid.
4. Ibid.
5. Ibid.
6. ACIM: T-6.I.9:1–3 . . . 11:5–7
7. Helen Schucman, an unpublished autobiography.
8. Kenneth Wapnick, *Absence from Felicity: The Story of Helen Schucman and Her Scribing of* A Course in Miracles (Roscoe, NY: Foundation for "A Course in Miracles," 1991).
9. Bridget Winter (producer), "The Story of a Course in Miracles," a film documentary (Tiburon, CA: Foundation for Inner Peace, 1987).
10. Wapnick, *Absence from Felicity*.
11. ACIM: T-9.I.7:1
12. Wapnick, *Absence from Felicity*.
13. ACIM: T-31.VIII.12:1–8
14. From a version of Helen Schucman's autobiography appearing in Wapnick's *Absence from Felicity*.
15. Ibid.
16. Ibid.
17. ACIM: T-31.III.1:1–6
18. Helen Schucman quoted in "The Experience of Scribing the Course," *Miracles Magazine*, No. 3, Summer 1992.

19. Robert Skutch, *Journey Without Distance* (Berkeley, CA: Celestial Arts, 1984).
20. Although her full name is now Judith Skutch Whitson, she will be referred to as "Judy Skutch" throughout this book because that is the name by which she is historically associated with the Course.
21. Judith Skutch and Tamara Cohen, *Double Vision* (Berkeley, CA: Celestial Arts, 1985).
22. Ibid.
23. Ibid.
24. Ibid.

Chapter 2

1. Arthur Hastings, *With the Tongues of Men and Angels* (Fort Worth, TX: Holt, Rinehart & Winston, 1991).
2. Judy Skutch maintains that John Koffend originally wrote a manuscript (which he previewed with her) that was largely complimentary to the Course, and that the most critical comments, as well as the article's title, were written in later by Koffend's editor at the magazine. I was unable to locate the story editor to verify this account.
3. John Koffend, "The Gospel According to Helen," *Psychology Today,* Sept 1980.
4. Ted Schultz, "Voices from Beyond: The Age-Old Mystery of Channeling" in *The Fringes of Reason, A Whole Earth Catalog* edited by Ted Schultz (New York: Harmony Books, 1989).
5. Helen Schucman, an unpublished autobiography.
6. Ibid.
7. Ibid.
8. Ibid.
9. Ibid.
10. Ibid.
11. Ibid.
12. Ibid.
13. Ibid.
14. From "The Story of A Course in Miracles," a film documentary (Tiburon, CA: Foundation for Inner Peace, 1987).
15. Schucman, an unpublished autobiography.
16. Ibid.
17. This progression of dreams and visions is described in detail in Kenneth Wapnick's *Absence from Felicity* (Roscoe, NY: Foundation for "A Course in Miracles," 1991).
18. Wapnick, *Absence from Felicity.*

19. From a written record excerpted in Robert Skutch's *Journey Without Distance* (Berkeley, CA: Celestial Arts, 1984).
20. Ibid.
21. Ibid.
22. Ibid.
23. Ibid.
24. Wapnick, *Absence from Felicity*.
25. Alma and Dwayne Copp, "The Transformation of Bill Thetford," an interview with Jack and Eulalia Luckett, *Miracles Magazine* No. 3, Summer 1992.
26. Wapnick, *Absence from Felicity*.
27. Ibid.
28. Willis Harman in the Foreword to *Journey Without Distance*.

Chapter 3

1. ACIM: M-1.1:1–8
2. Judith Skutch quoted from "A Course in Miracles: A Balanced View" by D. Patrick Miller, *Free Spirit*, Dec 1990/Jan 1991.
3. Tara Singh quoted from "An Interview with Tara Singh" by Paul Ferrini in *Miracles Magazine* No. 7.
4. From a pamphlet distributed by the Foundation for Life Action.
5. Val Scott, "Freedom Now," a self-published booklet available from Freedom Now Associates, 5296 Crestview Drive, Nanaimo, BC, Canada V9T 5Z8.
6. From an open letter by Kalie Picone.
7. From a self-published booklet by Robert Lilly posted to an online ACIM discussion group.
8. *out of time*, an undated journal of the Endeavor Academy, Baraboo, Wisconsin.
9. Val Scott, *Freedom Now*.
10. From an online statement published by the Unity Movement Advisory Council.
11. Karen Casey, *Daily Meditations for Practicing the Course* (New York: Hazelden/HarperCollins, 1995).
12. Robert Roskind, *In the Spirit of Business* (Berkeley, CA: Celestial Arts, 1992).
13. Willis Harman, "Approaching the Millennium: Business as Vehicle for Global Transformation" in *The New Paradigm in Business*, Michael Ray & Alan Rinzler (eds.), (New York: Jeremy P. Tarcher/ Perigee Books, 1993).
14. Alan Reid, *Seeing Law Differently: Views from a Spiritual Path* (Ontario, Canada: Borderland Publishing, 1992).

15. Ibid.
16. Quoted from "The Story of a Course in Miracles," a film documentary (Tiburon, CA: Foundation for Inner Peace, 1987).
17. ACIM: Workbook Lesson #33.
18. ACIM: Workbook Lesson #34.
19. ACIM: Workbook Lesson #152.
20. Michael Stillwater, *A Course in Marigolds* (Kula, HI: Inner Harmony Press, 1988).
21. Ibid.

Chapter 4

1. Gerald G. Jampolsky, M.D., *Out of Darkness Into the Light* (New York: Bantam Books, 1989).
2. Gerald G. Jampolsky, M.D., *Good-bye to Guilt* (New York: Bantam Books, 1985).
3. "Helping," a segment of the CBS-TV newsmagazine *60 Minutes*, Dec. 9, 1979.
4. Quoted from Elena Oumano's *Marianne Williamson: Her Life, Her Message, Her Miracles* (New York: St. Martin's Press, 1992).
5. Marianne Williamson, *A Return to Love* (New York: HarperCollins, 1992).
6. Quoted from Oumano's *Marianne Williamson*.
7. Williamson, *A Return to Love*.
8. Ibid.
9. Ibid.
10. Quoted from "Marianne's Faithful" by Leslie Bennetts, *Vanity Fair*, June 1991.
11. Quoted from Oumano's *Marianne Williamson*.
12. Ibid.
13. Martha Smilgis, "Mother Teresa for the '90s?", *Time*, July 29, 1991.
14. Quoted from Paul Ferrini's interview with Marianne Williamson, *Miracles Magazine* No. 3, May 1993.
15. James Fallows, *Breaking the News* (New York: Pantheon Books/Random House, Inc., 1996).
16. Martha Sherrill, "A Course in Marianne," *Mirabella*, April 1993.
17. ACIM: M-in.5:5

Chapter 5

1. Kenneth Wapnick, *Absence from Felicity: The Story of Helen Schucman and Her Scribing of* A Course in Miracles (Roscoe, NY: Foundation for "A Course in Miracles," 1991).
2. Ibid.

3. Wapnick quoted in "The Miracles Interview with Ken Wapnick" by Paul Ferrini, *Miracles Magazine* Winter/Spring 1992.
4. ACIM: W-pII.3.2:1–4
5. Gloria and Kenneth Wapnick, "The Gulf War, Part II — A View from Above the Battleground," *The Lighthouse*, June 1991.
6. ACIM: T-18.VI.1:6
7. Robert Perry, "Liberalism and Conservatism in the Course Community," *Miracles Magazine*, January 1993.
8. Ibid.
9. Kenneth Wapnick, *Love Does Not Condemn* (Roscoe, NY: Foundation for *A Course in Miracles*, 1989).

Chapter 6

1. Roger Walsh, M.D., Ph.D., *The Spirit of Shamanism* (New York: Jeremy P. Tarcher/Perigee, 1990).
2. Roger Walsh, "The Perennial Wisdom of A Course in Miracles," *Common Boundary*, Jan/Feb 1989.
3. Ibid.
4. Ibid.
5. Ibid.
6. Ibid.
7. In the remainder of this chapter, the remarks of Roger Walsh are taken either from an original interview or his taped lecture "The Universal Course," available from Miracle Distribution Center.
8. ACIM: T-18.II.5:1–3 . . . 8 . . . 11–13
9. ACIM: M-20.4:8
10. ACIM: W-p1.124.12:2
11. ACIM: T-2.VI.4:6
12. ACIM: Workbook Lesson #128.
13. ACIM: T-30.VI.1:1–2
14. ACIM: Workbook Lesson #101.
15. ACIM: Workbook Lesson #126.
16. ACIM: P-1.1:1–5
17. Frances Vaughan, *The Inward Arc: Psychotherapy & Spirituality*, 2nd edition (Nevada City: Blue Dolphin Press, 1995).
18. ACIM: P-2.VI.1:3–8
19. ACIM: P-2.I.4:1–7
20. ACIM: P-1.5:1–10
21. ACIM: Workbook Lesson #268.
22. ACIM: P-2.II.3:1–5
23. ACIM: P-2.VI.7:1–5

Chapter 7

1. Kenneth Wapnick, Ph.D. and W. Norris Clarke, S.J., Ph.D., *A Course in Miracles and Christianity: A Dialogue* (Roscoe, NY: Foundation for *A Course in Miracles*, 1995).
2. Ibid.
3. Ibid.
4. M. Scott Peck, *Further Along the Road Less Traveled* (New York: Simon & Schuster, 1993).
5. Wapnick and Clarke, *A Dialogue*.
6. Ibid.
7. ACIM: W-pI.77.2:1–3
8. Wapnick and Clarke, *A Dialogue*.
9. Frances Adeney, "'Revisioning' Reality: A critique of *A Course in Miracles*," SCP Newsletter, June–July 1981.
10. Dean Halverson, "A Matter of Course: Conversation with Kenneth Wapnick," *SCP Journal* Vol. 7 No. 1, 1987.
11. Ken Wapnick, letter to *SCP Journal* Vol. 8 No. 1, 1988.
12. Halverson, *SCP Journal* Vol. 7 No. 1., 1987.
13. Ibid.
14. ACIM: Workbook Lesson #48.
15. This is an accurate quotation. The exact passage reads:
The ego analyzes, the Holy Spirit accepts. The appreciation of wholeness comes only through acceptance, for to analyze means to break down or separate out. The attempt to understand totality by breaking it down is clearly the characteristically contradictory approach of the ego to everything. The ego believes that power, understanding and truth lie in separation, and to establish this belief it must attack. ACIM: T-11.V.13:1–4
16. ACIM: T-3.I.1:8
17. ACIM: C-in.2:1–6
18. ACIM: T-8.VI.9:7

Chapter 8

1. James Hillman with Barbara Dunn, "A Course in Miracles: Spiritual Path or Omnipotent Fantasy?," *Common Boundary*, Sept–Oct 1989.
2. Ibid.
3. Ibid.
4. Ibid.
5. "Roger Walsh Responds," *Common Boundary*, Sept–Oct 1989.
6. Joel Kramer & Diana Alstad, *The Guru Papers: Masks of Authori-*

tarian Power (Berkeley, CA: Frog Ltd. Books, distributed by North Atlantic Books, 1993).

7. Ibid.
8. Ibid.
9. Ibid.
10. Ibid.
11. Ibid.
12. Ibid.
13. D. Patrick Miller, "Back to the Real World: Reflections on *A Course in Miracles*," *The Sun: A Magazine of Ideas*, August 1988.
14. Lesson 132 of the Course Workbook, which inspired my essay in *The Sun*, reads *"I loose the world from all I thought it was,"* and its text continues:

    What keeps the world in chains but your beliefs? And what can save the world except your Self? Belief is powerful indeed. The thoughts you hold are mighty, and illusions are as strong in their effects as is the truth. A madman thinks the world he sees is real, and does not doubt it. Nor can he be swayed by questioning his thoughts' effects. It is but when their source is raised to question that the hope of freedom comes to him at last.

15. Kramer and Alstad, *The Guru Papers*.
16. Letter by Seth Mirsky in *The Sun*, April 1995.
17. Martin Gardner, "Marianne Williamson and 'A Course in Miracles,' *The Skeptical Inquirer*, Fall 1992.
18. Richard Smoley, "Pitfalls of *A Course in Miracles*," *Gnosis*, Fall 1987.
19. Ibid.
20. Ibid.
21. Ibid.
22. Ibid.
23. ACIM: Workbook Lesson #136
24. ACIM: M-4.II.1:4–9 . . . 2:4
25. ACIM: T-15.IV.8:1–4 . . . 9:6–7
26. Jacob Needleman quoted from "In the Spirit of Philosophy," an interview by D. Patrick Miller in *The Sun*, June 1989.
27. Ibid.
28. "In Search of the Sacred," *Newsweek*, Nov 28, 1984.
29. "Religion, Spirituality, and American Families," *A Report from the Editors of Better Homes and Gardens* (Meredith Corporation, Jan 1988). This often overlooked survey of mainstream American spirituality surprised even its editors. After BH&G polled their readers in September 1987, the responses exceeded expectations

by 250%. A total of 80,000 people answered a 34-question survey, making it probably the largest poll of American religious and spiritual attitudes ever conducted.

30. Jacob Needleman, *The New Religions* (New York: Crossroad, 1984 [orig. edition, 1970]).

Chapter 9

1. Although Bill Thetford's parents were Christian Scientists, they lost faith in the creed after the death of a young daughter and Thetford himself grew up agnostic. Helen Schucman's mother dabbled in a variety of spiritual beliefs, but apparently she was not a significant influence on Schucman's own religious development. See Chapter 2 for more details. — *dpm*
2. ACIM: T-22.II.7:4
3. ACIM: Workbook Lesson #10
4. ACIM: T-15.XI.10:5–7

Chapter 10

1. Elaine Pagels, *The Gnostic Gospels* (New York: Vintage Books edition, 1979).
2. Ibid.
3. ACIM: T-4.in.1:6–8
4. ACIM: T-in.1:7
5. ACIM: T-15.IV.6:2
6. Jacob Needleman quoted from "In the Spirit of Philosophy," *The Sun.*
7. Ken Wapnick, *Love Does Not Condemn* (Roscoe, NY: Foundation for *A Course in Miracles*, 1989).
8. ACIM: W-ep.1:1–9 . . . 6:6–8

Index

Acknowledgments

In a project of this nature most of the quoted sources provide more information and assistance than show up on the printed page. It would take another book to describe all the ways in which the following people who figure in this book contributed to my effort to put together a coherent view of "the world of the Course." I'll have to settle for a simple list of their names and a nod to everyone on it for their advice, referrals, and insights: Paul Ferrini, Mike Gole, Ted Grabowski, Dean Halverson, Willis Harman, Jerry Jampolsky, Kalie Khalsa, Jonathan Kirsch, Beverly Hutchinson McNeff, Jon Mundy, Robert Perry, Tony Ponticello, Ted Poppe, Val Scott, Robert Skutch, Frances Vaughan, Roger Walsh, Kenneth and Gloria Wapnick, Allen Watson, Bill Whitson and Judith Skutch Whitson, and Marianne Williamson.

Behind the printed word, the following people offered valuable connections, suggestions, or ideas: Tal Brooke of the Spiritual Counterfeits Project, Melinda Elliott, David S. Eisenmann, editor Kay James of the *Wisconsin Dells Events*, Lois Louis at the Foundation for Inner Peace, Paul Norton of *The Capital Times* (Madison, Wisconsin), Pamela Parnell, Richard Pratt, Michelle Presley, Neil Purtell of the Federal Bureau of Investigation, Petrus J. Saaiman, Sy Safransky, Elizabeth Schmit at the Foundation for *A Course in Miracles*, David Thomson, and Vic Zarley.

For reading and commenting on the manuscript in progress I'd like to thank the Reverend William J. Kiser-Lowrance, Marc Polonsky, and Richard Smoley — as well as my brilliant wife and sweet-tempered agent Laurie Fox of the Linda Chester Literary Agency, who took this project off the back burner with Linda's enthusiastic support. Finally, I'm grateful to Stephanie Gunning, formerly of Dell Publishing, for agreeing with Laurie that the time was right for this book to be written, and for insightful comments through the first round of editing.

When fate firmly suggested that I should undertake the publication of this book myself, I was incredibly fortunate to encounter a series of generous helpers. Old friends from my graphic arts past stood me in good stead, especially Thomas Morris, Linda Davis, David Jouris, and Lory Poulson. Experienced and sometimes bracing advice was freely given by compatriots in the small press, including Malcolm Margolin of Heyday Books, Kathryn Leigh Scott of Pomegranate Press, Ltd., Robert Goodman of Silvercat Publications, Richard Grossinger of North Atlantic Books, Cor van Heumen of Cate Cumings Publicity & Promotion Group, Victoria Sutherland of The Jenkins Group, and Dan Poynter through the wide-ranging resources provided by ParaPublishing. Thanks to Eric Kampmann and Gail Kump of the "lean and mean" Midpoint Trade Books for taking on this property on very short notice. And I am especially grateful for the near-omniscient advice of distribution consultant Cierán Mercier, who facilitated several of the miracles required to transform *The Complete Story* from a manuscript on my desk into a book available in stores nationwide in a mere six months.

About the Author

D. PATRICK MILLER is a widely-published writer in the "journalism of consciousness," a reflective style of reportage focusing on psychological and spiritual subject matter. A Senior Writer for *Yoga Journal* since 1989, Miller is also a regular contributor to *The Sun: A Magazine of Ideas*. His articles have appeared in *Self, Mother Jones, New Age Journal, Gnosis, Intuition, The Utne Reader, The Columbia Journalism Review,* and many other periodicals. He is the author of *A Little Book of Forgiveness* and *The Book of Practical Faith* and co-author, with Tom Rusk, M.D., of *The Power of Ethical Persuasion* and *Instead of Therapy*. Miller is a member of the Authors Guild, American Society of Journalists and Authors, and Investigative Reporters and Editors. He is also the founder of Fearless Books.

A native of Charlotte, N.C., Miller has lived in California since 1976. He resides in Berkeley with his wife Laurie Fox.

Fearless Books will annually donate a percentage of profits from this title to the Healing Center for Survivors of Political Torture, sponsored by the California Institute of Integral Studies in San Francisco, California.